Open and Async

The collaborative software development playbook for remote and distributed teams

By **Ben Balter**

1.0.6 (19a4473a)

Open and Async: The collaborative software development playbook for remote and distributed teams

Version 1.0.6 (19a4473a)

ISBN 979-8-9957542-1-3 (paperback)

ISBN 979-8-9957542-0-6 (ebook)

Cover design by Matthew Morse.

Fine print

To the next generation of developers: May you never endure a meeting that should have been an ~~email~~ issue. I wish you contributions worth making, teams worth joining, and leaders who work in the open.

Introduction

Remote and hybrid work isn't just "traditional" work done on a computer. It's an entirely different way of working that demands new tools, processes, and mindsets—a shift from closed to open, synchronous to asynchronous, in-person to written, and face time to impact. For those who grew up with always-on connectivity, group chats, and social media, this isn't the future of work—it's the natural evolution of how they've always lived. For everyone else, it's a learnable skill with immediate payoffs.

Remote work that actually works

> **TL;DR:** Most companies just moved office habits online and called it remote work, but true remote success demands a shift to openness and asynchronous collaboration—without it, you're stuck with all the old frustrations plus new headaches. This chapter lays the groundwork so you can stop digitizing dysfunction and start building a team that actually thrives outside the office.

Your company survived the pandemic. Congratulations. Leadership shipped everyone a laptop, bolted Zoom onto existing workflows, and declared victory. *That wasn't remote work.* **That was office work in sweatpants**—the same meetings, the same approval chains, the same "quick sync" culture, just piped through a webcam.

They digitized office culture without rethinking it. At GitHub (the world's largest software development platform), we saw this repeatedly when companies tried to adopt our workflows—they'd add GitHub Issues (linkable threads for tracking and discussing work) to an existing hierarchy-driven approval process and wonder why nothing changed. Tools: right. Approval bottlenecks: intact. The result: Zoom fatigue plus all the old dysfunction, now faster.

There's a world of difference between being forced to work from home and intentionally building a distributed, async culture. **Working from home ≠ working remotely.**

This book is about that difference. Open and asynchronous (or "async") communication makes remote and distributed software development actually work. **Async is the operating system; remote is the hardware.** It's how the next generation of tech leaders already think.

> **Pro-Tip:** This book uses GitHub terminology—issues, pull requests, repositories—because that's the world these practices grew up in. The principles are platform-agnostic. If your team uses GitLab, read "merge request" for "pull request." If you're on Jira, read "ticket" for "issue." If you use Azure DevOps, Bitbucket, or Linear, the same patterns apply—swap in your own vocabulary and the workflows translate directly.

A generation of developers grew up building online communities, shipping open source projects from their bedrooms, and collaborating with people they'd never met in person. For everyone else, this book breaks async down into concrete, repeatable practices—no intuition required.

> **Pro-Tip:** Throughout this book, you'll see TL;DRs and Pro-Tips. TL;DRs are internet shorthand for "Too Long; Didn't Read"—quick summaries popularized across online forums and social media. Pro-Tips are actionable advice you can put to work right away. You'll also see callouts for managers or individual contributors where guidance differs by role.

Who this book is for

This book is for two audiences, both in remote and distributed software development:

> **For managers: Including engineering managers, directors, VPs,** and other execs—you've watched remote work evolve from "weird startup thing" to industry standard, and you've sat through more than one meeting about "bringing back the culture" by mandating return-to-office days. You've been both an IC (Individual Contributor) and a people manager, and you understand the grind from both sides. This book shows you how to lead remote organizations the way you've always wanted to work. Build cultures around transparency and async collaboration. Model the behaviors that make distributed teams actually work. Advance your career while creating environments where your team does their best work—not just looks busy on chat.

> If you're short on time, start with *Leadership* and *Adopting and Transitioning*—the chapters where the return on a few hours of reading is highest. Read the *Working in the Open* and *Async Communications* chapters to see the practices you'll need to model.

Whether you're leading teams or leading the work itself, these practices apply:

> - **For individual contributors: Including early-career engineers, senior software developers, product managers, tech leads, and staff+ engineers**—the line between IC and management blurs at the top, and many of you live on both sides of it. The way you've always communicated is finally how work gets done. You grew up on online communities, collaborative docs, and async communication. You shipped side projects with strangers across time zones before you shipped your first professional PR (Pull Request). This book shows you how to "lead the work" regardless of your title and build your reputation through transparent collaboration. Impact matters more than office presence. The skills you already have—async communication, digital collaboration, working in public—are exactly what remote work demands.
>
> If you're short on time, *Working in the Open* and *Async Communications* are where your day-to-day habits live. Then read *Leadership*—not for the management chapters, but to see how senior ICs lead

> through artifacts. Read across roles: managers benefit from understanding IC workflows, and ICs benefit from seeing how managers think about their teams.

This book assumes you're familiar with modern software development workflows. If you're new to software development, check out *Software development for non-technical roles* in the Appendix.

The **bold lines** throughout are the book's bumper stickers—each idea compressed to something you can drop in a channel or put on a slide. Steal them freely; the whole collection, with share-ready cards, lives at open-and-async.com/q.[1]

> **Pro-Tip:** "Shipping" is tech jargon for releasing or deploying—getting something out the door. Shipping culture thrives on small, frequent deliverables, not big reveals. Set a personal bar of sharing *something* tangible each week: a rough draft, a prototype, a documented decision. The cadence matters more than the size. Teams that ship small and often build momentum faster than teams that vanish for weeks and emerge with a grand unveiling—which invariably needs revision anyway.

The promise

You can *thrive* and *advance your career* in remote and distributed work. Along the way, you'll sharpen your written communication, async collaboration, and transparent decision-making—skills that compound over time and travel with you wherever you go. They're also what remote-first companies test for in interviews. Whether you're deepening your current practice or preparing for your next role, the investment pays off twice.

First, some vocabulary. "Remote," "distributed," "remote-first," "remote-friendly"—these sound interchangeable, but they represent distinct approaches with real implications for how you build your career and lead your team.

1. https://open-and-async.com/q

Defining Open, Async, and Remote-First Work

> **TL;DR:** If you don't nail down what "remote" and "distributed" actually mean in your company, you'll waste months propping up broken office habits online instead of reaping the benefits of proven, open source–style async collaboration. This chapter gives you the definitions—and the templates—you need to get it right from day one.

"Distributed," "remote-friendly," "hybrid," "flexible," "telework," and "remote-first" all get used as if they mean the same thing. They don't. Each describes a different operating model with different tradeoffs—and most of the dysfunction blamed on "remote work" comes from companies that picked one model in name and ran another in practice. So before going further:

- "**Distributed**" teams are spread across multiple locations—sometimes multiple offices, sometimes multiple continents. You can be distributed without anyone working from home.

- "**Remote-friendly**" (also called "flexible" work or "telework") means some people *can* work remotely either sometimes or all the time, but the defaults still favor whoever's in the room. Decisions drift back to hallway conversations, and remote folks piece things together after the fact.
- "**Hybrid**" splits time between office and remote, which sounds like the best of both worlds but often delivers the worst of each—neither the energy of co-location nor the discipline of async.
- "**Remote-first**" means the entire system—tools, norms, culture—assumes nobody is co-located, even when some people are. It's the only one of these that doesn't create second-class teammates.

This book focuses on remote-first because it's the only model that forces the right defaults. The principles still help the others—but the others don't force you to apply them.

Most organizations *adapted* to remote work during the COVID-19 pandemic rather than maturing into remote-first practices.[2] **Remote-first is a workflow refactor, not a workplace hotfix.**

> 🤔 **Common objection: "We tried remote work during the pandemic and it was a disaster."** No—you tried doing office work over Zoom during a global crisis, and what you got was trauma with a webcam. When the pandemic hit, plenty of thought

2. https://ma.tt/2020/04/five-levels-of-autonomy/

> pieces declared "remote culture seems broken—everyone's Zoomed out." The problem wasn't remote work; it was Zoom grafted onto an existing meeting-heavy culture. A company *already* trying to reduce meetings had an easier time adapting. If your "remote experiment" was eight hours of video calls, no documented decisions, and managers pinging people to prove they were online, you didn't test remote-first. You stress-tested your existing dysfunction on a new platform. The failure mode wasn't the location—it was the workflow.

Remote work often gets dismissed—especially by management—over concerns about productivity, collaboration, work-life balance, and burnout, not to mention sunk real estate costs. But the difference between being *able* to work remotely and thriving remotely[3] isn't better tooling—it's working *openly* and *asynchronously*. No amount of digitizing old workflows will get you there.

Beyond Cold War workflows

Traditional corporate workflows haven't evolved much from their Cold War–era predecessors. We've replaced typewriters with laptops, interoffice mail with email, and in-person meetings with video conferencing—but how work and information actually flow has barely changed in seventy-plus years. It's the organizational

3. https://web.archive.org/web/20200302200947/https://www.thegreatcodeadventure.com/my-long-distance-relationship-with-github/

equivalent of porting legacy code to a new platform without rearchitecting it: all the technical debt, few of the benefits.

The internet was a genuine disruption, but most organizations never reckoned with what that meant. Communication technology evolved in two directions: *asynchronous* written media—from stone tablets and the printing press to carbon copies—expanded reach and preserved fidelity, while *synchronous* tech like the telegraph, telephone, and radio compressed time.

The internet combined both for the first time: unprecedented speed *and* reach. Most organizations optimized for speed alone—instant messaging, constant email, back-to-back video calls—and ignored the reach. **We got the internet and sent memos faster.** Modern businesses make the same mistake as the scientists of *Jurassic Park*: they're so preoccupied with whether they *could* work faster, they don't stop to think if they *should*.

What open source figured out first

While most organizations digitized their office rituals, another community quietly worked out how to build complex things together without sharing a room, a time zone, or even a conversation. The open source community cracked this decades ago. Today, you can't get through a day without touching open source software—your phone, car, bank, and government all run on it. The twist? Open source often produces better software than its closed-source counterparts, faster and more securely.[4]

> **Pro-Tip:** Open source is a software development model where anyone can view, use, and modify a project's source code—and it's been remote since before remote work had a name. Popular projects often have thousands of contributors, and many are backed (or run) by the biggest companies in tech.

Open source differs from traditional software development in three ways:

- **Transparent processes**: Discussions and decisions happen in public forums where anyone can follow along, contribute, and verify. Trust comes from transparency, not authority.

4. For a brief overview, see Why open source (https://ben.balter.com/2015/11/23/why-open-source/); for a more comprehensive look, see David A. Wheeler's canonical Why Open Source? Look at the Numbers! (https://dwheeler.com/oss_fs_why.html).

- **Asynchronous development:** Contributors work on their own schedules across time zones. Nobody's locked out by geography or waking hours.
- **Collaborative problem-solving:** Because the work is open and asynchronous, a developer in Lagos can build on what someone in Portland started yesterday —no handoff meeting required.

Those principles apply to for-profit work, too—here's what "open" and "async" look like inside an organization:

Knowing the difference between "remote-friendly" and "remote-first" changes how you approach your work. These distinctions aren't academic—they're your negotiating vocabulary. When a manager says "we need more face time," push back: "Synchronous collaboration, or proximity-based oversight?" Understanding the difference makes you the person who clarifies confused conversations instead of getting lost in them.

> **For managers: Audit your workflows for proximity bias.** Pick any recurring meeting or approval process and ask: *does this require same-time, same-place interaction, or is that just how we've always done it?* If the answer is habit, redesign it for async. Start with the process that annoys your team most—you'll build credibility and momentum for the harder changes ahead.

If "open" and "async" sound idealistic, they're not. They're concrete, learnable practices—skills, not personality traits. **Remote-first skills are career insurance.**

Open: share early, share often

Working openly means making information and decisions as broadly accessible as the subject allows. You might share with your team, your department, your organization, or the public. Openness isn't publishing—publishing implies a higher bar for quality and completeness. Openness is sharing early and often, willing to iterate as you go. It's "here's my rough draft, poke holes in it?" rather than "here's my polished deliverable, admire it." Think of it like the difference between open source and closed-source software: **one invites contribution and inspection, while the other requires trust without verification.**

Openness matters most when you share the "how" and the "why." Showing your reasoning—not just your conclusion—lets people spot blind spots you missed and offer alternatives you hadn't considered. You don't need consensus or corporate democracy, but leaders need to explain their decisions and stay open to feedback and criticism.

Async: decouple when from where

Asynchronous work moves beyond the assembly-line-inspired, ad hoc workflows that still dominate most organizations. If you're a white-collar worker, you're likely a *knowledge worker*—someone whose output is intellectual rather than physical. Your deliverable at the end of each day exists primarily as electrical impulses in the cloud—you can't exactly point at a pile of widgets. You create organizational knowledge through meetings, discussions, decisions, and drafting—code, legal briefs, press releases, or whatever you do. Working asynchronously means:

- not requiring people to be in a specific place at a specific time, or to work on a specific thing at a specific time,
- allowing individuals to be productive without waiting for others to respond or complete a task,
- reducing batch size so that work can progress faster than its slowest component,
- minimizing unplanned interruptions and demands for immediate attention,
- decoupling work from communication, and
- trusting workers to autonomously pursue shared goals.

Making work naturally visible is the cheapest, highest-impact form of communication for distributed teams. It requires tooling that captures process without extra effort—and a culture where showing work-in-progress won't get you punished for not being "done."

The async expectation shift

If you're in an in-person meeting, on the phone, or on a video call with a colleague, you're working synchronously. Sure, there's technically a slight delay between speakers, but you *expect* responses in near real-time.

Asynchronous work resets that expectation. Delay is the whole point. When you send an email, you don't expect an immediate response—the recipient might take a day or more to reply. During a back-and-forth exchange, response time might shrink to minutes or seconds, but the expectation is different. You're not waiting; you're working on other things while the recipient responds thoughtfully. That's the *short* version of async work.

If you're an engineer, you already know this pattern by another name: event-driven architecture. Producers and consumers operate independently, processing messages when ready rather than blocking on immediate responses. Async communication works the same way—any exchange with a deliberate delay between sender and recipient.

> **Pro-Tip:** Want to learn more? Cali Ressler and Jody Thompson's *Why Work Sucks and How to Fix It*[5] (and its sequel *Why Managing Sucks and How to Fix It*) popularized the Results-Only Work Environment (ROWE)—the most comprehensive

5. https://en.wikipedia.org/wiki/ROWE

> framework I've seen for killing presenteeism and managing by outcomes instead of hours.

Openness and asynchronous work are intertwined—**open enables async; async demands open** regardless of industry. When you work in the open, async becomes natural because others can engage with your work on their own schedule. When you work asynchronously, openness becomes essential because you can't rely on real-time clarification.

> **For managers: Open and async won't take root without deliberate culture shift.** Set the expectation that decisions are documented, discussions happen in the open, and immediate responses are the exception—then enforce it by redirecting private threads to public channels. For practical strategies, see *Working in the Open* and *Core Practices for Async Communication*.

That same transparency works for individuals, too:

> **For individual contributors: Open and async gives you control over your own narrative.** Instead of hoping your manager notices your work, you're building a searchable, linkable record of contributions. See *Working in the Open* and *Work Loudly*.

These aren't abstract principles—companies have tested them at scale. GitHub, a company built by and for developers, turned open source collaboration patterns into the way the company itself ran. Its journey from scrappy startup to global platform shows what happens when open and async stop being ideals and become defaults.

History of Remote Work at GitHub

> **TL;DR:** GitHub used Issues, Pull Requests, and Markdown to run *everything*—code, legal, HR, even vacation policy—proving that open source workflows aren't just for open source. The practices that scaled a startup to a global platform are yours to replicate.

Most of the workday exists the way it does because that's how it's always been done. **We automated the bureaucracy and called it progress.**

A company that rethought the defaults

When I joined GitHub in 2013, I found a company that had systematically rethought the defaults. Remote-first. Widely reported to have no managers for most of its early history. Employees spread across the globe—60–75% remote for the better part of a decade; GitHub later went 100% remote.[6] This was unusual for startups, let alone large corporations. Depending on who you asked, it was either visionary or unhinged.

GitHub was dogmatic about "optimizing for developer happiness"—treating the internal development experience with the same care as the product. Inspired by open source workflows—the same workflows many GitHub developers grew up with—nearly everything was async. Between GitHub Issues, chat, and our trusty robot sidekick Hubot, GitHub practiced DevOps before it had a name. Remote work wasn't a concession; it was the culture. We ate our own cooking.[7]

> **Pro-Tip:** DevOps breaks down the wall between "people who write code" and "people who deploy it" by making both responsibilities visible and shared. One implementation—ChatOps—puts deployment (and cultural) commands in chat where everyone can see them—a natural audit trail that makes asynchronous collaboration the default.

Using GitHub to build GitHub

GitHub's development workflow didn't spring from any formal methodology—it grew organically out of open source culture. No mandatory daily standups, no sprint planning ceremonies, no fixed-cadence retrospectives. If

6. https://www.itpro.com/business/business-strategy/370043/github-shifts-to-fully-remote-working-model
7. https://zachholman.com/talk/how-github-uses-github-to-build-github/

you had to pin a label on it, the approach looked more like Kanban than Scrum—work moved through visible queues, passed through asynchronous review, and shipped when it was ready.

Flow-based approaches—work visible on a board, review happening asynchronously, delivery continuous—map naturally onto distributed teams. Ceremony-heavy frameworks that depend on everyone being in the same room (or the same time zone) fight that natural fit. The goal isn't to abandon structure, but to choose structure that makes work *visible* rather than *synchronous*—an idea *Lead Like an Engineer* takes further.

Concretely, that flow had loosely-defined gates. In my experience, GitHub never developed a permission-seeking or defensive CYA (cover-your-ass) culture; instead, the expectation was that you'd give the right teams a real chance to weigh in at four checkpoints—idea (~1%), proof of concept (~10%), staff ship (~50%), and final stages (~90%)—and keep moving between them. Silence meant consent, not absence. If the direction was wrong, the visibility of the work surfaced it long before launch.

> **For individual contributors: Flow-based workflows give you autonomy over *when* and *how* you work.** Instead of waiting for a standup to report progress or a sprint review to get feedback, your work is visible the moment you push it. That visibility is your career capital—every well-written PR

> description, every issue you close with context, is proof of your judgment that outlasts any status meeting.

The stack underneath was deliberately minimal. Issues to capture problems. Pull requests to propose changes. Markdown to write everything down. Hubot to automate the rest. Four primitives, infinitely composable. When I first joined, I was struck by how often I heard "put it on GitHub." That shorthand meant "make it transparent, discussable, linkable"—GitHub's culture in three words. It wasn't about the platform; it was about *how* you thought about work: things either existed in a way the team could find, discuss, and build on, or they didn't exist at all.

> **Pro-Tip:** Quick litmus test: if a task coordinates, reports on, or gates the actual work rather than advancing it, it's meta-work. Before adding a process step, ask: *could the tooling answer this question without a human in the loop?* If yes, automate it. If no, at least make it async.

Markdown's role wasn't arbitrary. It uses characters you already know—`#` for headings, `-` for bullets, `**` for bold—to format plain text that's readable without rendering. Unlike emailing word-processing documents back and forth with conflicting revision marks, Markdown files play nicely with version control and render cleanly in any modern tool. That killed the perennial "which version is current?" problem and made collaborative editing async by default.

> **Pro-Tip:** Markdown has since become AI-native too—large language models (LLMs) read and generate it natively, and its lightweight syntax uses fewer tokens than HTML or rich text. A format chosen for human collaboration turned out to be equally efficient for AI interaction. More on that in *Documentation as a Superpower*.

The real leap wasn't using these tools for code. **Every workflow is a pull request waiting to happen.**

Open source workflows for non-code work

GitHub used Issues, Pull Requests, and Markdown to manage internal policies, legal matters, HR, and sales. Need a contract reviewed? Open an issue, tag legal, and let the discussion happen in the open where anyone affected can chime in. Want to propose a change to the vacation policy? Submit a pull request against the handbook repository and let people debate the diff. Onboarding a new hire? A checklist issue with assignees for each step. Job descriptions, expense policies, the employee handbook, the code of conduct—all Markdown, all versioned, all reviewable.

Each choice creates a second-order payoff. When your HR policy lives in a Markdown file with complete change history, everyone can see not just what the policy is, but *why* it changed and who advocated for it.

When legal review happens in an issue thread, the reasoning is preserved for the next person with the same question—no meeting to rediscover what was already decided. When a proposed policy change is a pull request, dissent becomes structured feedback on a specific line rather than a grievance aired in passing.

I watched this pay off firsthand. Someone opened an issue asking Legal for a customer NDA (non-disclosure agreement)—the kind of routine request that normally waits on a lawyer's inbox. I'd been through that exact process a few weeks earlier, and because the ask was an issue I happened to see rather than an email I wasn't copied on, I dropped in a link to the prior thread before Legal's West Coast morning had even started.

The person was unblocked hours ahead of the first lawyer logging on. No meeting, no ticket queue, no rediscovering a decision that had already been made—just a question that was visible to whoever happened to have the answer (the "real" lawyers reviewed my advice a few hours later).

GitHub even ran its DMCA (Digital Millennium Copyright Act) takedown process this way: copyright notices moved through pull requests that eventually made it to a public repository. The lighter legal workflow doubled as a public record—anyone could see which projects were challenged and how GitHub responded. One design choice bought both less friction and more transparency.

Something subtler happens too: the walls between teams disappear. An engineer can read the sales playbook. A recruiter can comment on a design doc. A lawyer can file an issue against the marketing site. The work is *just there*—searchable, linkable, open by default. The gap between "tech" and "non-tech" turns out to be mostly a tooling choice.

This is the part skeptics get wrong. The magic wasn't the hoodies or the free lunches. It was that HR ran on a version control system. When you treat every policy, contract, and process as a document that can be branched, reviewed, and merged, "the way we work" stops being tribal knowledge locked in someone's inbox. It behaves like software: inspectable, improvable, forkable.

Intentionality over proximity

So the tools worked async—but what about the humans? GitHub had a physical office in San Francisco, but it was more hub than headquarters—meetups, events, coworking, not mandatory 9-to-5 attendance. Hubbers (GitHub employees) worked whenever and wherever they were most productive.

Remote didn't mean isolated. An annual company summit brought everyone together for a week. Smaller team mini-summits handled planning and the face-to-face trust that makes async work *easier* the other 51 weeks. The HQ was optimized for remote-first, with open cafés for drop-ins and streaming setups so distributed employees could join all-hands. Smaller teams ran

"Hack Houses" to ship complex projects together in person—a model that works at team scale even if it doesn't scale companywide.

Here's the thing about office serendipity—those hallway conversations, the overheard brainstorm, the coffee-machine epiphany—it was never accidental. It was *proximity-dependent*. And proximity is just one way to create those moments—an expensive, exclusionary way. Remote work doesn't end serendipity; it forces you to design it. Optional social channels, virtual coffee roulettes, open-ended team threads—these are the distributed equivalent, and they include people who'd never have been in that hallway to begin with. **Design serendipity; don't outsource it to a floor plan.**

> **For managers: Serendipity is your responsibility now.** In an office, chance encounters happened without effort. Remotely, you have to engineer them—cross-team channels, random pairing, open demo sessions. Carve out the time and attention deliberately; connection won't accrue on its own. The teams that feel most connected aren't lucky; they have managers who treat connection as a deliverable.

You'd think all this would weaken company culture. The opposite was true. Remote work forced GitHub to write down what most companies leave to hallway folklore—how decisions get made, what "done" looks like, who owns what. **Forced intentionality beats accidental culture.**

After the acquisition

Microsoft acquired GitHub in October 2018. The common worry—not just among Hubbers but across the broader developer community—was that the acquisition would revert everything unusual about the place. It mostly didn't. We took the work seriously but never ourselves. The emoji and GIFs never dried up, and Issues and Pull Requests kept doing the heavy lifting for engineering—even as non-engineering functions like HR, legal, and finance gradually migrated to purpose-built tools. Inclusive-language norms, time zone awareness, the relentless default to appreciating each other in public—all survived the transition.

The best way I can describe the result during my time at GitHub: **we kept the best parts of GitHub and learned what we could from Microsoft's scale.**

These patterns are yours to adapt

You don't need to be GitHub to work like GitHub. The tools are free, the workflows are documented, and the culture is a choice—not a perk of being a tech company.

> **Common objection: "This only works at GitHub—or tech companies like it."** Fair instinct, wrong conclusion. The patterns that made GitHub effective weren't perks or ping-pong tables—they were *workflow decisions*: write it down instead of saying it, make work visible instead of reporting on it, review asynchronously instead of scheduling a

> meeting. A law firm tracking contract revisions in pull requests, a marketing team running campaigns through issues, a nonprofit coordinating volunteers across time zones—none of that requires a hoodie or a San Francisco address. The advantage isn't being a tech company; it's being willing to rethink defaults.

> **For managers: Remote culture must be intentional.** What happened organically at 50 people requires deliberate effort at 500. Invest in codifying practices, building shared context, and maintaining the cultural elements that worked when you were smaller.

> **For individual contributors: GitHub's story is proof that these practices work at scale—but you can start at a team of one.** The habits that made GitHub effective—writing things down, defaulting to public channels, reviewing work asynchronously—didn't require a company mandate. They started with individual engineers who found better ways to collaborate. You can adopt the same patterns today, regardless of your org's official stance on remote work.

Over the years, GitHub practiced many of the principles in this book—imperfectly and not always simultaneously. It's a story of pursuing an ideal while occasionally falling short. Even so, GitHub remains the closest example I've seen of a company getting remote and distributed work "right," which is why many former Hubbers return after seeing how others do it.

Three ideas anchor everything that follows. *Remote-first* isn't a perk or a policy—it's a workflow refactor that assumes no one is co-located, so defaults work for everyone regardless of time zone. *Open* means sharing work early and often, making progress visible without being asked. *Async* means decoupling *when* from *where*, so a teammate in Toronto and a teammate in Bangalore can contribute to the same decision without scheduling a meeting at someone's midnight. Open enables async; async demands open. Two sides of the same coin.

Key takeaways

- Most companies just moved office habits online and called it remote work, but true remote success demands a shift to openness and asynchronous collaboration—without it, you're stuck with all the old frustrations plus new headaches.
- If you don't nail down what "remote" and "distributed" actually mean in your company, you'll waste months propping up broken office habits online instead of reaping the benefits of proven, open source–style async collaboration.
- GitHub used Issues, Pull Requests, and Markdown to run *everything*—code, legal, HR, even vacation policy—proving that open source workflows aren't just for open source. The practices that scaled a startup to a global platform are yours to replicate.

Making the Case for Open and Async Workflows

Open, async, remote-first, and the tools and workflows that support them aren't four separate trends you can adopt à la carte. They're a single interlocking system—and pulling on any one thread without the others is how "we tried remote work" becomes "remote work didn't work."

A product manager in Berlin opens an issue Monday morning with a proposal and three open questions. By the time she logs off, an engineer in São Paulo has answered two in the thread, linked to a prior decision that closes the third, and opened a draft pull request. An engineering manager in Seattle reads the exchange Tuesday morning, leaves a comment, and approves. No meeting. Three people, three continents, one durable artifact a new hire can still read two years later.

That isn't luck. That's *four things working at once*—openness, async, remote, and the tools that carry all three.

They sound like they could stand alone. They can't:

- **Openness** turns individual work into institutional intelligence. When reasoning is visible, colleagues course-correct early, newcomers onboard from the record, and nobody has to reconstruct a decision from a six-month-old calendar invite.
- **Async** gives that openness somewhere to land. Putting decisions in writing means the best idea wins, not the loudest voice at 2 PM Eastern Time (ET).
- **Remote and distributed work** makes the first two non-negotiable. The moment your team spans time zones, "I'll just grab you after standup" stops working. Distance is the forcing function that turns good habits into survival skills.
- **Tools and workflows** are the substrate the other three run on. Your culture will mirror the communication paths your tools support, whether you intend it or not.

Miss any one and the others collapse into caricature. **Openness without async is notification overload.** Async without openness is writing into the void. Remote without either is the office's worst habits rebuilt in your spare bedroom.

Put your team on email and you'll get long threads with buried decisions. Move that same team to Slack and you'll get fast answers that vanish in a week.

Shift the work to GitHub Issues and you'll get durable, linkable decisions with full context. Same team. Same talent. Wildly different outcomes—because **every tool is an opinion in disguise**. Programmer Melvin Conway named a version of this in 1967:[8] organizations tend to produce systems that reflect how they coordinate. Legend has it you could once crack open a PC and deduce the manufacturer's org chart from the chip layout on the motherboard. **New tools with old habits produce old results.**

> **Common objection: "We're already remote—isn't that enough?"** Remote is a location policy. Open and async is an operating model. Plenty of remote teams still pile into back-to-back video calls, make decisions in direct messages (DMs) that vanish, and treat "flexible hours" as "always on." The shift isn't about *where* people sit; it's about whether *how* you work actually benefits from the distance.

> **For managers: Make the case up, model the behavior down.** When pitching open and async to leadership, lead with business outcomes: reduced decision latency, faster onboarding, fewer single points of failure. When embedding it in your team, start with one practice—like moving decisions to

8. https://www.melconway.com/Home/Conways_Law.html

> issues—and let the results speak. Don't mandate a culture change; demonstrate one.

> **For individual contributors: You don't need organizational permission to start working more openly.** Post your work-in-progress in a public channel. Write down why you made a technical decision before anyone asks. These small moves make the case by example—and make your work visible to the people who decide promotions. The best argument for open and async is showing what it looks like in practice.

The next three chapters argue openness, async, and remote on their own terms—tools and workflows get a section of their own later. But the point doesn't change: **you don't get to pick two.** The *where* was never the hard part; the *how* is.

If "how" you work is what matters, visibility is where it starts. Working in the open isn't just about transparency for its own sake—it's how you avoid doing the same work twice, spot risks before they explode, and remember why you made choices in the first place.

Why You Should Work in the Open

> **TL;DR:** Work in private and you'll rediscover the same dead ends your teammates already hit—because nobody could see what anyone else was doing. Working in the open turns your process into something the team builds on instead of a mystery to reverse-engineer.

You spend a week refining an architecture proposal in a private doc, share it with the team, and discover that two people already explored—and rejected—the same approach three months ago. Nobody was hiding anything. You just couldn't see what they'd done, and they couldn't see what you were doing.

That's the tax on working in private by default—and duplicated effort is just the most visible line item. The subtler costs are silos that form when teams can't see each other's work, blind spots nobody notices until they become crises, and decisions made without context that existed somewhere but nobody could find. Modern collaboration tools make creating and sharing the same act —if you let them. This is a question of *visibility*—who can see your work and where it lives—the spatial dimension of collaboration, distinct from the temporal question of *when* people engage with that work.

The process is the product

Most organizations treat work like a magic trick—they only want to see the reveal. But the real value isn't the final deliverable; it's the trail of decisions, trade-offs, and reasoning that got you there. When that trail is visible, colleagues can course-correct early, new hires can learn from your thinking, and nobody has to reconstruct your reasoning six months later.

> **For managers: Make the trail visible by making it normal.** When your team sees you documenting your own reasoning—not just asking them to document theirs—the habit spreads. Link to your decision records in team channels. Reference past issues in new ones. The more you treat the trail as a living resource, the more your team will contribute to it without being asked.

> **Pro-Tip:** Ever inherited a project with no history? No recorded decisions, no rationale for the architecture, just artifacts and a prayer. You end up doing organizational archaeology—interviewing people who half-remember, reading between the lines of old Slack threads, and re-making decisions that were already made (sometimes badly). A visi-

> ble trail of reasoning isn't documentation busy-work—it's a gift to everyone who comes after you.

Show your work, own your impact

Working in the open lets you "show your work"—the same practice many of us learned in math class. **Open work is visible work, and visible work gets recognized.** When you make a decision, people have questions: they want to resolve ambiguity or understand your reasoning. When work happens privately, those questions go unanswered or surface as churn weeks later. Showing your work means capturing who decided what, when, and—concisely—why. Here's what you get:

Your team's knowledge will outlive any one person's tenure

Share context deliberately and you eliminate the "you had to be there" problem. Think of it like a well-maintained git history: future contributors can trace how the codebase evolved, understand why the team chose certain approaches, and build on that foundation rather than second-guessing every decision. **Knowledge should live with the organization, not the individual.**

> **Common objection: "If I document everything I know, I become replaceable."** You've got the causation backwards. People who hoard knowledge don't become indispensable—they become bottlenecks. And bottlenecks don't get promoted; they get

> worked around. The engineers I've seen advance fastest are the ones who documented themselves *out* of their current role, freeing themselves to take on bigger problems. Your value isn't what you know—it's your ability to keep learning and solving new things.

Let others learn by watching

What's routine to you is novel to someone in another role or at a different seniority level. Junior developers regularly watch code reviews (peer feedback on proposed changes) on pull requests—that's how they internalize the team's standards and conventions. Make other types of knowledge work equally transparent, and newer team members learn the same way—by watching and gradually jumping in. Open work makes the *content* available; async work gives people the *time* to absorb it at their own pace.

Culture lives in the decisions you make

An organization's culture and values come from the assumptions its members fall back on when resolving ambiguity. Should we be iterative or precise? Process-driven or outcome-oriented? Do we serve end users or execs? Showing your work reveals how your organization actually makes decisions—and surfaces the assumptions that usually stay unwritten.

Engaged teams speak up

I'll take a passionate (even critical) team over an uninterested one any day. Transparency gives people agency, context about what's happening around them, and a stake in the outcome—which means better ideas and more honest pushback. Showing your work is like the traditional comment box in the break room, but with far more reach and far less friction.

Accountability raises everyone's game

Scientists have reproducibility. Mathematicians have proofs. Developers have open source. Most corporate decisions have... a meeting invite that expired six months ago. Showing your work sets the expectation that decisions come with reasoning—raising the bar for how your organization operates. Just as code destined for review needs to be cleaner than code you keep to yourself, work you do in the open rises to a higher standard because others will see it.

> **For individual contributors: Open work is your portfolio in real-time.** You don't need a performance review to demonstrate impact when your contributions are already visible. The issue you triaged, the design decision you challenged, the doc you updated—that's all findable by anyone

> evaluating your work. Treat every public artifact as a line on your résumé that writes itself.

> **Pro-Tip:** If you think working in the open is a Silicon Valley affectation that won't translate to your organization, look at who's already doing it. When I worked in the US federal government, I saw a contract that required code to be delivered on physical disks in triplicate, in case one was lost or damaged. A decade later, the first commit from the Consumer Financial Protection Bureau (CFPB) landed on GitHub; not long after, the first commit from the White House; and eventually hundreds of government agencies were modernizing how they served citizens across thousands of public repositories. **If federal agencies can work in the open, your team's objection is a preference, not a constraint.**

What you lose when work stays hidden

Hidden work doesn't just cost you duplicated effort—those costs are covered above. The deeper problem is structural: hidden work makes your organization *illegible*. When decisions travel through DMs and hallway conversations, the organization becomes a system nobody can fully inspect. You can't challenge a decision you didn't know anyone made. You can't build on context that lives in someone's head. You can't safely change a process when no one can tell you why it exists. It's like walking into a building with no blueprints—you can see the walls, but you have no idea which ones are load-bearing until you start knocking them down.

Organizations that struggle most with remote work never had strong documentation habits to begin with. They relied on proximity and institutional memory—two things that don't survive the transition to distributed teams, or, for that matter, a key person's two-week vacation. Working in the open isn't just better for remote teams; it reveals whether your organization has the communication habits that make any team successful.

> **Common objection: "We can't work in the open—it's too risky."** This conflates "open" with "public." Working in the open doesn't mean broadcasting everything to the world—it means making your work visible to the right people at the right time, defaulting to organizational transparency rather than secrecy. **The real risk isn't openness; it's opacity.**

Most resistance to working in the open comes from two fears: that visibility invites criticism, and that sharing early work damages your credibility. The opposite is true. Working in the open catches problems early—like Toyota's andon cord, which lets any worker stop the assembly line the moment they spot a defect (more on that in *The Andon Principle for Knowledge Work*)—before they become expensive. Hiding work until it's "ready" is like developing on a long-running feature branch—the longer you wait to merge, the more painful the conflicts become. Ideas work the same way: early sharing reduces friction, late sharing compounds it.

Organizations that default to openness build institutional memory without trying. Someone from a different team spots a connection to their own work. A new hire inherits context instead of mysteries. The effect compounds—teams get smarter with age instead of losing knowledge every time someone leaves. (For how to build the systems that make this automatic, see *Documentation as a Superpower*.)

> **For managers: Your transparency is the permission slip your team is waiting for.** If they never see you work through hard decisions publicly, ask for help, or share incomplete work, they'll assume openness is a trap—no matter what you say in meetings. Share one rough idea this week in a public channel. The first time your team sees you say "I'm not sure about this yet, but here's my thinking..." in an issue, you've done more for your team's culture than any transparency initiative ever could. For the practical mechanics, see *Leaders Show Their Work*.

> **For individual contributors: Openness compounds in ways closed work can't.** Every decision you document in an issue, every PR description you write thoughtfully, every design discussion

> you contribute to—it all becomes searchable, linkable evidence of your judgment. Six months from now, when someone asks "why did we choose this approach?" the answer is already there. That's the kind of institutional contribution that shows up in promotion packets—not because you promoted yourself, but because the record did it for you.

Visible work that nobody has time to read is just a well-organized secret. Making work open is half the equation—the other half is rethinking *when* and *how* people engage with it.

Why You Should Work Asynchronously

> **TL;DR:** Putting decisions in writing catches problems early, includes everyone regardless of time zone or meeting stamina, and stops you repeating avoidable mistakes. Keep relying on meetings and you're guaranteed to miss critical input and pay for it in costly rework.

The best comment on a product document I ever received came from a colleague in Japan. She'd spotted a fatal flaw that everyone in the original meeting had missed—because she wasn't *in* that meeting. She was asleep. But when she woke up eight hours later and read the document, she had time to think deeply over her morning matcha, catch the issue, and write a thoughtful response that saved us weeks of rework and protected countless users.

That's async working exactly as designed. Don't limit decisions to whoever happens to show up at 2 PM Eastern. **The best ideas don't arrive on schedule.**

Writing first trades interruption-driven "speed theater" for clarity, inclusion, and momentum. You can recreate[9] the in-person defaults—ambient context, quick questions, shared memory—with shared documents, decision logs, and public channels that outperform the originals because they're searchable and permanent. Done well, async catches problems early—when they're cheap to fix—and lets everyone contribute, regardless of time zone, personality type, or meeting stamina. It's the collaboration equivalent of "shifting left."

> **Pro-Tip: Shifting left** is a software development practice that means "catching bugs earlier in the process." The "left" refers to the left side of a timeline, where design and development happen, as opposed to the right side, where testing and production happen. By writing first, you catch design flaws before they turn into costly bugs in production.

Working in the open solves the *where*—making work visible. Async solves the *when*: decoupling contribution from the clock so people can protect the deep-focus time that produces their best thinking.

Everyone gets a voice

Done right, async is indifferent to time zones—no proximity bias, no information imbalances. There's no "you had to be there" when "there" is "online" and "anytime." You hear from everyone, not just the loudest, fastest to

9. https://ben.balter.com/2020/03/18/tips-for-working-remotely/

unmute, or most extroverted. It's more welcoming to neurodiverse folks, people who go quieter in large groups, or anyone who needs time to gather their thoughts.

> **Pro-Tip:** Inclusion doesn't happen automatically. If you're pitching async to your organization, expect pushback—sometimes explicit, sometimes subtle. And remember: not everyone feels comfortable commenting on documents or in the open, especially if they're worried about how others will react. You can't have successful async work without psychological safety.

Diverse perspectives only improve outcomes when people have room to develop them. Async provides that room.

Better thinking, faster results

Writing a proposal makes you think through edge cases; reviewers spot issues before you write any code (or roll out any new policies). The discipline of putting something in writing *before* executing catches problems when they're still easy to fix. It's like type-safe code or static analysis—you catch errors at "compile time" rather than "runtime," before the blast radius grows.

Sure, it feels slower at first. But writing first cuts ambiguity, imprecision, and churn, so teams ship better ideas faster. That upfront clarity compounds—fewer misunderstandings, less rework, and shared understanding instead of parallel interpretations. **Write it down now, or debug the miscommunication or ambiguity later.**

> **For managers: Writing-first culture starts with your proposals.** Proposals are the keyword there, not mandates or fiats. The next time you're drafting a policy change or team initiative, write it up as a document with a comment period instead of presenting it in a meeting. You'll get higher-quality feedback—people will have time to think rather than react—and you'll model the exact behavior you want from your team. (For how to make meetings the escalation rather than the default, see the async communications section.)

Your decisions don't disappear

Async work relies on written communication, so you document decisions instead of letting them disappear into forgotten meetings. Think of it as caching for organizational knowledge: **you compute the answer once, store it somewhere durable, and everyone after you can retrieve it instantly** instead of recalculating from scratch. How many times have you left a meeting only to discover, weeks later, that everyone "agreed" on something different? Meeting notes—if they exist at all—read like horoscopes: vague enough to support any interpretation. Open work makes decisions *findable*; async makes them *durable*. Visibility without persistence is a live demo nobody recorded.

> **For individual contributors: Durable decisions protect your time.** When past decisions are documented and linkable, you stop relitigating them. The next time someone asks "why did we choose this approach?" you send a URL instead of scheduling a meeting. That's time you get back for actual work.

Time to actually learn

Most of us don't learn at the speed of conversation. Async gives you space to watch, participate gradually, and reflect—on both the problem you're solving and the culture you're joining.

> **Common objection: "Junior engineers need real-time mentoring, not more documents to read."** They need both—and async actually helps. A junior engineer once told me she learned more from reading resolved Issues and PR reviews than from pair programming—she could pause, look things up, and learn at her own pace without someone watching. She could learn from every senior engineer on the team, not just her assigned mentor. A well-written PR review teaches not just one junior today, but every junior who reads it for years.

> Async doesn't replace mentoring—it gives it a longer shelf life.

Async preserves knowledge *and* protects the time to create it.

> **Pro-Tip:** One of my favorite examples came from GitHub's own 404 page. For years its source carried a giant inline comment telling the next engineer *not* to make the page DRY (Don't Repeat Yourself). It read: "I bet you're here to remove those nasty inline styles, DRY up these templates and make 'em nice and re-usable, right? Please, don't." The repetition was the point. External dependencies become a liability the moment something breaks, so a page that has to render even when everything else is down should stand on its own. No policy, no rule, no meeting—just an inline comment that passed the lesson forward to every engineer who opened that file for years to come.
>
> That's async knowledge transfer at its purest: write the lesson down where the next person will trip over it, and it teaches long after you've moved on.

Reclaim your calendar

Async eliminates the information-sharing meetings that eat your day, freeing knowledge workers (especially managers) to focus on hard problems instead of performative status updates. When was the last time you had an entire uninterrupted afternoon to just *think*? If you had to check your calendar to answer that, you already know the problem.

> **Common objection: "Async creates distance and disconnection."** This confuses *synchronous* with *connected*. Teams that rely on constant real-time communication burn out faster and feel *less* connected than async-first teams. Synchronous communication favors whoever's available, creating an always-on culture where stepping away feels like falling behind. Async, done well, replaces rapid-fire interruptions with considered responses—giving people time to contribute their best thinking, not just their fastest, and respecting their lives outside of work. The strongest professional relationships aren't built on constant availability—they're built on trust, follow-through, and respect for each other's time.

That respect for each other's time has structural consequences—ones explored in depth in *Parallelization and Flow*.

Unblock yourself and keep moving

Async requires non-blocking workflows—parallelizing work[10] and protecting flow states. Break work into smaller, independent pieces so no one's stuck waiting on someone else's output. Document decisions and con-

10. https://remote.com/resources/insights-center/why-you-should-be-doing-async-work

text upfront so the next person can pick up where you left off without scheduling a "quick sync." Post your draft, tag a reviewer, and move on to the next task instead of hovering—non-blocking reviews keep the whole team moving.

> **For managers: Champion async at the decision point, not in the abstract.** The next time you're about to schedule a meeting to share a decision or status update, write it up instead. Post it in a public channel with a clear deadline for questions. Your team will follow your lead—when they see writing replace meetings, the culture shifts one decision at a time.

> **For individual contributors: Async is the great equalizer for deep thinkers.** If your best ideas come after staring at a problem for an hour—not in a meeting where the loudest voice wins—async work lets you contribute at your peak. Use the flexibility to work when you're sharpest, batch your communication so it's high-signal, and let the quality of your written output speak louder than hours logged. For strategies on making your async work visible, see *Work Loudly*.

The how-to is straightforward. The mindset shift is harder. Async changes your expectations—you start noticing how many meetings could have been a document, how many "quick syncs" were status theater, how much better your thinking gets when you have time to *actually think*. Once you've shipped a major feature across three time zones without a single scheduled meeting, synchronous-by-default feels like dial-up—technically functional, but why would you go back? And once you stop requiring everyone to be online at the same time, a bigger question surfaces: why require them to be in the same place at all?

Async is powerful in any office. But its full potential clicks when you pair it with remote and distributed work—where async isn't a nice optimization but the only thing that scales across time zones and geographies.

Why Remote and Distributed Work Matters

> **TL;DR:** Remote and async work isn't a trend—it's how top teams win better talent, higher output, and lasting engagement by letting people work when and where they thrive. Stick with the old ways and you'll struggle to attract, retain, or get the best from your team.

Most "office jobs" already are remote jobs—badly. Your calendar is a patchwork of video calls with people in other buildings, other cities, other time zones. You commute ninety minutes to sit in an open-plan office and immediately put on headphones so you can concentrate. **The office isn't where the work happens; it's where the commute ends.** Remote work doesn't change what you do—it drops the pretense that geography matters and lets you optimize for the work itself.

Work when you're at your best

Remote work fits your peak hours—whether that's 6 AM or midnight. Without a physical office dictating the schedule, you can match your work to your energy instead of the other way around. A Stanford experiment[11] found a 13% productivity gain from working from home—suggestive on its own, and consistent with what most remote workers already know: flexibility improves performance, not just satisfaction. Design your own workspace—one optimized for how *you* work, not for maximum desks per square foot.

> 💻 **For individual contributors: Own your schedule, but make it legible.** Working when you're sharpest is the point—but share your working hours with your team so they know when to expect responses. A quick note in your profile or team doc ("I'm usually heads-down 6–10 AM, available for sync after lunch") removes guesswork and earns trust.

> 🤔 **Common objection: "Without supervision, people will just slack off."** This says more about your management style than your employees. If the only thing keeping someone productive is a manager physically watching them, you have a performance management problem, not a location problem. Study after study—from Stanford[12] to Microsoft[13] to

11. https://inequality.stanford.edu/publications/media/details/does-working-home-work-evidence-chinese-experiment

> Prodoscore[14]—shows remote workers log *more* hours, not fewer. The real risk isn't slacking off; it's burnout from never disconnecting.

Office space isn't free

Office space costs real money. Commercial real estate runs an estimated $10,000–$15,000 per employee annually[15] in major tech hubs—that's rent, utilities, office supplies, and facilities management. Go remote and you can redirect those savings into things that matter: higher salaries, better development tools, or new projects—not to mention swag and remote-friendly perks. **Every square foot you don't rent is a square foot you can invest in people.**

Productivity gains are nice. But the bigger unlock is *who* you get to work with.

Hire from anywhere, not just nearby

Go remote and you can recruit the best people from anywhere, not just within commuting distance. A team spread across continents has seen different problems, worked in different markets, and brings experiences you'd never find in a single metro area. Organizations

12. https://nbloom.people.stanford.edu/research
13. https://www.nature.com/articles/s41562-021-01196-4
14. https://www.prodoscore.com/workplace-productivity/
15. https://www.commercialcafe.com/office-market-trends/us/

that insist on office-only end up with teams that are less diverse geographically and demographically—and narrower perspectives yield narrower solutions.

> **For managers: A global talent pool demands a global hiring process.** Your existing process probably assumes local candidates—whiteboard interviews, in-office "culture fit" lunches, overlapping business hours. Rethink it: async take-home exercises, structured rubrics, and interview panels that work across time zones. Opening the aperture is the easy part; ensuring your process doesn't filter it right back down is the real work. For the full playbook, see *Hiring for Remote-First Teams* and *Remote Onboarding Done Right.*

> **For individual contributors:** You're no longer limited to jobs within commuting distance or forced to leave friends and family behind to accept that next offer. The best role for your skills might be three time zones away—and that's fine.

Talent pools matter at the org level. At the individual level, what matters is whether your job leaves room for your actual life.

A job that fits your life

Remote work lets people build jobs around their lives—not lives around their jobs. When was the last time you rearranged something that mattered—a doctor's appointment, a kid's recital, a midday run—because it conflicted with a meeting that could have been an email? That flexibility means less stress, less burnout, and people who stick around. **A job that fits your life outlasts one that fights it.**

Distance doesn't mean disconnected

In most offices, influence is a function of proximity. The engineer who sits near the VP of Engineering gets pulled into hallway conversations about strategy. The team at headquarters shapes the roadmap while satellite offices learn about it after the fact. Seating charts quietly become org charts—and the people furthest from power have the least voice, regardless of how good their ideas are.

Remote work breaks that pattern. When everyone joins from the same-sized video tile or the same shared channel, a developer in Buenos Aires has exactly the same access as one sitting next to the Chief Technology Officer (CTO). Geography stops being a proxy for organizational influence, and the best ideas surface from anywhere—not just the desks closest to the corner office.

GitHub didn't always work this way. Early on, the gravity of headquarters was real, especially for formal leaders—the unspoken assumption was that the closer you sat to the action in San Francisco, the faster you'd rise. One rapidly rising star believed it enough to move their entire family across the country to be there. And it worked: they earned a well-deserved promotion. But the more telling part came years later. As GitHub leaned further into remote and its leaders spread across the globe, proximity stopped being the price of advancement. That same person was able to move back to their hometown—no longer trading where they wanted to live for where they wanted their career to go.

> **Pro-Tip:** For several years, I was tapped to represent GitHub at the foreign press dinner during GitHub Universe, GitHub's flagship conference. More than once, it was just me and the CFO—the two of us at the table on behalf of the entire company. We rarely crossed paths the rest of the year beyond the occasional briefing, and yet sitting literally shoulder to shoulder with an executive never felt awkward. If anything, it was one of the best ways I found to connect. That's what working in the open does to hierarchy: when the default is a same-sized video tile and a shared channel, you get used to engaging across levels, so a dinner beside the CFO is just dinner.

> **Pro-Tip:** In my first role at GitHub, I spent more than half my time on the road—conferences, customer visits, agency meetings, a rolling calendar of airports and hotel rooms. I expected to fall behind: miss the unrecorded decisions, lose track of who was working on what, watch the stationary engineers quietly accumulate the context I couldn't.
>
> None of that happened. The work lived in issues and pull requests I could read from a plane; decisions were documented in threads I could catch up

> on at 6 AM in a new time zone; my colleagues didn't need me in a specific chair to include me. Remote work turned out to be the most travel-friendly arrangement I'd ever had—not despite being distributed, but *because* of it.

At GitHub, we tried a bunch of ways to create serendipity—random Slack pair threads, "get to know you" channels, virtual coffee roulettes. Some felt forced. But our annual summit—where you couldn't predict who you'd bump into because we deliberately mixed teams at meals—actually created the conversations that hallway proximity never guaranteed. We also had open Slack channels (`#peloton`, `#dogcom`, `#catops`, `#livemas`, etc.) where anyone could jump in, and that's where unexpected collaboration happened most. The tools and rituals that worked weren't the ones that mimicked the office; they were the ones that were *intentional*—that forced overlap in a structured way.

> **Pro-Tip:** Early at GitHub, there was a practice called "travel buddies": if you were headed to a conference to speak or staff the booth, you were encouraged to invite a colleague you didn't already work with closely to come along. I used it constantly during conference runs, and it was the single best tool I had for meeting the Hubbers I'd later end up collaborating with tightly. One of them showed up at the airport holding a hand-lettered sign with my GitHub handle on it—partly a joke,

> partly because they were genuinely that excited to finally meet in person. GitHub hasn't run that program for a while, but the shape of it is worth copying, especially with locals.

> 🤔 **Common objection: "Remote kills culture."** Remote work doesn't kill culture—it exposes what was actually culture versus what was just proximity. At GitHub, we did lose something: that random conversation with someone outside your org, the serendipitous run-in with someone from finance or legal. We had to be deliberate about replacing it. Some attempts worked; some didn't. But that loss forced us to be *intentional* about what we valued, rather than assuming the building itself created culture. The engineers who felt most connected to the organization weren't the ones closest to the office—they were the ones most plugged into the open, documented culture.
>
> Strong remote cultures run on shared values, clear communication, intentional connection, and demonstrated trust. Remote work forces you to articulate what your culture is, instead of assuming proximity creates it.

Culture is about what you value, not where you sit. And as it turns out, where you sit has costs of its own—literal ones.

Built to survive disruption

The COVID-19 pandemic stress-tested every organization's infrastructure at once. Teams already doing remote work kept shipping code while others scrambled to set up virtual private networks (VPNs), video conferencing, and the unmute button. A remote-first approach isn't just about pandemic preparedness—it's about building organizations that can handle whatever comes next.

> **Pro-Tip:** It doesn't take a pandemic to disrupt work. In 2026, a global oil crisis pushed countries across Europe and Asia to mandate work from home to curb fuel consumption, while severe weather routinely shuttered offices for days at a time. Distributed teams kept shipping through all of it. Remote work is resilient work.

Think of it like designing a distributed software system. You build in redundancy and fault tolerance so there's no single point of failure. Remote-first organizations work the same way—they keep running even when individual components face disruption. **Your office has a single point of failure: its address.** Remote-first doesn't.

> **For managers: Build continuity into your defaults, not your disaster plan.** If your team's ability to work remotely depends on a last-minute scramble, it's not resilience—it's luck. Test it: can a new hire onboard without visiting the office? Can your team ship a release if headquarters goes dark

> tomorrow? The answers reveal whether you have real business continuity or just a business continuity *document*.

> **For individual contributors:** Career resilience means your job doesn't depend on a building staying open. When disruption hits, you're already set up to keep delivering—and that stability compounds over time.

Less commuting, smaller footprint

The average American spends nearly an hour each day[16] sitting in traffic or on public transit. That's almost five hours a week—over 200 hours a year—that vanishes into commuting. Think what you could do with an extra month: ship that feature you've been putting off, finally learn that framework you bookmarked six months ago, or—radical thought—have a hobby.

Fewer commuters mean fewer emissions and less congestion. You get your life back, your company saves on office costs, and the planet gets a break. **Rare is the policy that's good for workers, good for business, and good for the atmosphere all at once.**

> **For managers: Organizations that resist remote work are competing on legacy hardware.** The

16. https://www.census.gov/topics/employment/commuting/guidance/acs-1yr.html

> talent market has changed—engineers increasingly expect remote work as a baseline, not a perk. Companies that demand full-time office presence compete for a smaller pool of candidates, often at higher salaries, while watching top performers leave for organizations that offer flexibility. And when a company reverses course and orders everyone back, that's an operating-model failure, not the real-estate decision it's dressed up as—a case I make in full in *Making the Most of In-Person Time*. The best talent has options now, and many of those options don't require pants.

Hiring great people and giving them flexibility gets you partway there. But the tools and workflows your team uses every day aren't neutral infrastructure—they actively shape the work that comes out the other end.

Four arguments, one operating system. Working in the open prevents duplicated effort and makes decisions auditable. Asynchronous communication frees teams from the tyranny of overlapping calendars. Remote and distributed work turns geography from a constraint into a hiring advantage. And *how* you work matters as much as *what* you work on—tools and processes designed for offices import their dysfunction along with them. The case isn't that any one of these works on its own; it's that together they form the substrate everything else in this book stands on.

Key takeaways

- Work in private and you'll rediscover the same dead ends your teammates already hit—because nobody could see what anyone else was doing. Working in the open turns your process into something the team builds on instead of a mystery to reverse-engineer.
- Putting decisions in writing catches problems early, includes everyone regardless of time zone or meeting stamina, and stops you repeating avoidable mistakes. Keep relying on meetings and you're guaranteed to miss critical input and pay for it in costly rework.
- Remote and async work isn't a trend—it's how top teams win better talent, higher output, and lasting engagement by letting people work when and where they thrive. Stick with the old ways and you'll struggle to attract, retain, or get the best from your team.

Core Principles of Open and Async-First Teams

Every distributed team needs an operating system—not tools, but principles that let people move fast without constant meetings. You can have your stack perfectly configured and still ship at half speed if your culture treats interruptions as normal and deep work as a luxury. Async doesn't mean slow or unresponsive. It means choosing when to respond, how to unblock others, and when real-time sync is the right escalation.

You've probably been on a team that had every tool imaginable—Slack, Jira, GitHub, Confluence, a wiki nobody updates—and still couldn't ship without three meetings and a DM thread. You've also been on a team that ran on email and a shared spreadsheet and somehow moved faster. The difference wasn't the tools. It was whether people shared a set of assumptions about how work should flow.

Those assumptions are what I mean by *principles*—not values posters, but the mental models your team reaches for when nobody's around to ask. Should I ping someone or open an issue? Wait for permission or ship the draft? Block on this review or pick up the next thing? Good principles make those answers conscious, consistent, and fast.

The three principles—parallelization and flow, impact over input, and developer happiness—form a system. Protecting flow without measuring impact gives people uninterrupted time to work on the wrong things. Measuring impact without protecting happiness burns people out. Optimizing for happiness without enabling flow means your team enjoys their jobs but can't ship. Each principle shores up the other two.

> **Common objection: "These sound great in theory, but my team has deadlines."** So does every team that's ever adopted these principles successfully. Async-first practices don't ask you to slow down—they ask you to stop doing what was already slowing you down. Status meetings that could be a written update. Decisions that get relitigated because nobody documented the first conversation. Blocked work because the one person with context is asleep. **Deadlines aren't the reason to skip these principles; they're the reason to adopt**

> **them. Async isn't slow; it's choosing your interrupts.**

> **For managers: Your job is to protect these principles when organizational pressure pushes against them.** It's easy to agree that impact matters more than input—until someone asks why your team isn't in more meetings. You'll need to defend deep focus time, measure outcomes instead of activity, and resist the gravitational pull of performative busyness. Hold the principles as engineering, not ideology.

> **For individual contributors: These principles are your shield and your argument.** When someone questions why you're not online at 9 AM or why you declined a meeting, you need language to explain—not defensively, but confidently. Know them well enough to advocate for the working conditions that produce your best work. You shouldn't need to justify deep focus any more than you need

> **to justify using a linter—the value is self-evident once you've seen the alternative.**

The next three chapters cover the specifics: what to optimize for, how to keep work flowing, and why the fastest teams meet least.

Carving out space for deep work in a world wired for constant interruption is the hard part—agreeing it matters is easy. The real trick is building systems where the default mode isn't "wait your turn"—it's relentless progress. That's where parallelization and flow come in.

Parallelization and Flow

> **TL;DR:** Async communication and parallel work streams defend the deep focus where your best work happens. Keep treating attention as interruptible and you trade real progress for constant busyness—and burn out your team doing it.

You're three hours into debugging a race condition—call stack in one tab, log output in another, a mental model of the threading behavior you've been building since lunch. Then: *ping*. A chat notification. Someone needs your input on a sprint-planning question *they* think is urgent. By the time you've context-switched and come back, the mental model is gone. You rebuild from scratch. Another thirty minutes lost. Interrupt-driven work culture, working exactly as designed. **Everyone else controls your time, not you.** And it's silently destroying your team's output.

In software, a non-blocking call lets other commands execute simultaneously. Async communication works the same way. That *parallelization* creates space for *flow state,* the uninterrupted stretches where real progress gets made.

> **Pro-Tip:** If your to-do list is a single-threaded queue, you're doing it wrong. Structure your work like an async runtime: one primary task in the foreground demanding deep focus, one or two secondary tasks you can yield to when the primary blocks, and a handful of small items to fill the gaps between meetings. The goal isn't multitasking—it's having ready work so you never stall.

Do more at once, not one thing at a time

Async mirrors the engineering concept of concurrency — `Promise.all()`, not `await` one-at-a-time—but for human workflows. Sent a message? Don't idle—switch to another task. Waiting on a code review? Pick up the next issue. External dependency blocking one thread? Keep moving on others. Think of your workday as an event loop: the goal isn't to process one request to completion before accepting the next—it's to keep the loop spinning, always making progress on *something* rather than stalling.

> **For managers: Design work to be parallelizable.** Break projects into small, independent pieces with

> clear interfaces. If every task requires a hand-off meeting or a blocking approval, your team can't parallelize—and you've become the bottleneck. Write clear acceptance criteria in issues, keep decisions documented, and let people pick up the next item without waiting for you to assign it.

> **Pro-Tip:** Software development evolved from "waterfall" (finish one phase completely before starting the next) to "agile" (iterate with frequent feedback). The same evolution applies to how *you* work: don't wait until your proposal is perfect to share it. Ship a rough draft, get feedback, iterate. If you find yourself sitting on work because "it's not ready yet," you're stuck in waterfall thinking (for more on the transition from waterfall to agile in large organizations, see Towards a More Agile Government).[17]

The magic of uninterrupted time

Parallelization only pays off if you can go deep on any single thread. Flow—that state where you're fully immersed in the task—is where the real gains live. **A two-hour block of focused time isn't the same as four thirty-minute blocks.** Think about the gym: if it takes 20 minutes to hit your stride but you only have 30, you might skip it entirely. Deep thinking works the same way—it doesn't have an on/off switch. It builds gradually

17. https://ben.balter.com/2011/11/29/towards-a-more-agile-government/

and shatters instantly. In systems terms, constant context-switching is like memory paging in an overwhelmed system—the overhead of swapping state in and out costs more than the work itself.

Protect uninterrupted time

A former colleague once said,[18] "Chat is inherently asynchronous; tapping me on my shoulder is inherently being a jerk." Research[19] backs him up: knowledge workers spend only about 12 minutes on a task before switching, and once interrupted, take more than 25 minutes—after juggling other tasks—to return to it. Every "quick question" carries a hidden tax: the context switch, the rebuild of mental state, the loss of flow. **Interruptions don't steal minutes; they steal hours.**

Don't "walk over" to a coworker's desk, virtual or otherwise. Use tickets, issues, and chat instead of "just-in-time" interruptions. Your question can wait. Their flow state can't. (Yes, even if you think it can't. It almost certainly can.)

> 🤨 **Common objection: "But we need to stay connected and know what everyone's working on."** Connection doesn't require interruption. The most effective remote teams stay connected through shared work artifacts—issues, pull requests, documents—not constant pings. You'll learn more from

18. https://speakerdeck.com/holman/how-github-works-v2
19. https://ics.uci.edu/~gmark/CHI2005.pdf

> their public work than from interrupting them to ask. Open source proves this: thousands of contributors stay connected through shared artifacts, not synchronous check-ins.

Teams that optimize for flow end up *more* connected than teams that optimize for constant communication. **Visibility beats interruption.** What someone's working on, why they chose an approach, how far along they are —it's all legible in the work itself, there whenever you need it instead of only when you can both get on a call.

Getting there takes practice. Default to public channels instead of DMs. Write things down instead of having hallway conversations. Trust people to catch up on their own schedule rather than pulling them into real-time discussions. The payoff? Everyone gets focus time back *and* sees more of each other's work.

Turn off notifications—especially email

Your email client is not a chat app. Email was designed with a cultural expectation of delay—it's correspondence, not conversation. Yet somewhere along the way, every inbox grew a badge counter, every message spawned a desktop pop-up, and what was once asynchronous became *why haven't you responded to my email from 20 minutes ago?* That pop-up notification isn't a feature—it's an engagement antipattern. Email and chat apps are optimized for *their* engagement metrics, not *your* productivity. Turning off desktop notifications isn't radical—it's refusing to let someone else's engagement KPI (Key Performance Indicator) dictate your attention.

Slack is trickier. Chat carries a stronger expectation of responsiveness—which is part of what makes it useful. But "available" doesn't mean "monitoring every channel in real-time." The fix isn't quitting Slack; it's checking it on your terms. Close the window during focused work. Turn on Do Not Disturb. Let notifications queue up rather than burst-interrupt you every 11 minutes.

The underlying shift is from *interrupt handler* to *cron job*. An interrupt handler treats every notification as a demand on attention—the inbox as a runqueue that other people manage for you. A cron job checks at intentional intervals: between tasks, at the top of the hour, before and after lunch. The messages get answered. But the deep work gets done *first,* with the full cognitive resources it requires. **Check your inbox like a cron job, not an interrupt handler.**

> **For individual contributors: Treat notification settings as part of your development environment.** Engineers will spend a weekend tuning `.vimrc`, fine-tuning IDE keybindings, and remapping caps lock to escape—then run Slack and Gmail on factory defaults. The tools that interrupt you most often get the least configuration. Apply the same rigor to your communication tools: mute channels you only need to check weekly, set key-

> words for topics that actually require your attention, and batch everything else into a triage window.

Speed up by slowing down to think

> 🤔 **Common objection: "Brainstorming and creative work require real-time interaction."** Real-time brainstorming often favors the loudest, fastest voices, not the best ideas. Async brainstorming gives everyone time to think deeply and contribute equally. Introverts and careful thinkers can shine. The "energy" of live sessions often produces shallow ideas that sound exciting in the moment but don't survive written scrutiny. Pair an async brainstorm with a synchronous discussion for real-time creative energy *and* the depth of written reflection.

A longer cycle time actually speeds things up. A single batch might *feel* slower because you're waiting for a thoughtful reply instead of stream-of-consciousness chat. But the team ships faster because you're batching communication like database transactions—committing ten operations at once instead of after every single write. You're:

- parallelizing work to reduce blockers,

- reducing decision churn through clarity, thoroughness, and forward-thinking (fast thinking vs. slow thinking),[20]
- shifting from sender-optimized messages to one-to-many communication that serves the long tail of recipients, and
- building shared context that increases the team's tempo, quality, and resilience.

> **For managers: Protect your team's focus time like you'd protect your budget.** Declare "no-meeting mornings" or block team-wide focus hours on the shared calendar—and actually enforce them. Batch your own questions into a single async message instead of five separate pings throughout the day. Mark recurring status meetings as optional and cancel them when the agenda is empty. If you're the one interrupting deep work, no amount of "focus time" policies will save your team's flow.

Managers protect the team's time. ICs protect their own:

> **For individual contributors: Your best work happens in uninterrupted blocks.** Schedule focused time on your calendar and defend it. Use status indicators honestly—"busy" should mean something. Turn off desktop notifications during deep work; your phone can handle true emergencies. When blocked, switch to parallel tasks rather

20. https://en.wikipedia.org/wiki/Thinking,_Fast_and_Slow

> than waiting. Document work-in-progress so others can continue where you left off—and so you can pick it back up after context switches. Responsiveness and productivity aren't the same thing, and the colleagues who matter will respect your focus time.

Parallelization and flow aren't productivity hacks—they're how teams ship without burning out. Synchronous cultures optimize for *responsiveness*; async cultures optimize for *throughput*. By the time a sync team has scheduled a meeting to discuss a problem, an async team has already solved it. Protect uninterrupted time, keep multiple work streams moving, and measure impact by what ships—not hours logged.

Impact Over Input

> **TL;DR:** The correlation between hours worked and value created isn't just weak for knowledge work—past a point, more hours produce less. Optimizing for what people deliver rather than how long they're online produces better work, prevents burnout, and frees both managers and ICs from the performance theater that quietly kills remote teams.

Here's a dirty secret about knowledge work: your best idea this month might arrive at 2 AM while you're half-asleep. Your worst week might be the one where you logged the most hours. **Hours worked ≠ value created.** Everyone nods along with this in the abstract—but remote work is where the principle actually gets tested, because the old substitute for measurement (watching people sit at desks) disappears entirely.

Remote work killed the clock

The eight-hour workday[21] made sense when output scaled with time on the factory floor. Remote work didn't just challenge that norm—it removed the enforcement mechanism. You can't watch butts in seats when seats are distributed across the globe. Suddenly, organizations that had been measuring presence instead of output had to confront the question they'd been avoiding: how do we actually know if someone is productive? Measuring productivity by hours worked is like measuring code quality by lines of code or number of commits —a vanity metric that tells you nothing about value and is easily gamed by smart engineers.

> **For managers: Stop counting hours—start counting outcomes.** If you're still approving time-off requests or tracking "core hours," ask yourself what signal those controls actually give you. Replace activity proxies with delivery metrics: what shipped, what unblocked others, what improved outcomes. When someone on your team delivers a week's worth of impact in three days, celebrate it—don't wonder what they're doing the other two days.

21. https://en.wikipedia.org/wiki/Eight-hour_day

Not every manager has made this shift yet. If yours hasn't:

> **For individual contributors: If your manager still values hours, make impact impossible to ignore.** Keep a running log of what you shipped, what you unblocked, and what you improved—even if nobody asked for it. Quantify where you can—reduced build times, improved reliability, shipped features that moved metrics. At reviews, lead with "here's what I delivered and what it meant for the team," not "here's how many hours I worked." You're training your organization to evaluate you on the right axis.

Hours are a terrible proxy. But so is *when* those hours happen.

What you deliver matters more than when you deliver it

Async work makes this principle operational. When your team spans six time zones, enforcing 9-to-5 is either impossible or it means "9-to-5 in headquarters' time zone"—exporting one office's commute to people who never agreed to it. Sometimes the fix is obvious at 3 PM your time. Sometimes the answer clicks during a morning run while your colleagues are asleep. The goal isn't to control *when* work happens but to ensure *what* ships matters.

> **Common objection: "How do I know remote workers are actually working?"** This is the wrong question—and a red flag when managers ask it. The right question is: "How do I know they're delivering value?" If you can't answer that for remote workers, you couldn't answer it for office workers either—you were just substituting presence for measurement. That's theater, not management. Impact-over-input thinking forces you to define what success looks like and measure whether your team achieves it. That's better management, regardless of where people sit.

Every manager *should* define what "done" (and "good") looks like and measure whether their team achieves it—but few bother until remote work forces the issue.

> **For managers:** As a manager, **I don't track my team's hours.** Tracking hours signals distrust rather than good management. I care that they deliver quality work, meet deadlines, and support their colleagues. If someone thrives on a 30-hour week—great. If they're most productive starting at noon and working until 8 PM because that's what their time zone or their life demands, fine. What I *do* expect: responsiveness, availability, and a con-

> sistently high bar for quality. **Trust outcomes, not appearances.**

Some roles—on-call rotations, customer-facing support, coordinated releases—genuinely require availability during set hours. Impact over input doesn't abolish schedules; it refuses to confuse *presence* with *productivity*.

> **Pro-Tip:** A security leader I worked with lived this in the clearest way I've seen. His team caught a steady stream of incidents that ate nights and weekends—the shape of the job, not an exception to it. Rather than let the extra hours quietly accumulate, he made an explicit agreement with his team and his manager: since he was consistently working well past forty hours, he'd take Fridays off in any week without an active incident. The arrangement was written down, manager-endorsed, and visible to his peers so nobody had to guess why he was offline. Once proven, this practice was extended to the entire team as a norm.
>
> That's what impact-over-input looks like operationalized: match the work schedule to the *actual shape* of the job rather than to a default rectangle that has nothing to do with either.

The measurement challenge holds regardless of schedule: what does "impact" actually mean for each role, and how do you make it legible?

> **For managers: Make "impact" concrete, not abstract.** Define what impact looks like at each level and make those expectations visible—especially across time zones where managers can't rely on osmosis to communicate standards. During performance reviews, ask yourself: Am I evaluating what this person achieved, or how much effort they appeared to spend?

> **For individual contributors: Lean into your natural rhythms.** Remote work lets you step away when inspiration wanes—take that walk, run errands, reset. Nobody benefits from desk-warming. If you can exceed expectations by working odd hours that suit your time zone and your life, do it. Now you have the language to advocate for it.

None of this matters if impact stays invisible.

Making results visible

Impact-over-input thinking only works if impact is visible—and visibility is exactly what remote teams struggle with. "Trust me, I'm doing great work" isn't a system—it's a hope. For engineering teams, that means tracking indicators like **cycle time** (start to ship), **throughput** (work shipped per period), and **quality indicators** (bugs, incidents, rework). These metrics work across time zones and don't require a manager to be in the room watching.

What you *don't* need to measure: whether everyone attended standup, how accurately teams estimated stories, or how many retrospective sticky notes your team generated. Think of it like monitoring a production system—you track request latency, error rates, and throughput, not how many times someone SSH'd into the server. **Measure the system's outputs, not its rituals.**

> **Pro-Tip:** At GitHub, engineering performance ran on a career ladder paired with self-assessment and peer feedback—not seat time, not PR count, not hours online. The rubric asked what your work *did*, not how much of it there was.
>
> More than once, I watched it cut the wrong way. One quarter, a program manager spent every cycle on the unglamorous work nobody was watching—hiring pipelines during a hiring slowdown, internal mobility, cross-training across teams so we wouldn't be stuck when headcount opened back up. Quietly critical work. It didn't ship a feature. It didn't show up in a launch post.
>
> Meanwhile, a peer who'd picked a less structurally important but visibly shipping project that aligned with company priorities in the moment came out ahead at calibration. Same quarter. Same effort. Different legibility. **Impact isn't just output; it's output aimed at what matters—*and* documented**

> **so the people doing calibration can see it.** Once you're measuring the right thing, hours stop being even a useful proxy.

> ■ **For individual contributors: Translate your work into the language of impact.** When preparing for performance reviews, lead with outcomes: problems solved, value created, colleagues helped. "I refactored the auth module" is activity. "I reduced auth-related incidents by 40% and cut onboarding time for new engineers by a week" is impact. In remote organizations where your manager can't observe your effort firsthand, this framing is how you make your work legible.
>
> **Ruthless prioritization is how impact scales.** Write down the three to five things that matter most this quarter, stack-rank them by impact, and draw a line. Every minute spent below that line is stolen from above it.

Impact over input doesn't stop at metrics—it reshapes how you work day-to-day. When results matter more than hours, you start protecting the conditions that produce them: focused time, fewer meetings, tooling that doesn't fight you, and people who aren't grinding through bureaucracy on the way to the actual work. **Optimize for outcomes long enough and you'll find yourself optimizing for the people producing them.**

Optimize for Developer Happiness

> **TL;DR:** A happy engineer isn't bribed with snacks; they're one whose laptop boots, whose calendar has a four-hour block on Tuesday, and whose pull requests get reviewed within a day. Lose any one of those and the rest of this book is decoration.

Burnout and friction show up in velocity—the clever fix nobody attempts, the gnarly bug nobody volunteers for—long before they show up in resignation letters. **Happy developers aren't a perk; they're a leading indicator.** By the time someone quits, you've been paying for it for months.

The causal chain is unsentimental. When I interviewed at GitHub, the founders described their philosophy like this: happy developers make great software, great software makes happy customers, happy customers make happy shareholders. It was a table flip of every business school deck I'd sat through. Shareholder value wasn't the starting point—it was the *output* of treating the people doing the work as though their experience mattered.

I signed up because I believed the chain—and then spent the next dozen-plus years watching it hold up, sometimes in absurd ways.

> **Pro-Tip:** The most over-engineered internal app I ever saw was a reservation system a Hubber built so visiting colleagues could snag tickets to Giants games when they were in San Francisco. Nobody asked for it. It had queues, fairness rules, the works. That's what "happy developers" looks like in practice: people who care enough to over-build the silly thing, because the culture treated their time as theirs to spend. You can't fake that with a ping-pong table and a slogan.

The reason the chain holds is biological, not idealistic. You can't coerce a clever fix for a race condition the way you can coerce a widget onto a conveyor belt. Creative problem-solving runs on engagement, and engagement runs on the absence of friction. Burn people out and you don't just lose them—you lose the work they would have shipped while they were quietly stewing. Gallup's *State of the Global Workplace*[22] puts the global price tag at roughly $10 trillion in lost productivity a year—about 9% of GDP.

> **Common objection: "Developer happiness sounds like an excuse to be unproductive."** It's the

22. https://www.gallup.com/workplace/349484/state-of-the-global-workplace.aspx

> opposite. Removing friction, protecting autonomy, and treating people as creative professionals instead of interchangeable resources—that's what drives shipping speed, retention, and quality. **Happiness is the precondition for productivity in creative work.**

Happiness isn't one thing, though. It's three, owned by three different people.

What organizations do

Organizations set the structural conditions. In distributed teams, these choices echo louder—there's no office culture to mask a hostile system.

Invest in tools—especially the ones that bridge distance

For distributed teams, tooling isn't just a productivity lever—it's the connective tissue replacing physical proximity. Unreliable dev environments, broken chat integrations, and laggy video calls don't just slow people down; they make remote workers feel like second-class citizens.

At GitHub we called these "culture tools" and designed them with the same rigor as GitHub.com itself. We had a `/office me` ChatOps command any Hubber could run before visiting HQ—it collected your comfort foods, the small things that made travel easier. I like sourdough pretzels. They were there every single time I walked in, in every kitchen on every floor. That's a "small" culture tool by any rational accounting. It's also the kind of detail remote employees tell their friends about for years and one that made me feel on equal footing with the locals.

Not every culture tool was that whimsical. GitHub's support team used Halp, a home-grown ticketing app that amounted to GitHub for support requests—emoji, @mentions, and cross-references between related tickets, the same collaboration primitives Hubbers already lived in, pointed at account management instead of a pull request. We could have bought something off the shelf. We built Halp instead because no commercial offering at the time was as obsessed with the developers filing the tickets—internal and external alike—as a tool built by the people who'd answer them. Years after it was retired, Hubbers still miss it.

> **For individual contributors: Don't wait for the org to fix your tooling—start small.** If a broken tool is slowing you down, document the friction and propose a fix. A one-page write-up showing "this costs the team X hours per week, here's an alternative" travels further in async organizations than a complaint in chat. You're the one feeling the pain; you're the best person to articulate it. *Be the PR you want to see in the world.*

Protect autonomy—async-first defaults do this automatically

Autonomy is one of the strongest predictors of engagement in knowledge work, and async-first practices protect it most effectively. When the default is "write it down" instead of "schedule a meeting," you eliminate the approval chains and "alignment" rituals that fragment focus. As a former colleague once put it, **never take no from someone who can't say yes.** Give teams clear outcomes, protect large unbroken blocks of quiet time, and bias toward writing things down instead of convening.

What managers do

Organizations set the stage; managers decide whether a distributed team actually ships or just attends meetings about shipping.

Remove blockers—and use async to absorb the bureaucratic hit

The most valuable thing a remote manager does is usually invisible: the async message that kills a pointless meeting, the escalation that unsticks a cross-team dependency, the "I'll handle that review cycle, you keep coding." If a status report can be satisfied with a link to an issue, send the link. Every piece of organizational noise you filter asynchronously is a synchronous interruption your team never has to absorb.

Protect focus, not attendance

Presence is not progress. A manager who measures engagement by green Slack dots and meeting attendance is measuring compliance—and compliance is the floor, not the ceiling. Default to async. Cancel the meeting that could have been a doc. When an engineer is deep in a hard problem, keep their calendar clear for the next four hours—don't check in to see how it's going.

> **For managers: Audit your team's calendar the way you'd audit a slow query.** Which meetings recur because they're useful, and which recur because nobody's canceled them? Kill one recurring meeting this month and replace it with a written update. Watch what happens to your team's shipping velocity.

Amplify wins out loud

Work that goes unseen may as well not have happened. When an engineer ships something good, say so—in the channel where their skip-level lurks, in the written weekly update, in the promotion packet you're quietly building six months early. Credit costs you nothing and motivates like almost nothing else. Hoarding it, or letting it drift upward to whoever presented last, is malpractice.

> **For managers: In remote teams, amplification is half the job.** Your ICs can't rely on hallway visibili-

> ty to get noticed by leadership. You are the bridge. Make it a weekly habit: find one thing someone on your team shipped and surface it in a public channel, a written update, or a skip-level note. It takes five minutes and compounds into career outcomes. Consider weekly sparkles or shoutouts in your team meetings or weekly reports. **Amplify wins, and do it in a way that makes them visible to the people who can reward them.**

What ICs do for themselves

Here's the part nobody tells you in onboarding: remote work gives you more control over your happiness than any office job—but you have to actually use it.

Set boundaries before you need them

The most burned-out remote engineers I've worked with didn't burn out in a single bad week. They burned out by slowly letting the edges erode—answering one Slack after dinner, then three, then picking up a Saturday incident nobody asked them to handle. Remote work blurs the line between "home" and "office" because they're the same place. Decide, in advance, what your working hours are. Put them in your status. Enforce them when it's inconvenient, because boundaries you only honor when it's easy aren't boundaries.

Protect your own flow—and skip the theater

Block focus time and defend it like a meeting with your skip-level. Batch shallow work—code review, Slack triage, email—into one or two windows instead of letting it fragment every hour. And learn to recognize the remote-specific flavor of productivity theater: the meeting you don't need to attend, the status update that already exists in the issue, the performance of being "available" via green dot instead of doing actual work. Quietly stop performing. The people whose opinion matters are watching what you ship, not how busy you looked while not shipping it.

> **Pro-Tip:** For years, I blocked off the first hour of my day as "triage." I'd go through GitHub and chat notifications, answer the easy ones, and prioritize the harder ones alongside my goals for the day. It kept me in control of my work, instead of letting it control me.

Advocate for what you need, with receipts

"Our tools are bad" is a complaint. "Our build takes fourteen minutes, I run it twenty times a day, and here's a two-week spike that would cut it to three" is a proposal.

Quantify friction. Propose fixes. In distributed teams, this kind of written, evidence-based advocacy travels further than hallway complaints ever could.

> **For individual contributors: If you've pulled every lever available and the environment still makes you miserable, that's signal too.** Sometimes the most important optimization is choosing a team that values developer happiness rather than one that merely claims to. Exit is also a form of advocacy.

The three layers reinforce each other

None of these layers works alone—and in distributed organizations, the gaps between them are more visible. A great manager can't out-hustle broken tooling that makes remote developers feel like second-class citizens. An IC can't boundary their way out of a culture that equates "online" with "productive." But when all three align—structural conditions that bridge distance, managers who protect focus across time zones, and ICs who show up engaged and honest about what they need—the gains stack. Not a perk. A shipping advantage that compounds quarter after quarter.

Three ideas run through this section, and they're more connected than they first appear. Async workflows protect deep focus by treating communication as non-blocking I/O—you stay connected through artifacts, not pings. Impact-over-input thinking frees teams from performance theater that makes remote work feel like surveillance with better Wi-Fi. And developer happiness isn't a budget line for bean bags—it's the leading indicator that tells you whether the first two principles are actually working. Get any one wrong, and friction compounds across the other two.

Together, they form an operating system for distributed teams: protect focus, measure what matters, and keep the people doing the work from burning out while you're busy measuring the wrong things.

Key takeaways

- Async communication and parallel work streams defend the deep focus where your best work happens. Keep treating attention as interruptible and you trade real progress for constant busyness—and burn out your team doing it.
- The correlation between hours worked and value created isn't just weak for knowledge work—past a point, more hours produce less. Optimizing for what people deliver rather than how long they're online produces better work, prevents burnout, and frees both managers and ICs from the performance theater that quietly kills remote teams.
- A happy engineer isn't bribed with snacks; they're one whose laptop boots, whose calendar has a four-hour block on Tuesday, and whose pull requests get reviewed within a day. Lose any one of those and the rest of this book is decoration.

These principles answer *what* to optimize for. The next section—working in the open—answers *how*. Protecting flow and measuring impact only work if the work itself is visible: decisions need permanent addresses, progress needs narration, and institutional memory can't live in someone's head. Principles without practices are poster slogans. Time to make them concrete.

Working in the Open

Working in the open isn't about sharing finished work—it's about making the process, context, and decisions visible from the start, turning individual effort into shared knowledge that compounds. If you've contributed to open source or built in public, you already get it—now apply the same instinct at work.

Most engineers do this naturally outside work. You file a public issue against an open source library before you patch around the bug locally. You write a Stack Overflow answer in the open instead of replying to one person's email. You push a sketch to a side-project repo before it's "ready," because that's how you find out if anyone else cares. The internet trained an entire generation to default-public.

Then we walk into our day jobs and immediately default-private—decisions in DMs, designs in our heads, debates over coffee. Open source contributors figured out decades ago what distributed companies are still relearning: when contributors span every time zone and have never met, the only thing holding the work together is a visible, durable record of what's happening and why. Not ideology—physics. Private knowledge doesn't scale past a handful of people in the same room.

Your company isn't an open source project. But your distributed team faces the same constraint: **if work isn't visible, it might as well not exist.** You can't collaborate asynchronously on something you can't see. You can't give feedback on a decision you didn't know was being made. Async communication is the *mechanism*; openness is the *prerequisite*. Without it, async just means waiting in the dark.

Five practices carry the load: give everything a permanent address, treat documentation as a force multiplier, build your team's andon cord, narrate your work as it happens, and eliminate surprises. The throughline is building institutional memory that survives someone going on vacation—or leaving the company entirely. **Institutional memory shouldn't depend on individual memory.**

> **Common objection: "Won't sharing everything just create noise and slow us down?"** The risk most teams face is not over-sharing; it's invisible work. When work happens behind closed doors—in private channels, local branches, or someone's head—

> teams duplicate effort, miss context, and rediscover the same dead ends. Openness doesn't mean firehosing every Slack channel with your stream of consciousness. It means making work *discoverable* so the right people can find it when they need it, not just when you remember to tell them.

> **For managers: Make openness concrete with a single action this week.** Pick a decision you'd normally make over DMs or in a 1:1—say, a priority change or a technical direction call—and post it as an issue or discussion instead, with your reasoning. "Be more transparent" isn't an actionable instruction; "post your next decision in #team-eng with a two-day comment window" is.

> **For individual contributors: Narrate your work before anyone asks you to.** Post updates to shared channels, document decisions in issues, and make your in-progress work discoverable. If you wait to be asked, the asking *is* the failure mode.

> **Pro-Tip:** I have a personal goal of having a colleague complain that I "over-communicate." A decade+ of working this way, and it has yet to happen. When in doubt, communicate more.

Permanent addresses first. Everything else builds on them.

Why Everything Should Have a URL

> **TL;DR:** If a decision, process, or artifact doesn't have a URL, it effectively doesn't exist—you're one departure, one reorg, or one Slack retention policy away from losing it forever. Linkable doesn't mean public; it means findable, shareable, and durable enough to outlast the person who created it.

You're three months into a new role when you hit a design decision that doesn't make sense. You ask around. "Oh yeah—Alex and Jordan worked that out over lunch last summer." Cool. Alex left in October and Jordan doesn't remember. The reasoning behind a decision that shaped the entire architecture is just *gone*—not because anyone was irresponsible, but because it was never written down. No document, no issue thread, no link. It might as well have never happened.

Throughout GitHub's history, there was an ironically unwritten mantra: "everything should have a URL" (also phrased "URL or it didn't happen," or my personal favorite "if you liked it then you should have put a URL on it"). Hyperbole, sure—but it points at something real.

Systems that naturally capture and expose process make organizational context time-, location-, and person-agnostic. **Unlinkable knowledge has a bus factor of one**—a bus factor being the number of people who'd need to disappear before critical knowledge is lost—**if one person leaves, the knowledge leaves with them.**

Let your tools do the remembering

AI can transcribe every meeting and hallway conversation. But recording everything isn't the same as knowing anything. A firehose of raw transcripts—no structure, no curation, no signal about what mattered—just relocates the problem.

The better move is to adopt systems that generate documentation as a byproduct of doing the work—issue trackers, pull requests, decision logs—where doing the work *is* documenting it. These tools force you to structure your thinking, address a specific audience, and leave a permanent, linkable artifact behind. That's the difference between dumping your desk drawers into a box and organizing a library—one hoards information, the other makes it findable.

> **Pro-Tip:** Think camera roll versus curated album. A camera roll captures *everything*; finding signal requires serious scrolling. A curated album selects what matters and is actually worth revisiting. Optimize knowledge management for the per-

> son searching six months from now, not the person snapping away today.

Some conversations—interpersonal conflicts, brainstorming, 1:1s—belong in higher-fidelity media. But most work communication, especially technical decisions, belongs in async tools that leave a trail.

> 🤔 **Common objection: "Everyone was there."** Were they? Think about the last decision your team made in a meeting. Now list everyone who'll be affected by it over the next year—the new hire starting next month, the partner team that depends on your API, the you-from-six-months-from-now who can't remember *why* you chose Option B. "Everyone" was never in that room. And even for the people who *were*, memory is unreliable—ask three attendees what was decided and you'll get three different answers. The meeting isn't the record. The URL is.

The consumer/producer disconnect

Every piece of information you *consume* comes with a URL—the news you read, the videos you watch, the products you buy. But inside most organizations, the work you *produce* lives in email threads, chat rooms, and shared drives—without permanent addresses. We've adopted URLs as consumers while rejecting them as creators. Your cat video has a permanent address. Your architecture decision doesn't.

> **For individual contributors: Start giving your work addresses.** The next time you solve a problem in a DM or explain a decision over a call, ask yourself: does this answer have a URL? If not, take five minutes to post it in an issue or a doc. You're not creating busywork—you're creating a findable artifact that proves you solved the problem and saves the next person from having to solve it again.

> **Pro-Tip:** Early in my civic-tech work, I watched a federal agency review pull requests submitted by citizens to a public repo by *printing them out*. A small team gathered on a weekly cadence around a stereotypical government conference table covered in stapled printouts, went through diffs line by line, and left with action items: someone to merge, someone to reply in the browser afterward, someone to ping the contributor.
>
> It worked, in the sense that the code eventually shipped. It also defeated every reason URLs exist. A pull request *is* the conversation—inline comments, linked commits, threaded replies, a permanent record anyone can read later. Flatten it to paper and you've traded a living artifact for a photocopy of one, added a week of calendar dance to

> every review, and guaranteed that nobody who wasn't in the room will ever see what was said. **If you have to print a URL to discuss it, you've already lost the game.**

The compound returns of linkable work

You know what was decided—and why

No more "you had to be there." A decision with a URL gives you the reasoning, the alternatives rejected, and the people involved—at one address. Top-down decisions can't hide behind "because I said so" when the URL shows the deliberation. The next person with the same bright idea you rejected six months ago can find out *why*, instead of burning a week rediscovering the same dead end. **Decisions without URLs get relitigated forever.**

> **For managers: Link to the why, not just the what.** When you announce a decision, include the URL where the reasoning lives. "We're going with Option B—here's the discussion" with a link to the original thread kills the back-channel relitigating before it starts and signals that your team's decisions are traceable, not arbitrary.

Linkable writing is better writing

Writing destined for a URL—permanent, discoverable, potentially read by people you've never met—hits differently from a dashed-off chat message. When your words will outlast your tenure, you write with more care. You anticipate objections and make reasoning explicit instead of assuming shared context. And once written, that output scales as meetings never can: a conference room fits thirty people across two time zones; a URL reaches anyone, anywhere, on their own schedule.

Everything connects to everything else

Once decisions have URLs, they reference one another—like academic papers or case law, each citation adding context. "Person X would want us to do Y" becomes "here's what person X actually said." For technical matters, charts and data in the discussion anchor debate in facts rather than opinions.

People can dig as deep as they want

A policy memo blasted out as a PDF gives those affected the outcome and nothing else—no why, no how. Post the same decision to an internal discussion board, linked to the forum where the team worked through it, and anyone—delighted or disgruntled—can opt in to as much or as little context as they want. That's how you earn genuine support instead of grudging compliance.

Async and distributed become possible

> **Pro-Tip:** Give *concepts* URLs, not just outcomes. Each team should have one, as should each project, document, meeting, and employee. At GitHub, we used an in-house app called `team` to give every Hubber a profile behind a predictable URL: who

> they were, what they worked on, how to reach them. It killed the "who owns this?" guessing game in the first week on the job.

The same principle drove the roadmap from the customer side. GitHub kept an internal customer-feedback repo—one issue per requested feature, with the accounts that had asked linked in the thread. Product managers worked it like any other queue. The roadmap wasn't whatever the loudest sales call demanded; it was whatever the receipts said the market wanted most. "The account team on this call wants [X]" loses force when the adjacent issue shows forty other accounts asking for [Y]. **Give every feature request a URL, and prioritization stops being political.**

> **Common objection: "A URL for every meeting and every employee? That's overkill."** It sounds extreme until you've spent an afternoon hunting for who owns a project or what was decided in last month's architecture review. You don't need to hand-craft artisanal pages—most tools generate URLs automatically. A calendar invite already has one; so does a Slack channel or a GitHub team. The goal isn't busywork; it's making "go ask Person X" unnecessary by making context self-serve. One way this showed up at GitHub was the Service Catalog, an app that gave each service a URL, along with a link to its durable owner.

Linkable doesn't mean public

Giving a decision the respect of a URL doesn't mean broadcasting it to the world. A URL is distinct from who sees it—you can share one with one person, a hundred, or six billion, just as you already do with bank accounts, photos, and intranets.

Some links are read-only

A chat transcript linked six months later gives context without inviting new replies. Set expectations: are you communicating a decision or inviting discussion?

Scope limits exposure

Salary negotiations stay with the employee, HR, and the direct supervisor. Legal decisions stay inside legal. The URL's value is the same regardless of audience size. A digital record of who decided, how, and why—available to the right people—beats hallway chatter that a memory lapse erases.

Time shifts exposure

Security teams disclose vulnerabilities once a patch is ready. Executives can make a sensitive call in private, then share the deliberation alongside the announcement. You can document a decision today and publish it next quarter. Think of it like a photograph: you take it to capture the moment, but who sees it—and when—is up to you. What matters is that the record exists.

> **For managers: Build the infrastructure for URL-centric work.** Adopt tools that naturally give concepts addresses. Make linking to prior decisions a team habit, not a personal quirk. When URLs become the default way teams share context, you stop losing institutional knowledge every time someone changes roles.

> **For individual contributors: Give your work URLs.** Document decisions, share work-in-progress, and create linkable artifacts. When you reference something, include the link—you'll save others from hunting for the same context. Six months from now, the person most grateful for that link will probably be you.

"Everything must have a URL" doesn't mean everything must be public, or that everyone gets to critique every decision. It's shorthand for: adopt systems that naturally produce linkable records, and share context as widely as the subject matter allows. You can argue against memorializing every decision—but not that your organization would be better off memorializing none.

A URL is only as valuable as the documentation it surfaces.

Documentation as a Superpower

> **TL;DR:** You're the go-to person everyone Slacks with the same three questions, and every answer disappears the moment the conversation ends. Writing it down once—in the right tool, structured so people can actually find it—turns 25 hours of repeated explanations into a two-hour investment you make once and draw on indefinitely.

It's 2 AM and your pager goes off. The payment-processing service is down. The team that built it has turned over completely. Nobody knows why the retry logic works the way it does, why there's a hardcoded timeout of 47 seconds, or which downstream systems will break if you change it. The original design? Explained verbally to someone who summarized it in a Slack thread that got buried eighteen months ago. You spend four hours reverse-engineering what a five-minute doc would have told you.

Every remote team hits this wall. The same questions keep surfacing. New hires spend weeks ramping up. Tribal knowledge—expertise trapped in people's heads—

walks out the door when they do. And outdated wikis, sprawling Confluence spaces, and scattered Google Docs make it worse, not better—they create the illusion of knowledge while burying what's actually accurate. The fix isn't more meetings or longer Slack threads. It's documentation—written in the right tools, structured for the people who'll need it, and kept close enough to the work that it stays true.

> **Pro-Tip:** Early in my career, I learned the only way to scale my impact was through URLs. I made myself a rule: **If I answer the same question more than twice, I document the answer** and respond with a URL the third time. That one habit changed how I worked. Instead of being a single point of failure, my knowledge lived on in documentation that others could find and use without me.

Write it once, use it forever

Think of documentation as code that runs on human brains. Write it once, call it thousands of times. **No other work habit scales like this.**

Do the math: explaining a process takes 30 minutes and you'd explain it 50 times a year—that's 25 hours. Spend two hours documenting it instead, and you've saved 23 hours—plus the time saved by everyone who finds the answer without asking. Documentation keeps paying off long after you've moved on.

I experienced this firsthand as a new hire at GitHub. An early peer had built up a stack of documentation for their program—what they'd tried, what had worked, what hadn't, where the pitfalls were. When I picked up a program with a similar shape, I didn't start from zero; I copied their previous year's plan and adapted it. That alone saved me the full first year of beginner mistakes. One peer's patient writing replaced a year of my re-learning. **Documentation is how you give next year's version of your role a one-year head start.**

> **Common objection: "Documentation takes too much time—I'd rather just get the work done."** Short-term thinking that costs you far more over time. Every time you answer a question verbally, that knowledge disappears the moment the conversation ends. Multiply that by everyone who will ever have the same question. The two hours you "saved" by not documenting become dozens of hours of repeated explanations, inconsistent answers, and new hires who can't find what they need. Documentation isn't separate from the work—it's the work, scaled. Ship the doc alongside the feature, and future-you will be grateful.

Most teams treat documentation as separate from "real work"—something you do *after* the feature ships. That framing is backwards. Documentation isn't overhead; it's how you think through the problem, explain your approach, and hand off context.

Architects don't build first and draw blueprints later. The blueprints *are* part of the building process. Writing forces you to identify gaps, surface unstated assumptions, and pressure-test your approach before you've invested weeks in implementation. There's a reason it's called "reducing something to writing"—**writing compresses thinking.** It forces you to maximize signal-to-noise and focus on what matters. And once in written form, ideas scale: the effort to articulate an idea to one person is the same as to a thousand, regardless of time or location. Documenting doesn't slow you down; it prevents the rework that would have slowed you down more.

> **For managers: Every process you document is a decision you won't have to re-explain.** Document how decisions are made, who owns what, and what "good" looks like—you're building the operating system for your team and freeing yourself to focus on work that only you can do.

> **For individual contributors: Documentation amplifies your impact.** When you write the authoritative guide to something, you become the go-to expert—even after you've moved on. Well-documented work is visible work, and that expertise compounds over time.

Documentation reduces what programmers call "interrupt-driven work"—the constant context-switching from being the go-to person for tribal knowledge. Good documentation is a self-service API for your team's knowledge—anyone can query it without blocking the author. Every question a doc answers is an interruption you don't have to recover from.

Documentation habits only go so far if your tools work against you—word processors designed for printouts, opaque file formats, and collaboration workflows built for an era of emailed attachments. For a deeper look at why those tools hold your team back and what to use instead, see *Retool Your Documents*.

How to write docs people actually read

If the biggest documentation problem is that it doesn't exist, the second is that nobody reads it when it does.

Get to the point first, then make it skimmable

Don't bury the important information at the end. Busy people skim; give them what they need first, then fill in detail. Think newspaper article: headline, summary, then details. Use headings, bullet points, and short paragraphs. Break complex procedures into numbered steps, put commands in code blocks, and let readers find what they need without reading every word.

> **Pro-Tip:** If you haven't noticed, I'm a big fan of TL;DRs. You may also hear them called BLUFs (bottom line up front), or more traditionally, executive summaries. They force you to distill your point

> into a few sentences, which makes people far more likely to read and retain it.

Write headings that promise something, for readers who don't share your context

A heading does more than break up the page—it makes a promise. "Background" tells you nothing; "Deprecating the V1 API" tells you exactly what follows. Descriptive headings let readers triage content without reading every word and make documents searchable by the questions people actually ask. Each heading also becomes a shareable anchor—a direct URL fragment like `#restoring-from-backup`—so you can point a colleague to the right section. Clear, specific heading text is also what screen readers and AI assistants use to navigate and summarize your documents.

Then assume no other context. Define acronyms on first use. Link to background material. Remember that your reader is probably stressed, busy, and unfamiliar with your mental model.

> **Pro-Tip:** Write headings as questions or action phrases: "How do I reset my password?" or "Reset your password." When headings mirror how people search, your docs surface at the right moment—whether someone's using the search bar or asking an AI assistant. On the internet, nobody reads anything—they skim, scroll, and move on. The "inverted pyramid" technique works *with* that

> reality: start with the most important information, then add layers of detail. Readers can stop at any point and still walk away with the core message.

Update or delete stale docs

Documentation has a half-life. Build maintenance into your workflows: review docs when related code changes, update runbooks after incidents, archive irrelevant pages. Stale docs actively mislead—like a deprecated API that still shows up in search results but throws errors when called. They erode trust in *all* your docs.

> **Pro-Tip:** GitHub's security incident response team (SIRT) had an impressive `PIR` pattern. During an incident, anyone could react to a chat message with the `:pir:` emoji to flag an action item for the post-incident review. Easily searchable, it was a low-cost way to capture "we should fix this" without interrupting the flow of the incident response.

Make it easy to find

The best documentation is useless if no one can find it. Use consistent naming, good search, and logical organization. Link generously. If someone asks where something is, that's a signal your information architecture needs work.

> **Pro-Tip:** Apply the "3 AM test": Could someone responding to an incident at 3 AM find and follow this documentation without any other context? If the answer is no, simplify and clarify.

Consistently passing that test isn't about individual heroics—it's about how your team treats documentation day-to-day.

Make documentation part of how you work

Documentation isn't a solo activity—it's a team habit woven into how you work, not an afterthought.

Document while the context is fresh

The best time to document is while you're doing the work—the context is fresh, and you'll capture details that seem obvious now but won't in six months. (Nothing is as temporary as a developer's certainty about what they'll remember.)

> **Pro-Tip:** Point your AI tools at your team's docs—via MCP (Model Context Protocol) servers, repository indexing, or custom instructions—and watch

> the difference. Teams with well-structured, up-to-date documentation get noticeably better AI-assisted answers because the model can find relevant context. Teams with scattered tribal knowledge get generic responses. Your documentation quality *is* your AI quality now.

When you learn something new, write it down. Solve a tricky problem? Capture the solution. Answer a question in chat? Ask whether that answer belongs somewhere others can find it.

Your README is your project's constitution

Every repository, service, and internal tool should have a README at the front door. **A good README doesn't just explain what and how; it explains *why*.** Ship it with the project's purpose, the problems it solves (and the ones it explicitly doesn't), how to run it, and how to contribute. Done well, the README becomes your project's constitution—the document every future contributor reads first, the one you point to when scope creep arrives with a pull request, and the durable statement of intent that outlives any individual maintainer. When a feature request lands outside the project's charter, you don't argue taste—you link the README.

Your pull requests are documentation, too

I've lost count of the times I've spelunked historical pull requests to understand why a feature works the way it does. Most teams treat PRs purely as a review mechanism, but they're also organic documentation—some of the most valuable your team produces. A PR captures not just *what* changed, but who made it, why, and what alternatives were considered. The discussion *around* the change—trade-offs weighed, approaches rejected, edge cases debated—is often more valuable than the diff.

Unlike a wiki page someone has to remember to update, PRs create documentation as a side effect of doing the work. Write every PR description with two audiences in mind: the reviewers who need to approve it today, and the stranger who'll land on it from a search result two years from now. A descriptive title, a brief summary of the "what," an explanation of the "why," and links to related context turn every merge into a searchable decision record—no extra process required.

Let anyone fix it

Documentation should be as easy to improve as code. Use version control, pull requests, and low-friction editing. When someone finds an error or gap, they should be able to fix it—not file a ticket and hope.

At GitHub, the employee handbook lived in a Markdown repo anyone could open a pull request against. Benefits policy evolved meaningfully through PR discussion: employees proposing changes, people-ops reviewing in-thread, the resulting conversation preserved as the commit log. Company policy became a diff, not a decree—which is exactly the point of letting anyone fix the docs.

Treat documentation like a real contribution

Documentation is invisible work at most companies. Fight this:

> **For managers: Write your team's first ADR (architecture decision record) yourself.** Document a recent technical decision—what you chose, what you rejected, and why—then put it where your team can find it. Add "docs updated?" as a checkbox on your pull request template, and call out documentation contributions in sprint reviews the same way you'd highlight a shipped feature. If docs aren't in your team's definition of "done," they'll always lose to the next ticket. And credit documentation in performance reviews—when someone ships the runbook that cuts your team's on-call burden, name it in their written review and promotion packets. People optimize for what gets rewarded.

> **For individual contributors: Treat docs like shipped features in your self-reviews.** Include doc updates in your pull requests, and call them out in weekly updates and performance reviews—not as an afterthought but as evidence of impact. The engineer who writes the authoritative onboarding guide or the definitive runbook builds a reputation that outlasts any single feature.

Getting credit for writing docs matters—but people *finding* those docs matters more.

Think about the person searching for this later

Every time you document something, ask: could someone find it six months from now without knowing where to look? A little more work up front saves everyone downstream from reinventing the answer—the same async-as-cache principle that makes written decisions durable.

> **Pro-Tip:** Apply SEO (search engine optimization) thinking to your internal docs, too. Use clear, descriptive titles and headings that match the language your team uses when asking questions. Link related documents to create a web of knowledge that search can navigate. The easier it is to find the right document, the more likely people are to read it.

Small habits that help

- **Build time to update documentation** into your work plans (and if a document's maintenance outweighs its benefits, delete or simplify it)
- **Block focus time on your calendar** for writing and reading so synchronous time stays reserved for high-value conversations
- **Ensure every meeting has an agenda** document (bonus points if it's a discussion post) shared ahead of time to collect input from team members who can't attend live—and post pass-down notes after the call

- **Make big announcements ahead of (not during) synchronous meetings** so the whole team has access to the announcement, even if they can't attend the call, and they have time to process the information and collect their questions

Start small: the next time you answer a question, write it down. The next time you make a decision, record your reasoning. The next time you learn something new, share it. One document at a time, you're building the infrastructure that lets your team work asynchronously and ship—no matter where or when.

Documentation makes work visible—and visible work has a second payoff: it surfaces problems early. When everything is written down and shared, hidden issues lose their hiding places.

The Andon Principle for Knowledge Work

> **TL;DR:** When work is invisible, small problems hide until they become expensive outages. Make work visible and reward early signals, and you'll catch issues while they're still cheap to fix.

A junior engineer spots something off in a production config but stays quiet—unsure if it's a real problem, afraid of slowing the team down. Two weeks later, the same config takes down the search backend for four hours. The fix takes twenty minutes. Toyota solved this problem on its factory floors seventy-plus years ago—and its solution is worth stealing for knowledge work.

Both lean manufacturing and, decades later, Agile software development drew on what Toyota worked out on its production floors. The Toyota Production System,[23] documented in Jeffrey K. Liker's The Toyota Way[24] and

23. https://en.wikipedia.org/wiki/Toyota_Production_System
24. https://en.wikipedia.org/wiki/The_Toyota_Way

the inspiration behind lean manufacturing,[25] introduced the andon[26]—a principle worth stealing if you want to catch problems before they become incidents.

> **Pro-Tip:** The Toyota Production System (TPS)—which happens to share its initials with the "TPS Report" from the 1999 workplace satire *Office Space* —wasn't about bureaucratic reports. It was about empowering any worker on the line to halt production the moment they spotted a defect. Unlike the film, Toyota's version was the opposite of pointless paperwork.

Let anyone stop the line

An andon is a system of lights and signals that lets workers alert managers and colleagues to production defects. With the pull of a cord or the press of a button, any worker can halt the entire line. Letting *anyone* stop production seems counterintuitive, but catching a defect early costs a fraction of shipping it downstream. The approach has been so successful that Toyota—and most car manufacturers—still use it today.

Workers stop the line, identify root causes, and apply fixes—rather than letting issues slide or assuming someone else will handle them. The andon isn't a process bolt-on; it signals that the organization trusts its work-

25. https://en.wikipedia.org/wiki/Lean_manufacturing
26. https://en.wikipedia.org/wiki/Andon_(manufacturing)

ers' judgment. In programming terms, it's "fail fast" for organizations—surface errors immediately rather than letting them propagate silently.

> **For managers: Make stopping the line a rewarded behavior.** If someone on your team surfaces a problem early and your first reaction is frustration—even privately—you've just taught them to stay quiet next time. Publicly thank people who flag issues before they escalate, and make "caught it early" a data point in performance conversations.

Transparency is your team's andon cord

Transparency does for knowledge work what the andon does on a production line. When your work is visible, anyone can spot trouble before it compounds—and the right people can talk about a fix before the next standup. Co-located teams get this without trying: problems surface in hallway conversations and over-the-shoulder code reviews. Distributed teams don't. Without transparent work, the same problems hide until they're expensive crises. **Invisible work hides invisible problems.**

The andon cord only works if workers can *see* the production line. Toyota designed its factory floors for maximum visibility—open layouts, status boards at every station, color-coded signals visible from across the plant. Knowledge work has the opposite default. Work happens in local branches, private channels, and someone's head. Often just someone's head. A team member could be stuck on the wrong approach for days, and nobody would know until the sprint review—the knowledge-work equivalent of a defective part reaching the end of the assembly line.

For knowledge workers, the andon cord is working loudly—making your work visible enough that others spot problems before they escalate. When your team spans time zones, defaulting to visible means someone in Singapore can catch issues in your work before you wake up in Denver—turning time zone differences from a coordination headache into a quality advantage. The goal isn't surveillance; it's building the open factory floor that makes the andon cord worth pulling. In async environments, "pulling the cord" means posting in the right channel or opening an issue—not waiting for the next standup (for more on how and when, see *The Rule of No Surprises*).

> **For individual contributors: Your visibility *is* the team's early-warning system.** When you push work-in-progress to a branch, post a draft PR, or share your thinking in an issue, you're giving colleagues in other time zones the chance to catch problems while you sleep. That's not over-sharing—it's distributed quality assurance.

Feedback is cheapest when it's early

The cost of fixing a problem grows exponentially[27] the later you find it—a pattern Barry Boehm documented in *Software Engineering Economics*. **Problems don't age well; they age expensively.** A design flaw caught during review is a conversation; the same flaw caught in production is an incident. A misaligned assumption caught in a draft RFC (request for comments) is a paragraph edit; the same assumption caught after launch is a rollback, a postmortem, and a quarter of lost momentum. Seek feedback at every stage—prototype, test, and experiment to challenge your assumptions before the blast radius grows.

> **For managers: Create psychological safety for pulling the cord.** Reward surfacing problems early, even when it's uncomfortable. Run blameless postmortems—focused on systemic fixes, not individual fault—and feed findings back into retrospectives so your team spots the next issue faster. Your response to raised issues determines whether your team keeps raising them—or starts hiding them.

> **For individual contributors: When you hit a blocker, open an issue immediately—don't wait for standup.** Title it clearly ("API rate limiting causing staging deploy failures"), describe what you've already tried, and tag the most relevant person.

27. https://en.wikipedia.org/wiki/Barry_Boehm

> Frame it as "here's what I know and where I'm stuck" rather than "this is broken, please fix." A well-written issue that says "I've narrowed this to a connection timeout after the Redis migration—@sarah, does this match what you saw last sprint?" gets fast help without looking like you're shifting blame.

Spotting problems early is only the first step; the rest is making sure people hear about them. It's not enough to notice red flags—you've got to make your work (and your worries) visible, or risk silence letting avoidable mistakes slide by.

Work Loudly

> **TL;DR:** Silent work is a rework factory: you keep your head down for three weeks, then a stakeholder sees the result and says "that's not what I meant." Working loudly—sharing progress, surfacing risks, including people early—turns surprise feedback into course corrections before they get expensive.

You've pitched an idea. The response? Silence. No enthusiastic endorsement, no outright rejection—just... crickets. Should you wait for permission, or forge ahead and risk looking foolish?

This ambiguity paralyzes more good work than any explicit rejection ever could. You ship nothing while you wait for a signal that never comes, and three months later someone with more audacity—not more talent—

launches the thing you were too polite to build. The fix isn't reading minds better. It's refusing to let silence be the decision-maker.

> **Common objection: "Won't I be annoying if I share too much?"** This fear keeps valuable work invisible. People have filters—they'll tune out what doesn't apply to them. The cost of over-communicating is mild noise; the cost of under-communicating is duplicated work, missed chances to collaborate, and being blindsided by feedback that comes too late. Make your updates opt-in rather than opt-out (post to a channel, not DMs), and let others choose their engagement level. Nobody ever got fired for keeping stakeholders informed. The risk isn't being too visible—it's being invisible when it matters.

Whether you're launching a project, floating an untested idea, or wandering into organizational territory where nobody's drawn a map, the prescription is the same. The single best piece of advice I give my team when working under ambiguity: "work loudly." Think of it as "building in public" or "showing the receipts"—proof that you did the work to get the right people involved.

What does silence actually mean?

That silence stings, but it rarely means what you think. Maybe your idea genuinely misses the mark, or the timing's off and your coworkers don't know how to say so. When stakeholders believe the organization shouldn't do something, they speak up.

More likely, those you're looking to for feedback are busy, have other priorities, or have nothing to add. Don't read their silence as an implicit "No"—**silence is not consent; it's invisibility.** Do the opposite: move forward as if you have their support, but do so *loudly*.

Show your work in real-time

Hike through bear country and the last thing you want is to surprise one—startled bears attack. So you clip bells to your pack. As you walk, the jingling announces your presence. Bears hear you coming and clear out. No confrontation necessary.

Working loudly is the same principle applied to knowledge work: proceed with more transparency than anyone expects, especially without explicit sign-off. Share progress with your team, stakeholders, and anyone your work might affect. You're building observability into your work—emitting structured logs so anyone who needs to follow along can, without interrupting you.

When you work loudly, you're not keeping your head down and hoping for the best—you're inviting scrutiny on your own terms. Stakeholder feedback arrives early and actionable, not as a surprise at the end—the *andon cord* for knowledge work, surfacing problems while they're still cheap to fix. If the work *does* catch someone off guard, you'll have the receipts showing you were seeking feedback all along.

Make the work tangible

Here's the thing about status updates and proposals: nobody reads them. They're the terms and conditions of the corporate world—technically available, universally skipped. Too abstract, too divorced from actual work. A five-page design doc is someone's interpretation of what they *plan* to build. A working prototype—even a rough one—shows what they're *actually* building. When you share **demos, not memos**, you give people something concrete to react to.

This is where open and async work has a superpower. Drop a screen recording into an issue, push a proof-of-concept branch, or deploy a rough prototype to staging. Feedback shifts from "I think this approach might work" to "I clicked the button and it broke." People poke around on their own time and come back with specific, actionable input that never emerges from a document review. Better still, when your demo is a branch or a deployed environment, collaborators can fork it, extend it, or build on it directly. You're not just showing your work—you're inviting others into it.

A two-minute video showing your half-baked user interface (UI) says more than ten pages explaining what you *might* build. A feature branch with messy commits beats a perfectly formatted proposal every time. Show the thing. Let people touch it. A rough draft shared on day two catches fundamental misunderstandings. A polished presentation shared on day thirty reveals them too late to matter.

> **Pro-Tip:** For most of my career at GitHub, I made more prototypes than decks. When I wanted to argue for a direction, I'd send the room an ugly-but-working URL instead of a slide. A link you can click outruns a deck you have to sit through—every time. The prototype doesn't need to be pretty; it needs to exist. AI has lowered the bar even further: the cost of producing something clickable has collapsed, which means the excuse of "we don't have time to build it" has collapsed too. **An ugly working URL beats a beautiful deck.** If you're still opening PowerPoint to make your case, you're doing more work to say less.

> **Common objection: "This is just self-promotion dressed up as teamwork."** There's a difference between broadcasting your brilliance and making your work legible to others. Self-promotion says "look how great I am." Working loudly says "here's what I'm building—does anyone see a problem?" One seeks applause; the other seeks course correction. And introverts often *prefer* this model: a shared document or a screen recording lets you communicate on your terms, without performing

> in a meeting or lobbying in a hallway. Quiet people thrive when visibility doesn't require volume.

The clearest example I ever watched play out at GitHub was an engineer who was, by his own description, deeply introverted—meetings cost him, hallway small talk cost him, "executive presence" as traditionally defined was never going to be his medium. He became the public face of the company's internal AI adoption anyway. Not in spite of being introverted, but because of how he worked. He built in the open. He posted tight, well-reasoned write-ups in widely-read channels the moment he had something worth reading. By the time the broader organization needed someone to anchor a high-visibility initiative, his name was the obvious choice—not because he'd campaigned for it, but because a year of quietly-excellent-in-public work had already made the case.

Async visibility is an equalizer. Quiet people with something to say don't have to out-shout anyone. They just have to out-write the room, consistently, where the room can read along. **Share early, share often—and let the receipts do the lobbying.**

> **Pro-Tip:** Working loudly doesn't stop at your company's walls. Some of the most durable influence I've had at GitHub came from things I wrote publicly on my own blog. A 2018 post I published arguing against adding a Contributor License Agreement (CLA) to open source projects[28] still gets cited in project-governance debates years later —by people I've never met, at companies I don't work for, making decisions I'll never be in the room for.
>
> That's the durable reach public writing gives you. A blog post is a pull request against the industry's defaults. It doesn't need sign-off from a committee to ship, and if the reasoning holds, it keeps running long after the meeting that would have debated it has been forgotten. **Writing in public is the cheapest durable reach you have—someone can find it, link it, and use it without ever meeting you.**

28. https://ben.balter.com/2018/01/02/why-you-probably-shouldnt-add-a-cla-to-your-open-source-project/

The show-and-tell dividend

Sharing a demo in an issue is a good start. Making it a regular team ritual is something else entirely.

Internal show-and-tell sessions—recurring, low-stakes demos where anyone can walk through something they've built, learned, or half-figured-out—are worth more than most formal training programs a distributed team will ever run. They look informal. They feel optional. But they quietly do two things at once. **Show-and-tell is both a broadcast and a lesson.**

For the presenter, it's the least awkward form of visibility that exists. You're not writing a brag document, lobbying for credit in a performance review, or angling for a mention in someone's status report (though it helps with all of those—see *Corporate Self-Care*). You're clicking through the thing you built and explaining how it works. The impact is concrete, and it doesn't feel like self-promotion because it isn't. Just the work, out in the open.

For everyone watching, it's accidental education. When a colleague demos the GitHub Actions workflow they built to auto-close stale issues, or walks through how they used a command-line interface (CLI) tool to cut a two-hour manual process to thirty seconds, everyone picks up a pattern or technique they wouldn't have found on their own. No curriculum required. Just someone showing their work while others pay attention.

The format matters less than the frequency. Weekly or bi-weekly works. Fifteen to thirty minutes. No formal agenda—just a standing invitation: *built something? learned something? show it.* Work-in-progress counts. Rough counts. The goal isn't polish; it's momentum. A half-finished feature with a sharp edge to discuss beats a finished feature nobody knows about. Done consistently, these sessions become the team's institutional memory—searchable if you record them, actually *watched* because they're interesting.

> **Pro-Tip:** What you show doesn't have to be strictly limited to work. When I was at one US federal government agency, we had a weekly Friday "hootenanny" (a term that evokes a fun, informal, often improvised gathering) where anyone could share anything they wanted. Colleagues brought side projects, new open source technologies they were hacking on, anything—and we all just geeked out and learned from one another, well beyond "here's what I shipped this sprint."

That's the dividend: each session deposits knowledge into the team's shared account. Someone demos a clever script this week; three people have added it to their workflow by next month. A junior engineer shows how they debugged a gnarly race condition; a senior engineer realizes they've been approaching similar problems the hard way for years. Share the code so others can build on it. The team levels up together without anyone writing a guide or declaring it a learning initiative.

> **For managers: Put it on the calendar and protect it.** A show-and-tell that only happens when someone has "something worth sharing" will never happen. Set a recurring slot, keep it even when the signup sheet is empty, and put your own name on it first. When managers demo their work—a new hiring process, a team dashboard, a decision they walked back—they signal that visibility isn't reserved for individual contributors. If sessions consistently get skipped or the signup stays blank, that's a signal too: something is making people feel their work isn't worth showing. Find out what.

> **For individual contributors: Don't wait until it's finished.** A rough demo before you've committed to an approach gets you feedback while it still matters. A polished one after the fact gets you applause that changes nothing. Show the messy middle—the partially built thing, the script you hacked together at midnight, the approach you're not sure about. That's impact over input, documented in real-time.

How to be visible without being obnoxious

Working loudly isn't about flooding every channel with noise. It's about sharing the right things with the right people:

- **Share progress**—Keep your team and stakeholders informed, even when you're unsure you're heading in the right direction. *Especially* then, actually.
- **Broadcast challenges**—If you're facing a technical hurdle or need input, share it in a public channel. You're not looking for permission—you're creating the surface area for someone to say "oh, I solved that last month" or "have you tried X?" You're inviting collaboration, not escalation. (For high-stakes risks and bad news, see *The Rule of No Surprises*.)
- **Celebrate wins**—When you hit a milestone, share it widely. Visible progress gives people a reason to care about what comes next.
- **Seek feedback**—Ask for feedback early and often. Even if it arrives late, you'll have the receipts to show you were actively seeking it all along.

> **Pro-Tip:** Two patterns from traditional project/program management that translate well to working loudly async are **decision logs** and **risk registers.** A decision log captures decisions, who made them, when, and why. A risk register tracks potential risks, their likelihood, impact, and mitigation strategies. Both create a paper trail that makes your work visible and accountable—bureaucratic receipts.

Sharing progress and wins is the easy part. The real test is whether you surface the *hard* stuff—risks, blockers, bad news—in those same channels, before anyone has to ask, letting the paper trail speak for itself.

Don't spam—signal

Notification hygiene matters. Think of it like log levels in production: not everything deserves a page. A typo fix is `DEBUG`-level; a new feature is `INFO`; a breaking change is `WARN`. Notifying a 500-person channel about a typo? `FATAL`. When in doubt, observe your peers. You don't want to be the person who notifies the entire company (at GitHub, that meant @mentioning a team containing all employees) for a minor bug report.

Network engineers have another useful mental model: unicast, multicast, and broadcast. A DM is unicast—one sender, one receiver. If five people need the same context, you send five separate messages. A channel post or issue is multicast—one sender, many receivers who opted in. And @channel? Broadcast—everyone gets it, want it or not. **Most people unicast when they should multicast, and broadcast when they should multicast.** Default to multicast: share once, in the open, and let the right people find it. A few tips for getting the signal right:

Let people opt in to your updates

Interested stakeholders should be able to opt in to updates. Say you prepare a weekly report. Rather than copying and pasting a list of @mentions each week, create a team people can join. Better still, place the weekly report in a dedicated repository people can subscribe to (and unsubscribe from).

Let people opt out, too

Avoid overusing forums with no opt-out mechanism. It's tempting to blast updates across chat channels, but absent an awkward conversation, there's no natural way for someone to say, "I don't want to receive these updates." Create a dedicated channel for updates that stakeholders can leave at will or a bot that can be muted.

Tell them why it matters

When sharing updates, lead with *why it matters*. Don't just post a link to a pull request—include a brief summary of what changed and why anyone should care. People can then quickly assess whether to dig deeper or move on.

Bundle updates into weekly summaries

At GitHub Engineering, we solved this with "rollups." Inspired by abridged mailing-list summaries, teams posted updates as discussion posts to the most logical repository. Once a week, a GitHub Actions automation rolled up all the posts from across Engineering with a given label, then posted the weekly summary to the Engineering repository with a brief TL;DR so you could skim the week's activity. Everyone could access the information, but not everyone got notified about every update.

Rollups and working loudly look different depending on your role:

> **For managers: Build the infrastructure that makes working loudly frictionless.** Establish weekly "rollup" patterns (at GitHub, we called them "snippets"), set up notifications for key repositories, and publicly recognize team members who share early. When someone posts an update, engage with it—a comment, a reaction, a follow-up question. Your attention signals that you value visibility.

Visibility compounds for individual contributors. Post a brief update each week on what you're working on, even if no one asked. When you hit a blocker, share it in a public channel before you've solved it—others might have the answer. Under the rule of no surprises, share news with stakeholders before they hear it elsewhere. You're building a paper trail that speaks for you when you're not in the room.

> **For individual contributors: Your weekly updates are your career receipts.** Each post documenting what you shipped, what you learned, and what you're tackling next becomes a searchable record of your contributions. Six months from now, your self-review writes itself—and anyone evaluating your impact can see it without asking. Pair every "for review" post with an explicit dead-

> line—"I'll move forward Friday at 5 p.m. ET unless I hear otherwise"—so a non-response becomes a clear green light to proceed rather than a sign you've been forgotten.

Next time you're facing ambiguity, clip on the bear bells. Make your progress visible, surface challenges early, and let the receipts do the talking.

When work is visible by default, teams spend less time asking "What's everyone working on?" and more time doing actual work—meetings become what they should be: escalation points for issues that need real-time discussion.

Working loudly means your written communication *is* your professional presence. Every update, every request for feedback, every shared decision becomes a record of your judgment. Make transparency a habit, and trust compounds—people vouch for you when it matters most.

The Rule of No Surprises

> **TL;DR:** If information would surprise someone when they discover it later, share it now—not when it's convenient, not when you have a solution. One blindside can undo months of trust, but consistent transparency earns you the autonomy that makes micromanagement unnecessary.

Your project's three weeks behind schedule. Your manager finds out during a steering committee meeting—when someone else asks about the launch date. Instead of problem-solving, you're explaining why you didn't say anything sooner. The actual delay becomes secondary to the trust issue you just created. **Surprises break trust faster than setbacks.**

In an office, surprises get defused through ambient awareness. Your manager sees you stressed, asks what's wrong, and you mention the delay before it becomes A Thing. Remote work strips away that safety net. Async communication amplifies the damage—by the time someone discovers the surprise, you're three time zones away or asleep. The emotional response festers with no chance to talk it through. What could have been a five-minute conversation becomes a day-long exchange of increasingly tense messages.

Surprises also violate the implicit contract of working loudly. When you broadcast progress and wins, people assume they're seeing the full picture. A surprise reveals a gap—and now they're not just reacting to the bad news; they're questioning every update you've shared before. *What else isn't in these updates?* One omission poisons the entire feed.

When you're unsure whether to share, apply one test: **if it would surprise them later, share it now.** Not when it's convenient. Not when you have a solution. Now.

What deserves a heads-up

The question isn't whether to share—it's when. Would discovering this later make someone feel blindsided?

Risks and blockers

Risks and blockers belong at the top of the list. That vendor who's gone silent? That dependency that's looking shaky? That migration that's been "almost done" for the third week running? Share it when it's a possibility, not when it's a crisis. "Hey, I'm watching this closely and wanted you to know it's on my radar" costs you nothing and buys you credibility.

Timeline changes

Timeline changes need immediate disclosure, even when you're not sure yet. *Especially* when you're not sure yet. "I'm seeing signals that we might slip by a week—still investigating, but wanted you to know" beats hoping you can make it up and revealing the slip later.

Scope decisions

Scope decisions you're making unilaterally—share those too. Even if you have the authority, stakeholders deserve to know you're making the call. "Under the rule of no surprises: I'm cutting feature X from the minimum viable product (MVP) to hit the date. Here's why, and here's the plan for adding it back in v2."

Changes in approach or strategy

Changes in approach or strategy, particularly after you've shared an earlier plan, need to be said out loud. People make decisions based on what they think you're doing. Pivot without telling them, and their decisions go stale—they look foolish for not knowing.

People issues

People issues you're handling—performance problems, team conflicts, someone threatening to quit—your manager needs to hear from you, not through back channels. Leaders can't support you or plan around problems they don't know exist.

> **Common objection: "If I share every potential problem, I'll look incompetent or create alarm."** This fear gets it backwards. Surprises make you look incompetent because they suggest you either didn't see the problem coming or saw it and hid it. Raising concerns early demonstrates awareness and judgment. Frame risks as risks, not certainties, and you'll be seen as thoughtful, not alarmist.

That framing—risk, not certainty—matters more than you'd think. So does delivery.

How to deliver bad news without making it worse

The rule doesn't mean dumping problems without context.

Lead with the headline, then the plan

"We're going to miss the deadline" or "The vendor backed out" or "I'm seeing higher-than-expected churn." Don't bury the news in preamble or soften it past recognition. People need to know what they're dealing with.

Follow with your assessment and plan: What's causing this? What are you doing about it? What do you need? This structure—headline, context, plan—keeps the conversation productive instead of degenerating into panic. Better yet, lead with the solution: instead of "We have a problem with the deployment," try "I've identified a deployment issue and here's my plan to fix it."

Be explicit about what you need. "Just a heads-up, no action needed" versus "I need a decision on X by Friday" versus "I need help navigating Y." Don't make people guess whether you're informing or asking.

Use the phrase directly: "Under the rule of no surprises, I wanted you to hear from me first that..." This signals deliberate transparency, not an accidental problem dump. It frames disclosure as a courtesy, not a crisis.

> **For managers: When an IC brings you bad news early, your reaction sets the tone for every future disclosure.** Resist the urge to problem-solve or assign blame immediately—start with "Thank you for flagging this," then ask how you can help. If you punish early warnings—even unintentionally, with visible frustration—you'll stop receiving them, and the surprises will get bigger and more expensive. Treat the early warning as a win, not a nuisance—it's the andon cord for knowledge work.

> **For individual contributors: Don't wait until you have a solution to surface a problem.** Your

> manager would rather hear about a potential issue on Monday than a confirmed one on Friday. You don't need a fix to earn trust—you need a clear description of what's happening and what you've ruled out so far. Early transparency is exactly what seasoned senior engineers do routinely.

Framing matters. So does timing.

> **Pro-Tip: Time bad news carefully within working hours, but don't wait for perfect timing.** Sending "We missed the target" at 11 PM on Friday is inconsiderate. But waiting three days for a meeting to share time-sensitive information is worse. Share news when people can reasonably process it, not when it's convenient for you.

Knowing when and how to share is the easy part. The hard part is making yourself actually do it.

Start small, build the habit

The hardest part isn't knowing what to share—it's overcoming the instinct to wait. We want to solve problems before revealing them. We want certainty before raising concerns. We want to control the narrative instead of exposing uncertainty. Really, we just don't want to look bad.

That's backwards.

Start with low-stakes practice. Share a minor risk that probably won't materialize. "Heads-up: the API provider had an outage last week, and while they say it's fixed, I'm watching it closely for the next sprint." Notice that nothing bad happens. In fact, if the API does go down, you look prescient instead of caught off guard.

Gradually increase the stakes. Share a timeline concern before it's certain. Disclose a decision people might question. Each time the world doesn't end, you build confidence that transparency works.

> **Pro-Tip: Make it routine.** Fold the habit into your weekly reporting with a standing "Watching Closely" or "Potential Risks" section. Raising concerns early becomes normal, not alarming—the rule of no surprises, baked into your workflow.

Same rule, different stakes

The rule applies to everyone. The stakes differ by role.

> **For individual contributors: Individual contributors** should focus on surprises that affect your team, your manager, and your stakeholders. You don't need to share every implementation detail or technical decision—that's working loudly, not surprise prevention. Focus on information that would make someone say "I wish I'd known this sooner."

> Your manager is your primary no-surprises stakeholder. Risks, blockers, timeline concerns, and anything that might bubble up to their level—share those proactively. When in doubt, overshare with your manager and let them filter what goes higher.
>
> For peer stakeholders, share information that affects their work or decisions. If the API you're building will be late and they're depending on it, they deserve advance notice. If you're deprecating a feature they use, tell them before you announce it broadly.

> **For managers: Brief up, brief down, brief across —on a schedule.** Send your manager a weekly async update covering three things: what shipped, what's at risk, and what you anticipate becoming a problem. Share that same update (minus anything confidential) with your team in a public channel so they see transparency in action. For peer leaders, flag cross-team dependencies and timeline changes the moment you learn about them—"Hey @platform-lead, our auth migration is slipping by two weeks; here's the updated timeline"—don't wait for the next staff meeting.

All of this proactive disclosure costs effort. Here's what it buys you.

The trust you earn by never blindsiding anyone

Most people treat the rule of no surprises as purely defensive—a way to avoid getting yelled at. They're underselling it. It's how you earn autonomy.

When you consistently surface concerns early, people stop micromanaging you—they trust you'll tell them if something goes wrong, so they trust your judgment calls too. That's how senior engineers earn real influence, how managers earn the latitude to run their teams without interference, how anyone at any level earns room to do their best work. Not by hiding problems until they're solved—which is mostly hoping nobody notices before you fix it—but by anticipating them and bringing people along when you do.

The flip side is just as real. One surprise—one thing someone discovers after the fact—can undo months of trust-building. They'll check your work more closely, question your judgment, ask for more frequent updates. You've signaled that they can't trust you to keep them informed.

I learned this the hard way. Early on at GitHub I shipped a breaking change to GitHub Pages—the decision to standardize on a single Markdown engine[29] that swapped the rendering stack and broke backwards compatibility for a non-trivial slice of the millions of sites hosted on the platform. It didn't surprise me—I'd been

29. https://github.blog/news-insights/the-library/a-look-behind-our-decision-to-standardize-on-a-single-markdown-engine-for-github-pages/

staring at the diff for days—but it surprised users, which meant it surprised the people users complain to, which meant it surprised leadership.

The pointed feedback wasn't really about the breakage. Breakages happen. It was about the fact that the first they'd heard of it was from someone on the outside, without context to defend or explain the decision. I'd written a good technical rationale in the wrong place, for the wrong audience, at the wrong time.

The correction was in writing, in public, and mine to make—acknowledging the surprise, explaining the call, and standing up a heads-up process for the next time the team changed behavior anyone depended on. The change survived. The trust took longer to rebuild than the feature took to ship. **The goal isn't never being wrong; it's never letting anyone find out you were wrong from someone else first.**

A skip-level ask compounds the problem. Early in the pandemic, two senior executives pulled my team into an urgent project—what shipped as Account Successors,[30] which I saw as a kind of open source supply chain continuity effort—and I assumed my own executive was in the loop. They weren't. The feature shipped; the team came under scrutiny for months because the first impression wasn't *what we built*, it was *that we built it without their knowledge*. **A request from above isn't a substitute for an update to your manager.**

30. https://github.blog/changelog/2020-05-11-account-successors/

Make it second nature

Internalize this rule until asking "Would this surprise someone?" becomes automatic. Before you send a status update, scan for surprises. Before you make a decision, consider who would want to know. Before the day ends, think about what you learned that your stakeholders haven't.

Use 1:1s as your safety valve. Keep a running list of potential surprises throughout the week, and triage them in your next 1:1. Some you'll realize aren't surprising. Others you'll share immediately instead of waiting. The habit keeps you calibrated on what's worth flagging.

Link it to your documentation habits. When you write down a decision or a risk, ask whether it would surprise someone. If yes, don't just file it—share it with the people who need to know.

The rule of no surprises is about respect—for people's time, because you're not forcing them to react to preventable blindsides; for their decision-making, because you're giving them information when they can still act on it; and for the relationship, because they deserve to hear important things from you first.

Six chapters, one principle applied at six scales. Give every decision a URL. Treat documentation as a force multiplier, not a chore. Pull the andon cord the moment something's broken instead of hoping it sorts itself. Narrate your work as you go so progress doesn't have to be requested. Tell your manager the bad news yourself before someone else does. None of these are revolutionary alone; together they're the difference between a team whose institutional memory lives in artifacts and one whose memory lives in whoever happened to be in the room.

Key takeaways

- If a decision, process, or artifact doesn't have a URL, it effectively doesn't exist—you're one departure, one reorg, or one Slack retention policy away from losing it forever. Linkable doesn't mean public; it means findable, shareable, and durable enough to outlast the person who created it.
- You're the go-to person everyone Slacks with the same three questions, and every answer disappears the moment the conversation ends. Writing it down once—in the right tool, structured so people can actually find it—turns 25 hours of repeated explanations into a two-hour investment you make once and draw on indefinitely.
- When work is invisible, small problems hide until they become expensive outages. Make work visible and reward early signals, and you'll catch issues while they're still cheap to fix.
- Silent work is a rework factory: you keep your head down for three weeks, then a stakeholder sees the result and says "that's not what I meant." Working loudly—sharing progress, surfacing risks, including people early—turns surprise feedback into course corrections before they get expensive.

- If information would surprise someone when they discover it later, share it now—not when it's convenient, not when you have a solution. One blindside can undo months of trust, but consistent transparency earns you the autonomy that makes micromanagement unnecessary.

Asynchronous Communications

Your team spans time zones, and that changes how you write, when you chat, and whether you meet. Clear, persuasive writing becomes the work itself. So does communicating like a human (not a fine-tuned corporate press release), using chat without burning out, respecting the etiquette of issues and pull requests, and treating meetings as escalation rather than the default. Async communication isn't about abandoning real-time interaction—it's about making written communication your primary mode and saving synchronous channels for when a live conversation genuinely adds something writing can't.

Openness without a communication strategy is just a fire hose pointed at your teammates' inboxes. A team can post every decision publicly, share every draft, narrate every design choice—but if it's all ad hoc Slack messages and "quick syncs" that eat three hours a day, the team is open *and* drowning. The missing piece isn't *whether* to communicate—it's *how*, *when,* and *where.* Think of it like the difference between a great codebase and a great continuous integration and continuous delivery (CI/CD) pipeline: the code matters, but without a reliable way to ship it, you're just accumulating files.

> **Common objection: "Async means everything takes longer."** It feels that way at first—because you notice the wait. What you don't notice are the hours you *didn't* spend in a meeting that could've been a comment, the context switches you avoided, and the decisions that stuck because someone actually wrote down the reasoning. Do async poorly and it's slow. Do it well and it's faster than synchronous work because it respects focus time, produces better artifacts, and doesn't bottleneck on whoever happens to be awake.

These chapters break async into its component skills: designing for time zone spread, sounding like a human, using chat without burning out, the unwritten rules of issues and PRs, meetings as escalation (and writing as the default), when sync genuinely wins, and matching work to medium.

> **For managers: Your team's async maturity is a direct reflection of yours.** Set the norm: all meetings require a written agenda 24 hours in advance. If someone struggles with written communication,

> invest in that skill like any other professional development—pair them with a strong writer for their first few issues. When you default to writing, your team follows.

> **For individual contributors: Treat async communication as a core professional skill.** Nobody gets promoted based on what they said in a meeting that wasn't recorded. They get promoted based on the artifacts they leave behind—the well-reasoned issue, the clear PR description, the proposal that anticipated objections before anyone raised them. Sharpen your written communication the way you'd sharpen any technical skill—it compounds.

Written-first communication isn't a constraint imposed by distance. It's a better way to work—clearer thinking, more durable decisions, and fewer hours spent in meetings where you're silently wondering if anyone would notice if you turned off your camera. **Async isn't waiting. It's working.**

If writing is the backbone of async, time zones are where its strength gets tested. Your team's ability to leave clear artifacts isn't just about clarity—it's about making progress while half the world sleeps. But clear artifacts are only half of it; the other half is keeping momentum when everyone's working on their own clock.

Working Across Time Zones

> **TL;DR:** A team spread across twelve time zones ships code around the clock—or grinds to a halt waiting for overlapping hours. The difference is whether you treat async handoffs as first-class workflows with documented context, or keep scheduling 8 AM standups that are someone else's midnight.

It's 5 PM in San Francisco, and a critical decision needs sign-off. London signed off hours ago. Tokyo won't be online for another six. The work sits there, aging like milk. **Time zone distribution isn't the problem—pretending everyone is in the same building is.**

Distributed teams that embrace their spread achieve something no co-located team can: true follow-the-sun coverage. A bug reported at end-of-day in San Francisco gets fixed by a colleague in Singapore before the original reporter wakes up. A document started in London gets reviewed and improved by the time the author returns the next morning. That's not a side effect—it's a competitive advantage.

The time zone spectrum

Overlapping hours (4+ hours of shared working time)

Teams with significant overlap can lean on synchronous communication more freely. Choose *which* hours to overlap—sometimes called "core hours"—and protect that time for work that genuinely needs real-time interaction.

Limited overlap (1–3 hours)

These teams need rigorous async habits but can still find windows for real-time work. The limited overlap is precious—use it for relationship building, complex decisions, and conversations where tone and body language matter. Protect it fiercely.

No overlap

Teams with zero shared working hours are async-first by necessity. Every process, decision, and piece of context must be documented. There's no "let me ping them real quick"—if it's not written down, it doesn't exist.

Most teams aren't purely one type. A team based in New York, London, and Tokyo has good overlap between New York and London, limited overlap between London and Tokyo, and virtually none between New York and Tokyo. This means different communication strategies for different pairings—even within the same team.

> **Common objection: "Time zones make collaboration impossible."** Only if you insist on synchro-

> nous collaboration as the default. Drop that assumption and the spread flips from liability to asset: urgent issues get eyes faster, and nobody sits through a meeting at 3 AM unless something is truly on fire.

> **Pro-Tip:** Map out your team's time zone overlaps visually. Tools like World Time Buddy or Every Time Zone can show you exactly which hours are shared across your team. This map becomes your guide for scheduling and setting expectations.

Designing for handoffs

The single most valuable practice for distributed teams: designing explicit handoffs. In a co-located office, handoffs happen naturally—you see a colleague putting on their coat, and a quick "heading out?" gives you organic context transfer. In a distributed team, what you don't write down doesn't transfer.

End-of-day summaries

Before you log off, spend five minutes documenting what you worked on, what's blocked, and what's next. This doesn't need to be formal—a quick update in an issue or team channel works. Colleagues in other time zones should be able to pick up without waiting for you to come back online.

> **Pro-Tip:** The support team had an elegant pattern of using a dedicated "shift log" emoji. They'd react to critical messages in Slack to add them to the "shift log." When Supportocats (as they were called) signed on, they could quickly scan the shift log for any critical issues that came up while they were offline. This made handoffs effortless and context-rich.

Status documentation

Keep running documents or issues updated with the current state of work in progress. Anyone who needs to pick up where you left off should understand the situation from the written record alone.

On one of my teams at GitHub—Community and Safety, as it was called at the time—we and our partners were spread across the US West and East coasts, Europe, and Japan: round-the-clock coverage with no required overlap and no standup. Our cross-functional handoff ran on dedicated issues: each active incident had a pinned thread that shift after shift updated with current state before signing off. A good handoff is explicit—a sentence that names what's in flight, what you tried, and what you're passing to whom.

Explicit blockers

If something is blocked and you need input from a specific person, say so—and provide enough context that they can respond without follow-up questions. A back-and-forth that takes ten minutes in a hallway can stretch to two days when each message crosses a 12-hour gap. Think of it like network latency: every round-trip across time zones adds delay.

The flip side is just as important: proactively *unblocking* others before you go offline. A colleague in London once noticed a pull request in their review queue late on the last working day before a four-day bank holiday. Rather than leave it sitting—knowing the rest of the team was online and waiting—they carved out twenty minutes to review and approve before signing off ("hey, I know I'm blocking on this, and I'm about to head out on holiday..."). The remaining reviewers finished their reviews that same day, and the fix shipped while London was still on holiday.

Without that forethought, the pull request would have stalled for nearly a week. The best distributed teammates think not just about what *they* need before logging off, but about what *others* need from them.

Be explicit about urgency

"Need this today" means different things across time zones. Say "Need this by 5 PM UTC" instead. The converse is also true. Sometimes "end of day" really means "end of day *in your time zone*" so it's ready when the next person starts their morning. When that's the case, say so—"Finish this before you sign off so Tokyo can pick it up" is clearer and often less stressful than a hard timestamp.

> **For managers: Make handoff documentation a habit, not a chore.** Build it into workflows so a quick end-of-day note feels as natural as committing code. Consider adding handoff updates to your team's definition of done for any work that spans time zones.

Good handoff habits benefit everyone on the team:

> **For individual contributors: Think of handoff notes as gifts to your future self and your colleagues.** Go beyond "what I did today"—include the dead ends, the debugging steps that didn't pan out, and the hypothesis you'd test next. Link directly to the branch, issue, or error log. The colleague who picks this up at 8 AM shouldn't need to retrace your steps to figure out where you left off.

Meeting strategies for global teams

Even async-first teams need synchronous meetings sometimes—but scheduling them across time zones takes care. The default approach—scheduling when it's convenient for the organizer (which, by pure coincidence, is always mid-afternoon in *their* time zone)—creates a "time zone tax" where the same people always take the early-morning or late-night hit.

Async standups

Default to communicating status asynchronously. Purpose-built tools like Geekbot, or even a scheduled recurring chat message, let team members share updates on their own schedule—no synchronous standup required.

Rotate meeting times

If a recurring meeting must include people across distant time zones, rotate the timing so that the burden is shared. One week it's early morning in Tokyo and afternoon in London; the next week it's evening in Tokyo and morning in London. Fair distribution matters more than perfect consistency. This is especially important for company-wide events like all-hands meetings, where the expectation is that everyone attends.

Record everything

Not everyone will attend every meeting. Record meetings by default, post clear summaries and action items afterward, and treat async participation as a first-class option, not an afterthought. As a bonus, ensure transcripts are available and easily accessible. Better still, commit them to a GitHub repo so they appear in search alongside other content.

> **Pro-Tip:** When a meeting's recorded, you can watch it at 1.5x or 2x speed to catch up faster. You effectively "attend" more meetings while focusing on the parts most relevant to you. Many Hubbers (myself included) caught up while on a treadmill or

> stationary bike, turning meeting catch-up into a mini workout.

Async-first agendas

Share meeting agendas in advance and invite async input before the meeting. People in inconvenient time zones can contribute even if they can't attend live. Often, the async discussion resolves issues before anyone joins the call.

Question the meeting

Before scheduling a synchronous meeting across time zones, ask whether it's necessary. A "quick sync" that requires someone to set an alarm for midnight is neither quick nor a sync. Most can be replaced with well-structured issues or documents. The higher the time zone burden, the higher the bar for requiring synchronous participation.

> **Pro-Tip: Normalize including a time zone whenever you reference a meeting time.** "2 PM Eastern Time (ET) / 7 PM Greenwich Mean Time (GMT) / 4 AM Japan Standard Time (JST, next day)" beats assuming everyone will do the math. Even better, use a tool that converts automatically.

Collaboration windows

For teams with limited overlap, shared hours are the scarcest resource you have. Guard them.

Identify your windows

Know exactly which hours overlap across your team. These might be the only times real-time collaboration is possible without someone working outside normal hours.

Protect synchronous time

Don't fill your overlap hours with one-on-ones or administrative meetings. Reserve at least some of this time for the whole team—it might be the only chance for real-time interaction.

Focus on high-bandwidth communication

Use overlap time for conversations that benefit from real-time interaction: complex problem-solving, relationship building, and resolving ambiguity. Status updates can happen async.

Don't over-schedule

Just because you *can* meet during overlap hours doesn't mean you *should*. Too many meetings during your only shared time leaves no room for spontaneous collaboration or focused work.

> **For managers: Audit how your team uses overlap time.** Is it filled with low-value status meetings? Create protected blocks for meaningful collaboration and enforce boundaries. Make clear that overlap hours belong to the team, not to headquarters claiming them as "their" business hours.

For individual contributors, overlap time is your chance for high-bandwidth collaboration:

> **For individual contributors: Be strategic about your overlap time.** Need to pair with a colleague, brainstorm a tricky problem, or build a relationship with someone new? Do it during shared hours. Save heads-down work for when you're the only one online—that's when you'll have the fewest interruptions anyway.

Let your tools do the math

Good tooling won't eliminate a twelve-hour gap, but it removes needless friction—mental arithmetic, scheduling tag, "wait, is that *my* Tuesday?":

Default calendars to open

Create a culture where calendars are open by default—team members can see availability at minimum, and ideally full details. When you're playing scheduling Tetris, knowing a "busy" block is "walking the dog" rather than "meeting with a customer" makes everyone more accommodating.

Time zone converters

Tools like World Time Buddy, Every Time Zone, or calendar apps with built-in time zone support show at a glance when colleagues are available. Many calendar apps now display multiple time zones simultaneously.

Smart scheduling

Tools like Calendly, Doodle, or Cal.com let participants see availability in their own time zone and find mutually workable times without endless back-and-forth.

Scheduled sends

Most email clients and chat platforms support scheduled sending. Write the message when it's fresh in your mind, but schedule it to arrive during your colleague's working hours so they don't feel pressure to respond immediately.

> **Common objection: That goes against letting people manage their own time.** True. If we say that some people are most productive at 3 AM, who are you to decide that they should get your message at 9 AM? If your tools (and socialized norms) support colleagues managing their notifications (office hours, do not disturb time, etc.), then scheduled sends become unnecessary. Without that culture, they help avoid the implicit expectation of instant response across time zones.

Status indicators

Use status features in chat to signal your availability. "Out of office (OOO), back online at 9 AM ET" or "In meetings until 3 PM Pacific Time (PT)" tells colleagues when to expect a response.

Time zones affect people, not just schedules

Late-night meetings, early-morning calls, and the persistent feeling of being slightly out of sync wear people down. Time zone distribution affects lives, not just productivity.

Respect boundaries

Someone's working hours are their working hours. Don't expect immediate responses outside those times, and don't create an implicit expectation that availability equals commitment. The best distributed teams make it safe to be offline.

Avoid the "always on" trap

When your colleagues are always online *somewhere*, it can feel like work never stops. (Technically, it doesn't—but *you* should.) Be explicit about expectations: async doesn't mean instant. Most things can wait until the next business day.

Build connection despite distance

Time zones make spontaneous interaction harder, so you have to build connection on purpose. Virtual coffee chats, team social channels, and occasional overlap time dedicated to non-work conversation help people feel like teammates rather than usernames.

Remote watch parties

For major company events or conferences, host regional watch parties where people in similar time zones gather virtually to watch together. This builds camaraderie and makes participation feasible without awkward hours.

Acknowledge the burden

If someone regularly attends meetings outside their normal hours, thank them. If one location always gets the awkward timing, acknowledge it and rotate the burden.

> **For managers: Protect your team from time zone tax.** Track who's bearing the burden of inconvenient meeting times and rotate fairly. Make it explicitly acceptable to decline meetings outside working hours. Set the example: don't send messages that imply you expect immediate responses across time zones. If you must send them, schedule delivery for their working hours.

> **For individual contributors: Be clear about your working hours and availability.** Put them in your calendar, your chat status, your email signature. Be flexible when occasional early or late meetings are necessary, but advocate for fair distribution over time. It's okay to say "I can do this once, but we need to rotate in the future."

Time zone distribution, like remote work itself, is only a challenge when you pretend it doesn't exist. Design around it—explicit handoffs, thoughtful scheduling, protected collaboration windows, genuine respect for boundaries—and distributed teams don't just cope with time zones. They turn them into an advantage.

Geographic spread shapes *when* you can collaborate, but *how* you communicate matters just as much. Written communication is the backbone of async work, and the difference between writing that lands and writing that confuses often comes down to one thing: sounding like a human being, not a corporate memo.

Speak Like a Human

> **TL;DR:** In async work, you *are* your writing—and nobody wants to collaborate with a corporate press release. Specificity, clarity, and a human voice aren't just nice to have; they're how you build trust, ship faster, and stand out in a sea of jargon.

"Per my previous email, I wanted to circle back and touch base regarding the action items we synergized on during our last alignment session. Please advise on the go-forward plan so we can leverage our learnings and optimize for key stakeholder engagement."

Did that make you cringe? Good. It should. That sentence says nothing while using 42 words to do it. Yet some variation lands in inboxes across the corporate world every day—and somewhere, a reply is being drafted that adds more of the same. In async work, where your writing *is* your professional presence, that reflex doesn't just waste a reader's time. It's how careers stall in plain sight.

Buzzwords and acronyms are everywhere in corporate life. We adapt our speech to fit the environment—"if that's the word they used, I should use it"—until nobody's saying anything real. Early in GitHub culture, we had the phrase "speak like a human." Years later, "speak human" has stuck with me. If you've ever cringed at a LinkedIn post dripping with "synergize" and "thought leadership," you already know what's wrong. Corporate buzzword culture feels fake because it *is* fake.

It's not just vibes. I noticed this pattern for years before I found research confirming it: the people who peppered their writing with the most buzzwords were also the ones who seemed to miss the obvious—overlooking simple solutions because they'd buried the actual problem under six layers of jargon.

Cornell cognitive psychologist Shane Littrell put numbers behind that pattern in *Personality and Individual Differences*,[31] introducing a "Corporate Bullshit Receptivity Scale" measuring susceptibility to impressive-but-empty rhetoric. Workers who rated computer-generated sentences like "We will actualize a renewed level of cradle-to-grave credentialing" as genuinely insightful scored lower on analytic thinking, cognitive reflection, and workplace decision-making—and were the most likely to spread the jargon themselves. Your instinct to cringe at buzzword-laden prose isn't just good taste—it's a reliable signal of critical thinking.

31. https://news.cornell.edu/stories/2026/03/workers-who-love-synergizing-paradigms-might-be-bad-their-jobs

Ditch the jargon

Professionalism is mastery of your craft—efficient, methodical, organized, focused on the task. Formality emphasizes strict adherence to rules and conventions, sometimes at the expense of efficiency—prioritizing ceremony over substance.

You can be professional without being formal. When responding to a pull request, chat message, or email, you can be tactful, helpful, and technically sharp without "Dear sir or madam, I am in receipt of your pull request..."

The best remote workers stay professional and reserve formality for when the situation demands it. Warmth and competence aren't opposites. A well-placed emoji or GIF can set tone better than a paragraph of caveats.

> **Pro-Tip:** Read your message aloud before sending. **If you wouldn't say it to a colleague in person, don't write it in an email.** Good written communication should feel natural, not stilted.

Even casual writing can hide behind vague, meaning-free words. Strip those out too.

Say what you actually mean

Buzzwords are the bureaucratic dialect of corporate life: "circling back," "touching base," "pinging"—phrases that became memes for good reason.

You've sat through this meeting: a screen share crammed with "alignment," "leverage," and "circle back"—corporate security blankets that mean nothing without context. Instead of "leverage," say "use." Instead of "resources," say "people" (because that's what they are). Instead of "touch base," say "check in." If a more precise word exists, use it.

> **Pro-Tip:** Try the "explain it to a new hire" test: rewrite your message as if the reader joined your team last week and doesn't know the internal shorthand. If you can't explain it in plain language, the buzzword is probably hiding a gap in your own thinking—not saving anyone time.

Overuse isn't even the worst part. Buzzwords actively obscure meaning. "Leverage synergies to optimize our workflow" uses three buzzwords to say nothing. What are you actually proposing? Share code between teams? Reduce duplicate effort? Use a new tool? Say that instead. **Jargon hides meaning; plain language reveals it.** Buzzwords are like magic numbers and vague variable names in code—they hide intent and make everything harder to maintain.

Here's the same project update, two ways:

> *Before: "Per our discussion, I wanted to circle back on the deliverables. We need to leverage cross-functional alignment to ensure we're tracking toward the Q4 OKRs. Let's sync offline to discuss next steps and action items."*

> *After: "The auth service migration is two days behind schedule. I need design review on the new login flow by Thursday. Can the frontend team look at PR #847?"*

The first version uses 35 words to say nothing specific. The second uses 28 to tell you exactly what's happening, what's needed, and where to look. In async work, that difference isn't stylistic—it's whether a teammate can act on your message or has to ping you for clarification eight hours later.

Writing *is* your connection to colleagues in remote work—your interface with the team. You can't fall back on tone of voice, body language, or real-time clarification. Every buzzword invites misunderstanding, and in an async environment, that misunderstanding might not surface for hours or days. Clear writing works like a good test suite: it catches confusion before deployment, not after someone builds three sprints of work on a misinterpretation.

> **Pro-Tip:** The worst buzzwords are fake indicators of inclusion—phrases like "we are committed to diversity," "we celebrate all backgrounds," or "we value uniqueness." They sound meaningful but substitute for action. When your team peppers its communication with "creating a safe space" or "ensuring everyone has a seat at the table" without specific, measurable commitments, you're not building inclusion—you're building skepticism.

> If you value inclusion, describe what you're doing: "We've restructured our interview process to reduce bias by using standardized questions" or "We promoted three engineers from underrepresented groups to senior roles this quarter." Actions speak louder than slogans.

Simple words work best

Clear writing respects your reader's time and mental energy. Your reader is smart—but also busy, potentially reading in a second or third language, and processing information at the end of a long day.

You don't need to prove your vocabulary. If "use" works as well as "utilize," use "use." A 40-word sentence broken into two 20-word sentences scans better than the original sounded smart. Think of it like clean code—readable, self-documenting prose beats heavily commented spaghetti every time.

Specifics carry the weight that adjectives can't. "We should improve our deployment process" could mean anything; "we should reduce deployment time from 45 minutes to 15 by parallelizing our test suite" tells your reader exactly what success looks like, and lets them disagree with something concrete rather than argue about abstractions. The same goes for hedges. "We might want to consider possibly updating the documentation" hides a decision behind four hedge words; "let's update the documentation" makes a call. Sometimes uncertainty is real and "perhaps" is honest—but most of the time it's filler that lets you avoid committing to anything.

And when you can, name who did what. "We deployed the feature" is clearer than "the feature was deployed." In a distributed team where the next person picks this up six months from now in a different time zone, accountability shouldn't be implied—it should be searchable.

> **For managers: Clear communication starts with you—then becomes a team norm.** When you avoid buzzwords and write plainly, you give your team permission to do the same. Make it safe to say "I don't understand" when someone uses jargon, and reward clarity over cleverness. Then make it stick: add time zones to every meeting invite, expand acronyms in team-wide announcements, and when you see jargon-heavy writing in a review, flag it as a readability concern for the whole team, not a nit-pick. Your writing is your leadership—make it count.

> **Pro-Tip:** The same way you'd run a linter before merging a PR, run one on your writing. This book's own prose pipeline uses Vale,[32] LanguageTool,[33] Harper.js,[34] proselint,[35] textlint,[36] and diction.[37]

32. https://vale.sh
33. https://languagetool.org/

> Together they catch passive voice, hedging language, clichés, and readability issues automatically. If your team produces a lot of documentation, wiring at least one of these into your CI pipeline pays for itself the first time it catches `it is important to note that` before it ships.

Write so everyone can understand

Remote teams are diverse teams. You're likely working with people from different countries, cultures, backgrounds, and native languages. What seems like common knowledge to you might be foreign to a colleague halfway around the world. In an office, a confused look prompts instant clarification. In async work, a misunderstood idiom, an ambiguous date format, or an inaccessible document creates friction that compounds silently across time zones.

I remember a German coworker who would "cosplay" as an American when communicating. Instead of saying a pull request was "fine," he'd describe it as "awesome" or "amazing." He'd picked up on the unwritten rule that Americans inflate adjectives—and overcorrected. What reads as enthusiastic to one person might feel excessive to another; what seems like directness might come across as rudeness.

34. https://writewithharper.com/
35. https://github.com/amperser/proselint
36. https://textlint.github.io/
37. https://www.gnu.org/software/diction/

Expand acronyms on first use

Acronyms are an unintentional form of exclusion. Don't use them without context. Even if you think everyone knows what API stands for, it takes seconds to write "Application Programming Interface (API)" the first time. That small effort makes your writing accessible to everyone who might encounter the acronym for the first time.

> **Pro-Tip:** At GitHub, we had a "glossary" repo with associated ChatOps. Encounter an unknown acronym, and ChatOps could explain it—or at least add it to the glossary for others once you learned what it meant.

Avoid cultural idioms

Phrases like "drop the ball" or "punt on this decision" are deeply rooted in American sports culture. To someone who didn't grow up watching baseball or football, these phrases are meaningless. Instead of "we hit a home run," say "we exceeded our goals." Instead of "let's touch base," say "let's check in." Be direct.

> **Pro-Tip:** Use GitHub Copilot code review to reinforce inclusive language norms on your team. Configure custom instructions—like avoiding gendered pronouns in documentation, flagging exclusionary idioms, or encouraging plain language—so every

> pull request gets consistent feedback that reflects your team's values.

Consider neurodiversity

Some people interpret language literally. Sarcasm, implied meanings, and subtle hints don't always translate well. Be explicit, especially in writing, where tone is harder to convey.

Use unambiguous date formats

Write "June 5" instead of "6/5," which could mean June 5 or the 6th of May depending on where you're from. When including times, always specify the time zone—"3 PM ET" takes two seconds to type and saves confusion. Better yet, include multiple time zones when scheduling across regions—for example, "3 PM ET / 9 PM UTC+1."

Write for accessibility

Screen readers rely on proper document structure to help users navigate content. When you use Markdown's semantic elements—headings for hierarchy, lists for enumeration, emphasis for actual emphasis—you make your writing usable for assistive technologies, not just prettier. Give images alt text and write descriptive link text rather than "click here."

> **Pro-Tip:** Run a document through a screen reader at least once (macOS has VoiceOver built in; Windows has Narrator). Five minutes of listening

> will reveal which "headings" are just bold text, which images lack alt text, and which "click here" links are meaningless without visual context. It catches accessibility problems that no style guide can.

Inclusive writing doesn't happen by accident—it takes reinforcement from both directions. When a manager expands an acronym, includes time zones in meeting invites, or writes accessible alt text, the team notices—and follows. And when an IC encounters unfamiliar jargon, inconvenient meeting times, or inaccessible content, speaking up isn't ignorance—it's a gift to everyone who was wondering the same thing but didn't want to ask.

Don't outsource your voice

Corporate jargon had a good run as the primary threat to clear communication. Then AI arrived and industrialized it. Large language models trained on the internet's corpus of corporate emails, marketing copy, and LinkedIn posts have internalized decades of every pattern this chapter warns against. Ask an AI to draft a status update, and you'll get something polished but written by committee:

> **For individual contributors: Your writing voice is a career asset—don't flatten it.** In async work, colleagues form impressions of you from your

> messages, not your meetings. The engineer whose issue comments have personality, specificity, and a clear point of view gets trusted faster than the one whose updates read like they were generated by a committee. Edit AI drafts until they sound like you, not like everyone.

"It's important to note that we've made significant progress on key deliverables, and moving forward, we're well-positioned to leverage our learnings."

That's not a communication style. **That's a style *absence*.**

The problem isn't that AI writes badly—it's that it writes *plausibly*. AI-generated text is fluent, grammatically correct, and structurally sound. The text hedges appropriately ("It's worth noting..."), transitions smoothly ("Furthermore..."), and summarizes confidently ("In summary..."). It reads like professional writing. It just doesn't read like *anyone's* writing. In async-first work—where your words are your professional identity—**a voice that belongs to everyone belongs to no one**. When every status update, design document, and pull request comment sounds generated by the same model, you lose what makes async collaboration work: the sense that you're engaging with real people who have real opinions.

You'd never ship a function you didn't understand just because it passed the test suite. Don't ship writing you didn't think through just because it reads cleanly. The value of writing isn't just the artifact—it's the thinking that producing it forces you to do.

> **Common objection: "But AI saves me so much time on writing."** It can—when used as a thinking tool rather than a ghostwriter. Use it to brainstorm, structure messy ideas, or draft a first pass when you're staring at a blank page. But treat AI output as raw material, not finished product. Edit ruthlessly. Inject your actual opinion. Delete the hedge words. Add the specific detail only you know. The time AI saves you on the first draft, spend on making the final version sound like you.

> **Pro-Tip:** Try the "anyone test" on AI-assisted writing: read it aloud and ask whether it could have been written by literally anyone on earth. If there's nothing in it that's distinctly *you*—no specific detail, no actual opinion, no hint of personality—rewrite it. Your colleagues can tell the difference between a message that was crafted and one that was generated. So can your manager.

Clear writing gets you promoted

People remember the colleague who writes clearly. Not because clear writing is flashy—it's the opposite. It disappears. The reader absorbs the idea without tripping over the words. That's the skill: making complex things feel simple, making async conversations feel real, making a person on the other side of the world feel like they're sitting next to you.

In a remote-first world, your writing is your professional presence. It's how people experience you in pull request reviews, design documents, Slack threads, and status updates. Every unclear message erodes trust; every clear one builds it. The engineer who writes "this PR refactors the auth middleware to reduce token validation from 200ms to 50ms" will always be more trusted —and more promotable—than the one who writes "made some improvements to the auth flow." The same applies to non-developers.

> **For individual contributors: Structure your async messages for scanning, not leisurely reading.** Lead with the ask or the decision, bold the key point, and keep paragraphs short. Your message competes with dozens of others in every channel—the person who writes clearly gets read, and the person who gets read gets influence. Treat every Slack message and issue comment like a tiny pull request for someone's attention.

Invest in your writing the way you'd invest in any other core skill. The clearest voice in the channel gets heard, gets trusted, and gets promoted.

Not all writing is long-form, though. Much of your day-to-day communication happens in chat—and chat has its own rules for staying clear without becoming a firehose.

Chat Responsibly

> **TL;DR:** Chat is your team's most abused collaboration tool. Every low-value message in a busy channel is a tiny denial-of-service attack on collective attention—so lead with context, use threads, structure your channels, and treat your teammates' focus as the finite, shared resource it is.

Your heart skips. A message from your boss: "Hey, got a minute?"

That's it. No context. No topic. Just three words that trigger an immediate spiral. *Am I in trouble? Is there a lay-off coming? Did I mess something up?* You spend the next 20 minutes catastrophizing instead of working. **"Got a minute?" is anxiety in three words.** The sender almost never meant to do that. They fired off a context-free ping because typing the actual question felt like it'd take too long—exporting their thirty-second convenience as their teammate's afternoon of dread. Multiply that by every channel, every DM, every team, and you've built an always-on culture out of habits nobody ever agreed to.

Chat isn't email

Chat is **ephemeral.** It's built for quick, real-time exchanges, not permanent archives. Retention logs are limited, messages are easy to miss, and nobody expects you to read days of back-scroll after vacation.

Chat lacks **filtering.** Email lets you flag, sort, and defer. Chat is an unbuffered stream—messages dump into your attention without queuing. An urgent message from your manager gets the same screen space as a GIF of a cat playing the piano.

Worst of all, chat creates an expectation of **urgency**. You feel compelled to keep it open all day "to show you're online," but the constant notifications and red badges interrupt relentlessly. Email has a built-in expectation of delay. Chat doesn't. You end up always-on, always-available, always-distracted. **Presence theater, not productivity.**

> **Common objection: "We need instant responses—chat keeps us connected."** Chat can keep you connected—and constantly interrupted. The dopamine hit of an immediate reply isn't collaboration—it's distraction theater. You wouldn't expect your friends to reply instantly to every text, so why expect that from coworkers?
>
> Real connection comes from reading someone's well-reasoned proposal, not speed-running their pings. The best remote teams use chat for what it's good at (quick coordination, social bonding,

> memes, urgent matters) and higher-fidelity async channels (issues, docs, pull requests) for everything else.
>
> Across time zones, it's worse. An off-hours ping forces a rushed, multitasked reply—and always-on expectations breed a habit of checking your phone before you've even opened your eyes.

The interruptions are bad enough when they come with context. Without it, they're worse.

"Can we chat?" is a recipe for interruption

When you send "Hey, got a second?" or "Can we talk?" you're knocking on someone's door and asking them to drop everything without telling them why—the remote-work equivalent of your manager saying "we need to talk" and then walking away, cruel even if unintentional. Stripped of body language and tone, that vacuum fills with worst-case scenarios, not good news.

The fix is simple: **always provide context with your ask.**

Instead of "Got a minute?" try "Got a minute to discuss the API change in PR #234?" Instead of a calendar invite with just "Sync," add a brief agenda: "Sync re: Q4 planning—want to align on priorities before Friday."

Even if the topic is sensitive, provide enough context to prevent spiraling: "I'd like to discuss feedback on the project timeline—nothing urgent, but want your input." Two seconds of typing saves your colleague hours of worry.

Meeting invites are no different. A calendar invitation without context is Schrödinger's meeting invite—simultaneously routine and career-ending until someone adds an agenda. Include what the meeting is about, what you hope to achieve, and what (if anything) they should prepare. Meetings with agendas run shorter and stay focused.

> **For managers: Every message you send teaches your team how to communicate.** Instead of "Let's chat about the project," try "Let's chat about the Q3 timeline—I'm thinking of pushing the launch by a week; thoughts by Thursday?" When you get "Hey, can we talk?" reply with "What's it about?" to normalize the pattern. A context-free ping from a manager lands differently than one from a peer.

> **For individual contributors: Build three chat habits that compound over time.** First, always reply in threads—it keeps the channel scannable and lets people opt into the conversation. Second, when a chat exchange passes five or six messages, move it to an issue with a summary and link back so the context isn't lost. Third, front-load your messages with context: instead of "the deploy is broken," write "the staging deploy is failing on the auth service—here's the error log and what I've tried so far." Every context-rich message saves your teammates a round-trip of follow-up questions.

Front-loading context means more than adding detail to your ask—it means leading *with* the ask.

Skip the "PING" and ask your question

Engineers have a stubborn chat antipattern: the belief that conversations must begin with a `PING` message. Not only is this rude—would you do that in person?—but it defeats the purpose of async communication. The same goes for a bare "hello" followed by silence while you wait for the conversation to go synchronous. Don't do that.[38] Unlike Transmission Control Protocol (TCP) handshakes, human communication doesn't require establishing a connection before transmitting the payload—just send the message.

Here's what that antipattern looks like in practice—and the async tax it creates:

> ***10:02 AM****—Dev A: "ping"*
> ***10:17 AM****—Dev B: "hey"*
> ***10:28 AM****—Dev A: "you around?"*
> ***10:33 AM****—Dev B: "yeah, what's up?"*
> ***10:35 AM****—Dev A: "can you look at the auth thing?"*
> ***10:36 AM****—Dev B: "which auth thing?"*

Thirty-four minutes, six messages, zero information transferred. A function that takes six arguments and returns `null`. Compare that with one message that could have been sent—and answered—asynchronously:

38. https://nohello.net

> ***10:02 AM**—Dev A: "@DevB Could you review the token refresh logic in PR #847? I'm not sure the validation handles expired sessions correctly—specifically this line.[39]"*

Just ask. Your colleague will know you have something to say because you just said it—and they can respond on their schedule, not yours.

Better still, post your question in a team channel rather than a DM. @mention them to push the question, not just the ping. Someone else might answer first, because you've exposed the question to the entire team rather than one person.

Your team's attention is a shared resource

It's natural to want your message to be seen—you're far more likely to hear "I didn't know about that" than "stop posting so much." But when everyone broadcasts without considering the audience, no one's message gets noticed. It's a digital tragedy of the commons—or in engineering terms, a denial-of-service attack on your team's collective attention. Rarely malicious, but it overwhelms the system's capacity to respond.

Your reader can only process so many words per minute or context-switch so many times per hour. Optimizing for *your* message being seen might work short-term, but it undermines everyone long-term.

Put a number on it: a message in a fifty-person channel takes roughly twenty seconds to process—notification, context switch, read, decide whether to respond. **That's**

over fifteen minutes of collective time for a single message. Scale that: ten low-value messages per channel per day across five active channels burn over twelve hours of collective attention daily—before anyone writes a line of code.

A time-sensitive heads-up or a genuine question? Worth every second. A "sounds good 👍" reply that could have been an emoji reaction? You just mass-interrupted fifty people for a thumbs-up. And `@channel` or `@here` in a large channel compounds the damage by an order of magnitude—the handful of genuine emergencies they exist for are vastly outnumbered by the reflexive uses. **A `@channel` ping should require a $1 donation to charity for every person it interrupts.** Only half joking.

Drive-through opinions are even more corrosive in chat. Someone drops into a thread, offers a hot take on a decision they have minimal context on, and vanishes—leaving the people actually doing the work to untangle whether the comment changes anything. In an issue, this is annoying but contained. In a fast-moving chat channel, it derails conversations in real-time—and the drive-through commenter won't stick around to follow up. Before weighing in, ask yourself: Am I one of the people closest to this problem? Do I have context the participants lack? If not, a 👍 or 👀 reaction will do.

39. https://github.com

Responsible chat usage looks different for each role:

> **For managers: Set explicit norms about chat expectations.** Make clear that team members aren't expected to monitor chat constantly or respond immediately. Consider "quiet hours" or encourage status indicators. Your behavior signals what's acceptable—if you send messages at all hours expecting responses, your team will feel obligated to stay connected.

> **For individual contributors: Treat chat like a buffered queue, not a live stream.** Check messages at natural breaks rather than responding instantly. Use threads religiously—they keep related conversations findable and reduce noise for everyone else. Set your status to signal when you're heads-down. Chat's always-on nature is a feature for the *channel*, not an expectation for *you*. For broader strategies on protecting deep work, see *Optimize for Flow, Not Face Time*.

Individual discipline only goes so far if the channels themselves are a mess—starting with your loudest megaphone.

An @mention is a page, not a shortcut

Every @mention triggers a notification—a vibration in someone's pocket, a banner on their screen, a break in their concentration. It's not a polite wave across the room; it's a tap on the shoulder that says "stop what you're doing and look at this." **Treat every @mention like paging someone on-call: warranted when you genuinely need their attention, rude when you don't.**

`@here` and `@channel` (or their platform equivalents) scale that page to everyone in the room. `@here` pings every active member; `@channel` pings *everyone*—including the teammate asleep three time zones away who wakes up to a red badge for something resolved hours ago. In a 200-person channel, that's 200 simultaneous shoulder taps. If that sounds excessive, it usually is.

Before reaching for an @mention, run through a quick mental checklist:

- **Do I need *this specific person*, or could anyone in the channel answer?** If anyone could help, just post the question—no @mention needed. The right person will see it.
- **Is this urgent enough to justify an interrupt?** If it can wait an hour or two, skip the mention. People check their channels; they'll find it.
- **Am I using `@here` or `@channel` because it's actually an emergency, or because I want a faster response?** Impatience isn't urgency. If the build is on fire, page away. If you want a status update, just ask—without the blast radius.

The real damage from over-mentioning isn't just the interruptions—it's the boy-who-cried-wolf effect. When everything is tagged `@here`, people stop treating `@here` as a signal and start treating it as noise. They mute the channel, disable notifications, or tune out entirely. Then, when a genuine emergency hits—a production outage, a security incident—your actual page lands in a graveyard of ignored alerts. **The team that @mentions everything effectively @mentions nothing.**

> **For managers: Set a team norm for @mention etiquette—and model it.** If you routinely `@channel` for non-urgent announcements, your team will mirror that behavior, and the signal-to-noise ratio will collapse. Reserve broadcast mentions for genuine emergencies and time-sensitive coordination. For everything else, post without the @mention and trust that your team reads their channels. Consider documenting your team's @mention policy alongside other chat norms—when `@here` is appropriate, when a direct mention is warranted, and when a plain message will do.

> **For individual contributors: Be surgical with your @mentions.** Mention the one person who can unblock you, not five people "just in case." If you're not sure who to ask, post the question without an @mention and let the right person self-select. And if you find yourself reaching for `@here` in a large channel, pause—could you post in a smaller, more targeted channel instead? A message in `#team-auth` reaches the people who care without paging the 150 people in `#engineering` who don't.

Structure your channels, not just your messages

Group DMs seem convenient—until you need to add someone three days in and realize it's a dead end. Named channels are discoverable, searchable, and expandable. Prefix temporary ones with `#tmp-` (like `#tmp-q4-launch-coordination`) so everyone knows they have a shelf life, and archive them once they've served their purpose.

> **Pro-Tip:** When a group DM grows past three people or lasts more than a day, move it to a named channel. Future you will never remember which combination of coworkers was in that thread—but you *will* be able to search for `#tmp-q4-pricing-discussion`.

Default to public channels unless privacy is genuinely required. The person who needs the information most is often someone you didn't think to invite. Keep channels specific, too—people engage more in `#proj-mobile-redesign` than in `#general-engineering`, where everything competes for attention and nothing wins.

The same goes for operational work. ChatOps—running commands like deploys and environment provisioning through chat rather than silently on your laptop—turns invisible work into a learning opportunity. A junior engineer watching a deployment in a channel absorbs context no onboarding doc could replicate. It's mentorship by osmosis, and it costs you nothing beyond choosing a channel over a terminal.

ChatOps also makes physical infrastructure legible to remote workers. Early GitHub had `.door me` to unlock the office front door from chat—no physical key required; anyone visiting could buzz themselves in. Hubbers traveling to HQ ran `.office me <snack>` the day before they arrived, and their favorite snack was waiting on the counter when they walked in (for me, it was sourdough pretzels). The commands look trivial, but the principle isn't: the office was a *service*, invoked through the same interface as a deploy. **If your physical infrastructure only responds to badge readers, it's telling your remote workers who the building is really for.**

Chat's lightness comes with a cost: without tone or body language, text is easily misread. A terse response reads as curt when you're just being efficient. A friendly joke lands flat—or worse, offends. The fix is to add context and warmth deliberately. A well-timed 😄, 👍, or 🎉 reaction can replace a reply that would only add noise.

Emoji and GIFs: digital body language

Tone is hard to capture in text—the thinking goes—but that sells us short. No body language doesn't mean no expression—it means being deliberate about conveying it. Emoji and animated GIFs are the facial expressions of online writing—and you've been communicating this way since you got your first phone. Keep it professional and respectful, sure—but not formal or sterile.

Internet culture runs on emoji and GIFs—not because GIFs of kittens are adorable, but because a 💁 is often the most efficient way to express sarcasm, and 💀 conveys "I'm dying laughing" in a way words can't. Emoji also make communication more inclusive, especially for neurodiverse team members and non-native English speakers.

The best custom emoji aren't decoration—they're shorthand for a shared story. GitHub's `:shipit:` squirrel started as an inside joke in Campfire, the company's internal chat before Slack existed. It wasn't designed by the brand team; it was recognized by the culture and promoted from meme to infrastructure. **Custom emoji become the petroglyphs of your team's inside jokes—the ones that survive become vocabulary.**

Use emoji reactions in discussions, issues, and chat to acknowledge you've read something—without adding noise. I ACK (acknowledge) chat messages to signal I've seen them, even when I can't respond yet. Not impolite. Among technologists, this is a nod to the SYN (Synchronize)/ACK handshake in TCP.

Why a 🎉 beats a thousand words

A "Thank you" becomes warmer with a 😊. A "Congratulations!" gains momentum with a 👏. A single 😃 conveys joy across every language and communication style.

Many platforms let you create custom emoji, building shared culture across distance. At GitHub, we had custom emoji like "Mona high five" and "Octocat party" to celebrate wins, plus "X intensifies" variants—adaptations of the popular internet meme where an emoji shakes for emphasis—that quickly became inside jokes.

GIFs: body language on loop

GIFs capture what text can't—the eye roll, the slow clap, the mic drop—on loop. Reply with a "That escalated quickly" GIF and you're connecting with anyone who gets the reference. A victory dance for a shipped feature, a dramatic "No!" from a soap opera for a build failure—they celebrate wins and commiserate over disasters in a way that `:tada:` alone can't match.

Don't overthink tone, either. A well-placed 😂 can lighten the mood, but a barrage of 🤣 might be overkill. If you use the red heart instead of the blue one or drop a reaction GIF from a PG-13 movie, you're unlikely to get a call from HR.

> 👔 **For managers: Use reactions to acknowledge contributions, especially for async work you can't comment on immediately.** A 👍 or 🎉 shows you've seen someone's work and value it. A 👀 signals you've noticed something without requiring a verbose response. Consider creating custom emoji that reflect your team's culture and inside jokes—these small touches build cohesion across distance. Don't agonize over emoji selection—just react.

Get chat right, and it's the glue that holds a distributed team together. Get it wrong, and it's the noise that drowns everything else out.

Chat is ephemeral by design—great for quick coordination, terrible for decisions that need to stick. For work that matters most, you need durable, structured channels with their own rules of engagement.

The Etiquette of Issues and Pull Requests

> **TL;DR:** Issues and pull requests have unwritten rules—open freely, @mention teams not people, and treat every comment as a tiny meeting you just called. Get the etiquette right and your work moves forward; get it wrong and you're the annoying new hire.

You join a new team: "We're async-first! Everything happens in issues and PRs." You're excited—this is how you like to work. Then you open your first issue and get... silence. Or worse, you comment on a thread and accidentally trigger a firestorm because you didn't know the unwritten rules. Or you @mention the wrong person, and suddenly you're "that annoying new hire."

Unwritten rules are broken rules—what follows are protocols for issues, pull requests, @mentions, and moving work forward without manufacturing drama.

Just open the issue already

Have a question? Open an issue. Have an idea? Open an issue. Notice something's a bit wonky? You guessed it, open an issue.

Issues are cheap—cheaper than the meeting someone will schedule if the question festers. They cost seconds to create and close just as quickly when they're duplicates. Issues start conversations, surface alternate viewpoints, and create permanent, searchable, linkable records—even when the answer is `wontfix` (a label maintainers apply to feature requests they decline).

Keep the barrier to opening an issue vanishingly low. If you're hesitating, you're thinking about it wrong. **Nobody gets fired for opening an issue.**

> 🤔 **Common objection: "We tried issues, but they just become a graveyard of stale tickets."** That's a symptom of treating issues like a formal system rather than a conversation. Issues aren't bureaucratic overhead—they're how you think out loud as a team. The problem isn't too many issues; it's issues without owners, without verbs in their titles, or without anyone willing to close them when the answer is "no."

A few nuances

- **Search before you open.** Opening a duplicate issue is a great way to embarrass yourself. Spend thirty seconds searching first.

- **Provide context.** Opening an issue comes with expectations: cross-reference relevant issues, document what you expected versus what happened, and give others enough context to reach a shared understanding.
- **Issues are constructive criticism.** Anything short of that is just complaining. If you're not proposing a path forward or asking a genuine question, it's not an issue—it's a vent.

Tag teams, not people

When you open an issue or pull request, copy all relevant teams—not individuals.

When I'm frequently mentioned by name on issues (or keep mentioning the same colleague), that's a red flag—a single point of failure waiting to happen. Humans tend to do silly things like get sick, sleep at night, or occasionally take a day off. An individual-based workflow also excludes anyone who hasn't built a broad social network.

Mention teams, not individuals, to distribute responsibility and awareness. Unless `CODEOWNERS` or similar mechanisms already handle it—by automatically requesting reviews from teams that own specific files—deliberately bring in the right groups.

> **Pro-Tip:** One design pattern we used extensively at GitHub was the idea of "First Responders"—a designated team member who was "on call" for a

> given week to be first to respond to any team mention during their normal business hours. The rotation keeps mentions from going unaddressed while sparing the rest of the team from constant interruptions.

In practice, this means creating many niche teams—teams for affinities as small as people who play board games or who are color-blind. If people can freely associate, the teams will populate quickly. It also means CC'ing the relevant teams when you're mentioned by name. The original poster will start mentioning the team instead.

Every comment has a cost

Every comment is a tiny meeting you just called—fifty subscribers means fifty context switches. (See *Chat Responsibly* for the math—the same scaling applies to issues and pull requests.)

Three things this means

- **Avoid drive-through opinions.** What issues can you contribute the most to? Which affect your role most directly? Think twice before weighing in outside your area of expertise, especially when you don't have the full context or aren't willing to follow through yourself.

- **Only post if you have something to add.** Many platforms let you react instead of posting—sharing sentiment without notification noise. Unless your response advances the discussion, react (or stay silent) rather than adding to it.

- **Always provide context.** Context-switching is expensive. Give teammates what they need to get up to speed and decide what to do. When CC'ing a team, absorb the complexity and make your ask explicit. Optimize for the reader who finds this thread six months from now, not the rush of hitting "send."

  The same applies to pull requests. A PR titled "a few edits" with no description forces every reviewer to reconstruct your intent from the diff—like reading code with no comments and no commit messages. Compare:

  - ✕ **Title:** "fix stuff" | **Description:** *(empty)*
  - ✓ **Title:** "Fix token refresh race condition causing spurious logouts" | **Description:** "Users on mobile were getting logged out mid-session because two concurrent refresh requests could invalidate each other's tokens. This change adds a mutex around the refresh flow. Resolves #1042."

    The second version takes thirty extra seconds to write and saves every reviewer minutes of detective work—and six months from now, when someone runs `git blame` (a command that shows who last changed each line of a file, and when) on that line, they'll understand *why* you made the change without mounting an archaeology expedition.

> **For managers: Your @mentions carry weight—be thoughtful about them.** Team members often feel obligated to respond immediately when

> pinged by a manager. Be explicit about urgency (or lack thereof) and encourage pushback on noisy threads. A "no rush, but when you get a chance" prefix costs you five seconds and saves your report an hour of anxiety.

> 💻 **For individual contributors: Curate your subscriptions ruthlessly.** Unwatch repositories and threads that don't need your attention. When you do comment, make it count—add information, ask clarifying questions, or move the discussion forward. "+1" comments are what emoji reactions are for. A 👍 costs nothing and adds no noise.

> **Pro-Tip:** Engineers call the drive-through opinion pattern "bikeshedding.[40]" The name comes from a famous observation:[41] give a committee a nuclear power plant to approve, and they'll spend most of their time debating what color to paint the staff bike shed—because that's the part everyone feels qualified to weigh in on. In async reviews, it's fixating on variable names while ignoring architecture. If you catch yourself debating the bike shed, ask whether you're contributing to the *structure* of the proposal or just its paint job.
>
> The dark-arts counterpart is worth naming too: the **bikeshed honeypot**—a trivial flaw you leave in a proposal on purpose to divert attention from the

40. https://bikeshed.com/

> parts you actually care about. Reviewers feel useful catching the obvious nit and rubber-stamp everything else. Use sparingly, and never on decisions that matter; but recognize it when it happens *to* you.

Turn blockers into checklists

The corporate world calls them "action items." In the GitHub cinematic universe, we called them task lists.[42] The intent is the same. Spell out what needs doing and who owns it.

> **For managers: Own the checklists for cross-team work.** When a project spans multiple teams, the task list in the coordinating issue is your substitute for a status meeting. Keep it updated, ensure every item has a named owner, and use it in your async updates. It's accountability without the calendar overhead.

An always-current task list at the top of an issue breaks complex problems into visible steps and keeps multi-issue projects on track. Link each action item to the associated issue, describe the task, and @mention the person or team responsible. On GitHub, you can have sub-issues and sub-sub-issues, all linked in a hierarchy. For example: `- [ ] @backend-team Review performance impact of proposed schema change by Friday`

41. https://en.wikipedia.org/wiki/Law_of_triviality
42. https://github.blog/news-insights/product-news/task-lists-in-gfm-issues-pulls-comments/

or `- [ ] @frontend-eng Open follow-up issue for mobile compatibility once browser support lands.` The checkbox is just structure; the real work is the clarity: who, what, by when.

Treat issues as your team's to-do list

Don't close issues until they're resolved. Issues represent actions the organization needs to take—or has decided not to take. Whether it's a bug, a feature, or a blog post, an issue stays open until someone acts on it or explicitly says "no."

Two things this means

- **Issue titles should contain at least one verb.** Borrowed from Getting Things Done:[43] if issues are organizational to-dos, the title should contain at least one verb so it's something the organization can act on. Compare these:
  - ❌ "Homepage"—✔ "Update homepage hero image for Q4 campaign"
  - ❌ "Login bug"—✔ "Fix session timeout causing logout after 5 minutes of inactivity"
  - ❌ "Performance"—✔ "Reduce dashboard load time from 4s to under 1s"
  - ❌ "Onboarding"—✔ "Add setup guide for new engineers joining the payments team"

43. https://en.wikipedia.org/wiki/Getting_Things_Done

- **Don't close issues prematurely.** Issues may stay open for months, even years, before anyone closes them. That's okay. A long tail of issues—pruned and organized—signals a healthy project. Premature closure just hides problems and forces the same conversation to reopen later.

How to politely follow up

Things get past people. If a pull request has sat too long without a relevant stakeholder weighing in, bump the thread. Publicly. Public follow-ups create visible accountability, and often someone else picks it up on their behalf.

The gentle bump

- **It's not the obnoxious bump.** Be sincere, explicit, and charming. "@benbalter, the gentlest of bumps on this. Got two minutes to look at this error? 😄" Your goal is to ensure they know about the request, not to trample their right to manage their own time.
- **No news isn't good news.** If you've proposed an idea or change and haven't heard back despite repeated follow-ups, read the silence as your answer. If your colleagues aren't opinionated enough to even comment on the proposal, that *is* their opinion.

- **An implicit promotion.** There's an art to knowing your coworkers, understanding how your organization works, and taking it upon yourself to hit that big green merge button. Often, that means you've just inherited a new responsibility—so merge wisely, and do so while working loudly.

> **Pro-Tip:** As a reviewer, build a reputation for monitoring your GitHub notifications. As a requester, avoid the temptation to build your own notification system by sending reviewers DMs. As a leader, foster a culture where DM follow-ups aren't necessary. Everyone manages their own time without unexpected interruptions, and work keeps moving.

One topic per thread

Unlike email, issues and pull requests can be split when topics diverge, keeping teams focused on shipping one thing at a time. Discrete topics reduce noise and speed up decisions—only the most relevant teams need to weigh in.

Discussions should have one purpose, defined by the title at the top of the page. When a concern not directly related to the thread's purpose arises—as it often does—open a new issue and encourage participants to continue the discussion there. If you see a teammate hijacking the discussion, do the same on their behalf. If the subtask is a blocker, note it as such and move on.

Change things through pull requests

Unless it's a minor typo—so irrefutable that no one would question it—the only way to change shared content is with a pull request: code, configuration, or internal policy.

Sometimes you'll submit pull requests you immediately self-merge just to notify teammates, or open longer discussions before merging. For ninety-nine percent of changes, committing directly to `main` is inappropriate. Yes, even that one. (If that becomes a problem, consider implementing branch protection rulesets.)

Not all pull requests are created equal

Not every PR needs a thorough, line-by-line review. Calibrate your approach—and your reviewers' expectations—based on the type of change:

- **Just a heads-up**—You've made a change so straightforward that no review is required, but you want teammates to know. Create the PR, merge it yourself, and let the notification do the work. Dependency bumps and minor configuration changes are classic use cases.
- **Quick check**—A small change, likely in unfamiliar territory, where you'd like a quick 👍 before merging. Wait briefly for a sniff test, then self-merge.
- **Draft pull request**—You've started something that isn't ready for review, but you want to signal intent and prevent duplicated effort. Open it as a draft[44] so reviewers know it's not actionable yet.

- **Early feedback**—You've spiked out a rough proof of concept. The code exists to convey the approach, not to ship. *Is this a good idea? Is there a better way?* Often starts as a draft and evolves into a full review.
- **Line-by-line review**—The change is feature-complete and ready to ship. You've CC'd the relevant teams and made it clear: unless you hear otherwise, you're hitting merge.

Knowing which type you're submitting—and stating it explicitly—prevents mismatched expectations. A reviewer who treats a heads-up like a line-by-line review wastes everyone's time. A reviewer who skims a feature-complete PR like a quick check misses real issues. **Tell reviewers what you need from them.**

Your PR belongs to the team now

When you hit the big green "submit pull request" button, your code is no longer your own. You're still responsible for seeing it through to merge, but getting there means steering discussion toward consensus—not defending "your" contribution.

That means it's bad form to title a pull request "@benbalter's edits." More broadly, you become the gracious host: answering questions, implementing suggestions, and pulling in the necessary teams. At GitHub, we primarily used branch-to-branch pull requests within the same repository, so don't be surprised if someone else jumps in and politely pushes a commit or two.

44. https://docs.github.com/en/pull-requests/collaborating-with-pull-requests/proposing-changes-to-your-work-with-pull-requests/about-pull-requests#draft-pull-requests

If you can't see the change, you can't review it

Pull requests—and by extension, diffs—are at the core of remote workflows. Whether you're changing code, configuration, policy, or prose, reviewers need to see exactly what you're proposing without downloading special software or leaving the browser. If they can't see the change, you can't seriously discuss its merits.

> **Pro-Tip:** A "diff" shows the line-by-line differences between two versions of a file—additions in green, deletions in red. Think of diff-friendliness as a format selection criterion: if a change can't be rendered as a readable diff, it's not suited for pull request review, and you'll need to compensate with screenshots or detailed descriptions. The collaborative power of pull requests is in the diff. If your change can't be diffed, you can't collaborate effectively.

Prefer formats like Markdown and CSV over proprietary or binary formats like Word or Excel, even at the drafting stage. Open formats let you diff changes and discuss them line by line. When binary formats are unavoidable—say, tweaking a site's design—provide before-and-after screenshots in the pull request body so reviewers can evaluate without downloading anything.

You're asking others to take time from their day to review your change. Optimize for their experience, not yours.

Email and DMs aren't collaboration

Email is a terrible collaboration medium and an even worse store of organizational knowledge. Direct messages in chat aren't much better. They offer no opt-in or opt-out, no ability to link or cross-reference discussions, and conversation history lives in a teammate's inbox (or chat app)—when they leave, so does the context.

> **For individual contributors: When you're tempted to DM, ask: does this need to be private?** Most "quick questions" belong in a public channel where others with the same question can benefit from the answer. Moving one conversation per day from DMs to a shared channel quietly builds your team's searchable knowledge base—and makes your contributions visible to people beyond the person you happened to message.

Use email and DMs sparingly, and only when issues or a public channel would be inappropriate. Reserve private channels for sensitive discussions—personnel matters, one-on-one feedback, external communication—and for conversations that don't need to be discoverable.

If you can have the conversation in a better medium, you should.

If it has a URL, link to it

If you reference something—a prior issue, the pull request that implemented a feature, a line in a file—and it has a URL, find it and link it.

You're infinitely more familiar with what you're referencing than your readers are. Given a comment read by fifty people, it's more efficient for you to look it up once than for each of them to search independently. **Link it once. Save fifty searches.**

On GitHub, linking to another issue or pull request creates a visible cross-reference—every link you add makes the next person's job easier.

None of this is arbitrary. These are hard-won habits from teams spread across time zones and continents—practices that become culture when leaders model them and teammates hold each other accountable.

Meetings Are a Point of Escalation

> **TL;DR:** Default to writing, escalate to a meeting only when you must. You save the team hours, leave a searchable record, and the meetings you do hold actually move work forward.

Meetings are where work goes to die—drowned in scheduling overhead, derailed by tangents, and forgotten the moment everyone closes the video call. We were all taught the opposite: meetings are where things get decided, where alignment happens, where the team comes together. They're not. If you've ever sat through one thinking "this could have been an email," you already know the problem. Default-to-meetings culture is a synchronous blocking call in code form: everything stops while you wait for everyone to be available, when an async approach would let work continue in parallel.

> **Common objection: "Some things just need a meeting."** True—but far less often than you think. Brainstorming, interpersonal conflict, rapport-

> building, and complex decisions where tone matters are genuinely better synchronously (see *When Async Isn't the Answer* for the full breakdown). Everything else? That's habit, not necessity. The question isn't "could this be a meeting?" but "must this be a meeting?" If the answer is no, don't schedule one. Think about how you handle things with friends: you don't schedule a call every time you need to share information—you send a message.

Even when you genuinely need a meeting, most teams don't account for what it actually costs.

The hidden cost of "let's just hop on a call"

Default-to-meetings culture persists because it feels efficient in the moment. Scheduling a 30-minute call seems faster than writing a document. But this ignores the total cost: scheduling overhead, calendar fragmentation, context switching, and the fact that only the people in the room benefit. When you write instead, that same 30 minutes creates an artifact hundreds of people can access asynchronously, without interrupting anyone's flow. **Writing scales; meetings don't.** Think of writing as `Gzip` compression for human-to-human communication—extra overhead on each end, but greater throughput and fewer "packets." You end up communicating *more, less frequently*.

> **Pro-Tip:** `Gzip` (similar to `.zip`) is a file compression format, common on the web, that trades compute time on each end for faster transmission across the wire. The same principle applies to thoughtful communication: a single well-written design document can preempt a dozen Slack threads, three "alignment meetings," and the inevitable "wait, I thought we agreed on something different" conversation two weeks later.

The real damage isn't to any single decision—it's to the organization's *tempo*. When every question, proposal, or decision requires a meeting, progress moves at the speed of scheduling, not the speed of thought. A straightforward technical decision that could resolve in an hour via a well-written issue instead sits idle for days while calendars align. Stretch that pattern across teams and projects, and **the organizational clock ticks in days and weeks, not hours.** It's like running a distributed system where every operation requires a global lock—technically correct, painfully slow, and completely avoidable.

My most expensive meeting ever was the weekly Fundamentals review. The premise: leaders gather on a cadence to review metrics. The practice: no decision was ever made. No option evaluated, no trade-off chosen. You've probably sat through your own version—the sprint retro where nothing changes, the all-hands where someone reads slides aloud. The only information transferred was "you are failing this thing"—delivered live, in front of peers, to people who already knew the number from a dashboard they could read on their own time.

The cost wasn't the hour on the calendar. It was converting a team's working hours into a ritualized performance of accountability that produced no learning, no course correction—only shame. If a meeting's entire output can be replaced by a chart and a two-sentence comment, the meeting wasn't a meeting—it was a pillory with a calendar invite. **A meeting whose only output is "you are failing" is a dashboard held hostage.**

Async communication (issues, pull requests, collaborative docs, and sometimes chat) should be the default (see why you should work *asynchronously*). Reserve synchronous time for conversations that genuinely require higher fidelity. Take "async-first" *literally*.

> **For individual contributors: Clear writing is the most powerful skill for your career.** It reduces back-and-forth, shows your thinking (not just your output), and makes it easy for others to build on your work. Before you book that meeting, open an issue. If someone requests time without context, ask for a read-ahead document first. Your deep work depends on your async discipline—and you'll be surprised how often "let's sync" becomes "actually, the issue answered my question."

That "write first" instinct scales best as a team-wide habit.

Write it down before you schedule a meeting

When starting a new initiative or collaborating with a colleague for the first time, it's tempting to "throw some time on their calendar" to "kick things off." These kick-off meetings are information downloads—context with a call to action or request for feedback. But information transfer is rarely the best use of synchronous time, given scheduling overhead (particularly across time zones), the producer-side scaling problem (one doc costs you O(1) to write and serves N readers; a meeting costs O(N)—you have to attend each instance), and the absence of a durable artifact. Not everyone absorbs information best in real-time conversation—some people need to read, re-read, and sit with an idea before responding.

Instead, transfer context asynchronously (via an issue or document) and schedule a meeting only if the conversation requires it. You'd be surprised how often it doesn't. A few minutes of reading or commenting on an issue often replaces days of scheduling and a 30-minute meeting.

When internal access to OpenAI-via-Azure was rolling out at GitHub, I got a stream of "quick call?" invites about the process. I'd already tracked the whole path—links, forms, checkboxes—as a public checklist issue. It was originally for myself, but there was no reason it couldn't benefit others. Instead of explaining the process in endless meetings, I replied to each meeting request with the link. The issue did the onboarding. I did other work. **The best meeting is the one a URL made unnecessary.**

> **Pro-Tip:** Thoughtful, written communication helps ideas scale—there's a reason the printing press accelerated the spread of ideas. It shifts communication from one-to-one to one-to-many. Next time you're about to "send a quick DM" or "schedule a quick chat," consider who might need this information in six months—and whether they'll find a DM thread or a meeting recording. Just like building a web app, "writes" are expensive, but "reads" should be "cheap," so avoid introducing mental N+1s into the system whenever possible.

The "radar" issue replaced another recurring meeting. Instead of a standup or weekly status meeting, automation opened an issue each week summarizing the week's activity—open issues, merged PRs, support tickets, and the like. Each member dropped a short comment whenever they had time: what's on my radar, what I'm worried about, what I need help on. No round-robin. No calendar invite. No interruption. Just a rolling thread that accumulated context, let peers react in their own time zone, and left a searchable trail.

The radar issue did what a standup pretends to do—surface concerns early—without charging a daily synchronous meeting against the team's most focused hours. Once one team showed their work, adjacent teams copied the pattern without being asked.

The best async leaders I've worked with modeled this in small, visible ways. One kept a large analog clock on the wall behind them, deliberately in frame on every video call—a silent reminder that the meter was running. Another declined, without apology, any meeting invitation that arrived without an agenda. Not passive-aggressively—politely, with a short note: "Happy to join once there's an agenda and a desired outcome. Until then, this belongs in an issue."

Both moves look like minor quirks until you watch them propagate. Within a quarter, meetings stayed on time, invites stopped arriving without agendas, and most would-be meetings resolved in issue threads before they hit a calendar. You don't need a policy document to fix your meeting culture. You need two or three people with enough standing to decline the bad meetings out loud—and a leader whose clock is visible.

Even after you've stripped out the information-download meetings, the calendar damage is real.

Real work happens between meetings

Meetings devour a large share of the modern workweek[45]—for many people, the better part of two days before they even start the "real work." I was curious, so I wrote a quick script to pull stats from my calendar.[46] In my first year at GitHub (2013), I had **16** internal meetings. Yes, we were smaller back then, but we were also *dogmatic* about being async-first, almost to a fault. I was worse than most—I'd always been allergic to meetings. As we grew, I had 43 meetings in my second year, and the number grew from there. By my tenth year, I had over **600** meetings.

The meetings had won—not because I stopped pushing back, but because pushing back became a full-time job on top of my actual job. Each new meeting felt harmless. None of them arrived with a sticker that said *this is the one that broke the calendar*. They rarely do.

No agenda? Push back

If you receive a meeting invite (or a request for one) without context, an agenda, explicit goals, or a read-ahead doc, politely decline—or at least ask for one. It's well within your rights (you can even send them noagendanomeeting.net[47]—yes, I built an entire website for this exact purpose—as a "get out of ~~jail~~ meeting free" card). A meeting without an agenda is like calling a function without documentation or type signatures—you don't know what inputs to prepare or what outputs to expect. After all, if the person requesting the meeting

45. https://hbr.org/2022/03/dear-manager-youre-holding-too-many-meetings
46. https://github.com/benbalter/gmail-and-google-calendar-stats
47. https://noagendanomeeting.net/

hasn't distilled their thoughts into writing, why should they get to decide how you spend your time (or spend your time doing their homework)?

> **Pro-Tip:** One pattern I've been enjoying, especially when presenting to executives: spend the first five minutes of the meeting in silence, reading a read-ahead doc together before the conversation starts. Everyone gets the context they need without having to "drain the deck" and spend time conveying information better suited for async reading.

Skip the intros, do your homework

The ritual of "going around the room" for introductions quietly wastes precious time. For internal meetings especially, those opening minutes of everyone stating their name, title, and team are pure overhead. You work together. You have an org chart. Instead, create a culture of pre-research. I would never walk into a meeting with someone I didn't know without first looking them up—either on an internal org chart or on LinkedIn. It takes 30 seconds and means you can skip the small talk and get to substance from minute one. As an added bonus, you can tailor your communication to the person's role and background, and find common ground to build rapport. At minimum, you look prepared.

Expecting others to do the same saves time. It's also a sign of respect—you valued the meeting enough to prepare.

This doesn't mean you can't acknowledge new faces. A quick "I see we have a few folks I haven't worked with before—great to have you" works fine. The difference is you're not burning five minutes on information anyone could have looked up beforehand.

Modeling async-first is half the battle. The other half is protecting boundaries:

> **For managers: Your calendar sets the team's culture—so default to writing.** Replace your next "let's sync" with a written proposal: post the update or decision rationale to a shared channel with a deadline for comments. Anything you'd present in slides, read aloud, or deliver as status belongs in a write-up, not on a calendar. When a meeting *is* warranted, require an agenda and a read-ahead—and decline, politely but consistently, the ones that arrive without either. Protect your team's time and they'll start protecting their own.

> **For individual contributors: You have more power over your calendar than you think.** Don't accept invites on autopilot—ask whether you're truly needed, or could weigh in asynchronously instead of attending. Put it to the test this week: pick one meeting where you'd mostly listen or give a status update, and post that as an issue instead. Notice how much time you reclaim—and how

> much more thoughtful the feedback is when people can respond on their own schedule.

Treat meetings as escalation points and your calendar opens up—deep work gets its time back. You're not being difficult. You're protecting your energy and attention in a work environment designed to fragment both.

Meet intentionally

You've decided this topic genuinely warrants synchronous time. Here's how to make that time count.

Start on time, end early

Start and end on time (consider starting five minutes after the hour to allow for transitions and bio-breaks). If you finish early, use the extra time to connect on a personal level or disband, rather than filling the slot.

If it's not written down, it didn't happen

Capture key points, decisions, and action items, and post them to a durable medium (for example, a GitHub issue, pull request, or team repository). The answer to "wait, what did we decide?" should be a link, not another meeting. Don't assume a meeting is the final word, especially on technical matters. *Write things down* and seek feedback from those who couldn't attend or have more context.

Make every voice count

Give people multiple ways to interact so they can choose the ones that make them most comfortable:

- Encourage hand raising and use of the meeting chat to avoid interruptions and keep the loudest voices from dominating.
- Keep your camera on whenever practical to accommodate those who rely on visual cues. To reduce video-call fatigue, try minimizing your meeting window or turning off your "self-view."
- Managers, be explicit about which meetings are mandatory and which they can skip (or catch up on via recording). Meeting loads pile up quickly, and sometimes it's hard to figure out what's required and what's just FYI.
- Check holidays and working hours across time zones before scheduling—what's Tuesday afternoon for you might be a national holiday for half your team.
- When referring to a meeting time, include the time zone, and avoid location-specific references like "this morning" or "in the spring." Prefer the ISO 8601 standard[48] (`YYYY-MM-DD`) to avoid date ambiguity across cultures.

> **For managers: Be explicit about mandatory versus optional meetings.** Record meetings and post summaries so team members can participate asynchronously. Rotate times across time zones rather than always favoring headquarters. When you act

48. https://en.wikipedia.org/wiki/ISO_8601

> on async feedback with the same weight as in-meeting comments, you signal that participation mode doesn't determine influence.

How much time you spend in meetings varies by role. Managers naturally require more synchronous time—1:1s with reports, cross-functional leadership meetings, coaching sessions—than individual contributors. The goal isn't zero meetings; it's making sure every meeting earns its spot on the calendar.

The retrospective deserves special attention—most teams run it synchronously, but few meetings convert to async as easily.

Make retrospectives async-first

Retrospectives suffer in remote environments when they try to replicate the spontaneity of in-person sessions. Sticky notes on virtual whiteboards rarely capture the candid feedback of a team comfortable in the same room. But async retrospectives have distinct advantages: more time to think, more equal participation, and a written record of improvements.

A process that works well for distributed teams:

1. **Async reflection period**—Give the team two to three days to add items to a shared document or issue. Categories might include "What went well," "What could improve," and "Questions or experiments to try."

2. **Synthesis**—Someone (often the team lead or a rotating facilitator) groups similar items and identifies themes.
3. **Discussion**—For items requiring real-time conversation, schedule focused time. Most items resolve through async comments.
4. **Action items**—Convert improvements into actual issues with owners and due dates. If an improvement isn't worth tracking, it probably wasn't important.

Retrospectives aren't about the meeting—they're about continuous improvement. When you track retro action items as issues alongside your regular work, they actually get done instead of vanishing into a shared whiteboard no one revisits.

Treat meetings as escalation, and you'll have fewer of them—but better ones. The meetings you *do* hold carry weight precisely because they're rare. The return on async-first isn't eliminating meetings—it's earning back every hour that was never a good use of your team's time.

When Async Isn't the Answer

> **TL;DR:** Async isn't a shortcut—use it when there's clear ownership and deadlines, but know when to switch to real-time conversations for crises, trust-building, or fast-moving decisions. Misusing async wastes time and creates confusion; this chapter shows you exactly when to choose each mode so your team actually gets things done.

Async gets a bad rap not because it fails, but because people misuse it as cover for disengagement. The goal isn't eliminating synchronous work—it's deliberately choosing when each mode earns its keep.

"Let's go async" shouldn't mean "let's do nothing"

The reasons vary—someone's heads-down on a project, the agenda's sparse, or they're just not feeling it—but the result is the same: "async" becomes a polite euphemism for "cancel." If that's what you mean, say so. Don't hide behind "async" when you mean "don't meet."

If you actually mean "let's go async," you're committing to something: everyone checks in *and engages* asynchronously—posting updates, asking questions, advancing the work—instead of sitting in a conference room.

When a coworker says they're "going to be working async today"—maybe a storm knocked out their power or childcare fell through—the same applies. Don't vanish when your coworkers expect you to be reachable. Async lets you work when it's best for you—use that flexibility loudly and proudly.

> **Common objection:** **"Async is slow."** Async *feels* slower because you notice the wait. But count the real cost of synchronous work: finding 30 minutes when six people are all free (three days of scheduling back-and-forth), the meeting itself (30 minutes × 6 people = 3 hours of company time), realizing you missed a stakeholder, scheduling again. That's easily a week of calendar time and 6+ hours of labor for a decision that a well-written proposal with a 48-hour comment window would have resolved in less total time—with a written record. Measure time-to-ship, not time-to-first-response.

True async work means being *more* engaged, not less—use the time you'd have spent in the meeting to move the threads you're on forward. Think of it like lazy evaluation in programming: you're deferring *when* the work happens, not *whether* it happens—**defer when, not whether.**

Sync isn't the enemy—misuse is

Some work genuinely resists async. It demands real-time interaction, immediate feedback, or rapid iteration that's hard to achieve across time zones. Spotting those situations isn't a failure of async—it's picking the right tool. (For how to structure synchronous moments well, see *Meet Intentionally*.)

When real-time actually earns its keep

A few situations demand immediate back-and-forth. Early brainstorming, when the problem space is wide open and no one knows the right question yet. Complex debugging—two engineers tracing through a stack together, watching state change live. Design workshops that build on each other's sketches in real-time. Crisis response, when coordination can't wait for time zones.

Don't assume something needs to be synchronous just because it's always been synchronous. "We always have a planning meeting" isn't a reason—it's a habit. But when you've tried async and it's consistently worse—when the work suffers from the delay—honor that signal.

If the same conversation stretches over several days in async channels, drifting further from consensus with each response, get on a call. Especially for interpersonal conflicts, where emotions add unintended tone to written words. Sometimes you just need to talk it out and move on.

> **Pro-Tip:** Even when you need synchronous collaboration, you can make it more inclusive. Record the session. Take good notes. Follow up with a written summary of decisions and action items. People who couldn't attend can catch up and contribute, and it creates the kind of artifact that makes async valuable.

Crisis and emergency situations

I've been the person reluctantly paging a colleague at 2 AM when production is down. You need people solving the problem together, not waiting for time zones. When a security vulnerability is being actively exploited or a critical bug surfaces hours before launch, synchronous coordination is the only sensible choice.

> **For managers: Build your crisis playbook during peacetime.** Define escalation paths, on-call rotations, and communication channels *before* the emergency. If your team's first experience with synchronous crisis response is an actual crisis, you've already lost time to confusion. Run a tabletop exercise once a quarter—it's cheap insurance for the 2 AM page that's coming eventually.

Here's the thing: actual crises are rare. If you're constantly in firefighting mode, you don't have a "should this be async?" problem—you have a reliability problem, and that's what needs fixing. The mistake isn't using sync during a real crisis—it's treating every situation like one. **Constant firefighting means the building's on fire.**

Early-stage teams building trust

When a team first forms—especially if members haven't met or worked together before—more synchronous interaction pays off. You're building working relationships, learning communication styles, and establishing shared context.

It's doubly true for remote teams spanning cultures, time zones, or organizational boundaries. A few video calls early on, some real-time pairing sessions, sometimes even a team gathering—these build trust that purely async interaction can't.

The emphasis matters: *early-stage* teams. Async works eventually—you just need runway. Start synchronous and shift toward async as the team matures.

> **For individual contributors: Invest in early sync to earn later async.** When you join a new team, lean into real-time interactions—pair programming, video 1:1s, casual conversations. The trust you build in those first weeks is what makes async collaboration work for the months that follow. Skip

> the relationship-building phase, and your async messages will land without context or goodwill.

Think of it like picking up a new sport. You might need an instructor in person at first, giving you immediate feedback on your form. But once you've mastered the basics, you can practice on your own, watch videos, and ask questions asynchronously.

When you need to think out loud together

Real-time conversation sparks ideas that written brainstorming doesn't—but only during the "what if we tried something completely different" phase, when you're exploring the problem space rather than solving a known problem. Someone says "yes, and..." and takes an idea in a direction no one expected.

Creative work feels this most acutely: design explorations, product strategy discussions, architectural brainstorming for greenfield projects. The divergent phase thrives on real-time; execution doesn't.

Recognize this as a *phase*, not a steady state. Once you've diverged and explored possibilities, you converge—and that's where async shines. The direction is documented, and people do the actual work asynchronously, regrouping when they need feedback.

A product team spends a few hours sketching ideas for a new feature, generating possibilities. They document the most promising directions, break them into concrete tasks, and work asynchronously over the next few weeks. When they need another round of creative exploration, they come back together.

> 🤔 **Common objection: "Our work is too complex for async communication. We need to be able to talk things through in real-time."**
>
> Complexity is an argument *for* async, not against it. Complex work demands written communication that people can read carefully, re-read, and respond to on their own schedule. Intricate technical problems and nuanced product decisions deserve time to think—really think—not the pressure of an immediate response in a meeting.
>
> What you probably mean is "our work requires significant collaboration," which is true. Collaboration doesn't have to be synchronous, though. Distributed, asynchronous teams built some of the most complex software systems in existence—the Linux kernel, Kubernetes, major scientific computing platforms. The complexity didn't prevent async collaboration; async practices made it manageable.
>
> If anything, complexity is a reason to slow down, document your thinking, and give people time to understand before they respond—which is exactly what async enables.

Choosing the right mode looks different depending on your role:

> 👔 **For managers: Show the difference between async work and disengagement.** When you "go async," overtly model active participation in written channels. Set clear expectations for response times and hold the team to them—"going async" can't be a euphemism for "nobody does anything." Before scheduling that meeting, ask: would real-time collaboration actually serve this better, or have we just never tried the async approach?

> 💻 **For individual contributors: Commit to genuine async engagement.** If you need to step away, say so —don't hide behind "working async." When you work asynchronously, show it: post updates, ask questions, move the work forward. Be the voice that suggests trying async-first, but recognize when the team needs to talk something through.

Judgment over dogma

Async is a default, not a dogma—the point is to work effectively as a distributed team, and that means picking the right mode for each situation.

When async isn't working, don't force it. But don't assume sync is the answer, either. Ask: does this genuinely need real-time interaction, or have we just defaulted to sync out of habit? Sometimes the answer is sync. Sometimes it's a better async pattern. The skill is telling one from the other.

> **Pro-Tip: Experimenting with async practices means some of them won't work. Ship it anyway. You can always revert.** The ritual I remember most clearly at GitHub for failing this test was "movie night." On paper, a reasonable async idea: pick a film, share your screen, watch over video chat. We ran it with *Jurassic Park* and *Sneakers*—crowd-pleasing films that should have worked. The ritual died anyway. Not because the films were wrong, not because participation was low.
>
> It died because we were taking a synchronous ritual and porting it over Wi-Fi. It was awkward getting a live stream of your colleagues eating popcorn, times were inconvenient across time zones, and it was a long commitment. We should have rethought the experience from first principles. **If you asynchronize the wrong part, you don't scale the experience—you erase it.**

Knowing *when* to go sync or async settles half the decision. The other half is *where* the conversation lives once you've chosen. A real-time crisis call still needs a written summary somewhere people can find it; an async proposal still needs to land in a channel that's searchable six months from now. Pick the right mode but the wrong medium, and you'll lose the decision anyway—buried in a chat thread or a meeting nobody recorded. Which turns the question from sync versus async to the tools that make either one stick.

Choosing the Right Collaboration Tools

> **TL;DR:** Chat is for now, issues are for later, and email is for outsiders—confuse them and your team spends Tuesday relitigating Monday's decision because nobody can find it. Pick tools that are linkable, searchable, and outlive the conversation, then make those defaults non-negotiable.

A teammate pings you on Slack with a three-paragraph technical proposal. You reply with questions. They respond. Someone else chimes in. Twenty messages later, you've built consensus in a medium designed for "hey, anyone want coffee?" Three months from now, when a new hire asks how that decision got made? Good luck finding the thread.

Every day you face dozens of these micro-decisions: chat message or issue? Video call or written doc? Email the team or post in the channel? The choices feel small. They compound. **Where you say it shapes what they hear—and whether anyone can find it later.** Get it right, and the work explains itself. Get it wrong, and your team spends more time hunting for "where did we land on that?" than doing the work.

The fix isn't knowing your tools. It's knowing *when* to use each one, and picking tools that reward the right defaults.

The medium shapes the message

Every collaboration medium is good at some things and terrible at others. Treat them as interchangeable and you'll pay in lost context, dropped decisions, and interrupted teammates. **Bad tools don't lose files—they lose decisions.**

Medium	Persistent?	Searchable?	Interrupt cost	Best for
Docs / wiki	Yes	Yes	None	Evergreen reference, runbooks, onboarding
Issue / PR / ticket	Yes	Yes	Low	Decisions, proposals, parallel discussion
Email	Kind of	Poorly	Low–medium	Formal announcements, external parties
Chat channel	Technically	Barely	Medium	Coordination, quick questions, social glue
Direct message	Technically	Only to you two	High	Genuinely 1:1, sensitive, or urgent
Video call (scheduled)	Only if recorded	Almost never	High	Nuance, rapport, unblocking a stuck thread
Video call (ad hoc)	No	No	Highest	Emergencies

Notice what chat isn't good at: being found later. Notice what docs aren't good at: urgency. Notice what meetings aren't good at: much of anything, really, except the rare case where tone and rapport genuinely matter (*Meetings Are a Point of Escalation*).

Pick the medium that matches the properties the work needs. Not the one that feels fastest in the moment.

A decision framework: persistence, audience, urgency

Three questions, in this order, get you to the right channel almost every time.

Will anyone need to find this later? If yes, it goes somewhere with a URL, a search index, and a stable history—an issue, a PR, a doc, a wiki page. **Chat is where information goes to die.** If you're explaining something complex in Slack, you're explaining it again next month to someone who wasn't in the channel—which, soon enough, includes *you*.

Who actually needs to weigh in? Two people can converse almost anywhere. Five or more people need structure. A DM that should have been a channel message excludes everyone who'd benefit. A channel message that should have been an issue excludes everyone in a different time zone. Default to the broadest medium your audience will tolerate—you can always narrow, but you can't retroactively include.

Does this need a response right now? "Right now" means minutes, not hours—production is down, a customer is blocked, a decision can't wait. Everything else? Not urgent. You just think it is. Genuine urgency warrants chat with explicit framing ("Need help now—production is down") or a phone call. Your curiosity about a project's status does not.

Chain the answers: *persistent + many people + not urgent* means issue or doc. *Ephemeral + few people + urgent* means chat or call. *Persistent + few people + not urgent* means issue, even if it feels like overkill. When in doubt, bias toward persistent and async. You can always escalate.

> **For managers:** You define "urgent" for your team through your behavior. If you Slack someone at 9 PM asking about a status update and expect an immediate response, you've told them status updates are urgent—no matter what your handbook says. Batch non-urgent questions into your next async check-in, and your team will follow suit.

> **Common objection: "Async takes too long—I just need a quick answer."** Most "quick answers" aren't quick. They interrupt someone's flow, require context-switching, and spawn follow-up questions. A well-written issue gets you a better answer in an hour than a "got a minute?" call gets you in ten minutes—and three other people learn from it, too. The real cost of the "quick" sync path—scheduling it, interrupting flow, reconvening when you miss someone—is almost always higher than the wait you were trying to avoid.

Where teams default wrong

Even with a framework, the same miscast shows up again and again: **chat as documentation.** If a conversation produces a decision, copy the takeaway into an issue or doc *immediately*. Thirty seconds now saves someone—probably you—thirty minutes of archaeology later.

> **Pro-Tip: Make it easy to do the right thing.** We had an `.xref` chatop that let you cross-reference chat content within an issue. More recently, the GitHub Slack/Teams app added a "Create issue" action on any message, which automatically copies the message content into the issue body and links back to the original message. The easier you make it to do the right thing, the more likely people are to do it.

> **For individual contributors: You have permission to redirect conversations—and scripts make it painless.** Two examples.
>
> When someone DMs a question others could benefit from, reply with something like: "Great question—mind posting in #team-eng so others can weigh in?"
>
> When someone requests a meeting for something that isn't yet written down, try: "Could you write up the key points first? I'll review async and we can meet if there are open questions."

> Redirect *and* explain why—people don't mind switching channels when they see the benefit.

> **Pro-Tip:** Establish a team norm around an emoji that means "can we move this to a public channel?" A single emoji is much less fraught than a message, and it gives the asker a chance to save face while learning the right default. On one of my teams, that was the `:yeet:` emoji.
>
> Many operating systems also allow for custom keyboard expansions, either natively or via third-party tools. For example, you could set up a shortcut like `;xref` that expands to "Great question—mind posting in #team-eng so others can weigh in?" That way, you can redirect conversations with a few memorable keystrokes.

Choosing the platforms underneath

The medium-matching framework only works if your platforms reward the right defaults. The real idea behind GitHub's internal mantra of "put it on GitHub" isn't GitHub-specific. It's about tools that consumerize open source norms:[49] reimagined for distributed work, not digitized paper processes. **Don't digitize the old process. Replace it.**

GitHub's own internal stack drifted over the years. Chat went from Campfire to an in-house tool called GitHub Chat (beloved, heavily Hubot-integrated) to Slack.

Project management took a longer road: teams used Trello, Airtable, and other third-party tools until GitHub Projects matured, then the "first-customer" principle pulled everyone back onto the first-party stack.

Good collaboration tools share four qualities[50] (adapted from Ryan Tomayko's open source process constraints):

Open

Contributors can opt in without being excluded by time zone, geography, title, or fear of being second-guessed. Shun secrecy unless essential. Openness extends to machines, too: programmatic access lets you build dashboards, mobile views, and expose context to AI through MCP servers. Developers feel at home on GitHub; lawyers and marketers often don't. APIs let you meet people where they are.[51]

Process-capturing

Good tools capture process automatically—not just *what* the team decided, but *who* decided, *what alternatives* they considered, and *why*. Chat captures text instantly, searchably, shareably. Audio and video capture none of that well. Try this: pick your team's last significant decision. Can you find, in under two minutes, where it was discussed, who participated, and what was considered? If not, your tools are forcing humans to be the institutional memory software should handle.

49. https://ben.balter.com/2013/02/06/the-next-big-thing-is-already-here/
50. https://web.archive.org/web/20220503063245/https://tomayko.com/blog/2012/adopt-an-open-source-process-constraints
51. https://ben.balter.com/2015/01/11/hacking-github/

Linkable

Every discussion, decision, and artifact has a unique address. The same link reaches one person or a hundred with no extra effort. Linkable work compounds in value —see Why Everything Should Have a URL.

Asynchronous

Tools let work move forward without everyone being in the same place at the same time. Async workflows all but require the first three qualities—and they make it trivial to weave in data and external sources, instead of "hold on, let me see if I can find that thing Bob emailed last year."

Not every tool needs to be the *same* tool. Sales teams use Salesforce; HR lives in Workday or BambooHR. The point isn't one platform—it's that whatever you pick meets these four criteria.

> **Common objection: "We've invested too much in our current tools to switch."** You don't have to rip and replace. Route one workflow—project proposals, design reviews, incident retros—through a tool that meets the four criteria. Once people experience the difference, switching costs start looking a lot smaller than staying-the-same costs.

Design patterns that separate good tools from bad

The four qualities are ideals. A few design patterns make them concrete:

- **@mentions** invite people into a conversation with equal footing and equal context.
- **Opt in, opt out.** You can subscribe to anything that interests you and mute anything that doesn't—unlike email, where the sender controls your inbox.
- **Single sign-on** keeps openness from dying due to lack of access.
- **Emoji** become your tone of voice when work moves from in-person to text. 😌 😄 🎉 do a thousand words of work.
- **Markdown** forces structured, semantic writing[52] and makes content portable across media.
- **Deep links** to a specific comment or line beat linking to a whole document readers won't consume.
- **Mobile** meets distributed teammates and travelers where they are.
- **APIs** avoid vendor lock-in and make information available in whatever format the reader needs.

Audit your stack against these patterns. The ones you're missing reveal exactly where context is getting lost.

52. https://ben.balter.com/2014/03/31/word-versus-markdown-more-than-mere-semantics

The goal isn't the perfect tool—it's conscious defaults

Comfortable isn't always effective. When you're about to send a message, schedule a meeting, or do what you've always done, pause: *persistence, audience, urgency.* Default to the least disruptive async medium that still fits, and escalate only when it doesn't. Pick platforms that reward those defaults rather than fighting them.

GitHub's Zen[53] prefers practicality over purity. A perfect workflow on paper doesn't stick with a team that's only ever used email, Word, and standing meetings. Even if you're not the person choosing the tools, you shape how they're used. ICs who master search, notifications, cross-references, and automation become the de facto standard-setters for their team.

> **For managers:** Create team norms for which work belongs in which channel, write them down, and model them yourself. But don't be dogmatic—sometimes the right answer is to ignore the framework and pick up the phone. **The framework exists to make exceptions explicit, not to outlaw judgment.**

> **For individual contributors:** Learn your team's tools deeply. Most adoption failures aren't tool failures—they're people not knowing how to use the

53. https://ben.balter.com/2015/08/12/the-zen-of-github/

> tool well. Fluency is influence. "I'm not a developer" is no excuse for not mastering your team's tools, especially when they don't involve code.

The right tools won't transform your team overnight. **The wrong ones—closed, synchronous, context-destroying—will hold you back indefinitely.** Choose tools that make openness the path of least resistance, build the habit of matching work to medium, and the rest of this book becomes the default instead of the exception.

Seven chapters, one operating principle: structure beats spontaneity. Async communication isn't about typing slower or replacing meetings with chat threads. It's about choosing the medium that fits the message, designing for interruption instead of reacting to it, and treating attention as the team's rarest resource. The chapters cover the practices, the channels, and the escalation path for when sync is the right answer. Get this layer right and a team spread across six time zones stops paying a coordination tax just to talk to itself.

Key takeaways

- A team spread across twelve time zones ships code around the clock—or grinds to a halt waiting for overlapping hours. The difference is whether you treat async handoffs as first-class workflows with documented context, or keep scheduling 8 AM standups that are someone else's midnight.

- In async work, you *are* your writing—and nobody wants to collaborate with a corporate press release. Specificity, clarity, and a human voice aren't just nice to have; they're how you build trust, ship faster, and stand out in a sea of jargon.
- Chat is your team's most abused collaboration tool. Every low-value message in a busy channel is a tiny denial-of-service attack on collective attention—so lead with context, use threads, structure your channels, and treat your teammates' focus as the finite, shared resource it is.
- Issues and pull requests have unwritten rules—open freely, @mention teams not people, and treat every comment as a tiny meeting you just called. Get the etiquette right and your work moves forward; get it wrong and you're the annoying new hire.
- Default to writing, escalate to a meeting only when you must. You save the team hours, leave a searchable record, and the meetings you do hold actually move work forward.
- Async isn't a shortcut—use it when there's clear ownership and deadlines, but know when to switch to real-time conversations for crises, trust-building, or fast-moving decisions.
- Chat is for now, issues are for later, and email is for outsiders—confuse them and your team spends Tuesday relitigating Monday's decision because nobody can find it. Pick tools that are linkable, searchable, and outlive the conversation, then make those defaults non-negotiable.

Transitioning to Distributed and Remote-First

Remote-first is a mindset, not a mailing address. Going from "the way we've always done it" to a sustainable, remote-first way of working isn't a single leap—mindset shifts come first, then practical changes, then sustained habits. Mindset shifts arrive in weeks, not days. Practices take months to feel automatic, not training-session afternoons. And most teams backslide somewhere in the middle, when the novelty wears off and sync meetings creep back in—so don't expect a straight line.

You've nodded along to the principles of async communication, working in the open, and measuring impact over hours logged. Now comes the part where most organizations quietly fail: actually making the switch.

The gap between "we believe in remote work" and "we practice remote work" is the same gap between understanding how a codebase *should* be structured and actually refactoring the tangled monolith you inherited. **You can't declare yourself remote-first any more than you can declare yourself tech debt-free**—and the transition doesn't happen by swapping your office lease for a Zoom subscription.

I've watched this go wrong at companies that genuinely wanted it to succeed. The failure mode is almost always the same: teams treat "going remote" as a single event—a policy announcement, a Slack rollout, maybe a half-day workshop—instead of an ongoing process of rethinking how work actually happens. They bolt webcams onto office rituals, wonder why everyone's exhausted, and conclude that remote work "doesn't work for us." **It worked fine. The transition didn't.**

> **For managers: Frame the transition around what your team gains, not what it gives up.** "We're going async" sounds like a constraint. "We're eliminating the meetings that waste your afternoons so you can ship the work that matters" sounds like a gift. Write your decisions down, default to public channels, and stop calling meetings for things that could be an issue comment. When your team sees you working this way—not just talking about it—

> the transition stops being a mandate and starts being contagious.

> **For individual contributors: Transitions are uncomfortable—use that discomfort as a career advantage.** While others wait for the dust to settle, you can be the person who already knows how to work across time zones, write clear async proposals, and ship without daily standups. The engineers who thrive during transitions aren't the ones who resist change or passively comply—they're the ones who start practicing the new way before it's required and help teammates make the shift. That initiative gets noticed.

Changing habits is hard enough; changing the assumptions baked into them is harder. Before anything improves, you've got to take apart the workflows holding your team back and ask whether they make sense outside the office at all. That's where the refactor starts.

Refactoring for Remote

> **TL;DR:** Don't just move your meetings online—overhaul your workflows to prioritize trust, accountability, and asynchronous collaboration, or your remote team will fail for the same reasons office habits did. By the end, you'll be able to spot and replace legacy "presence theater" with concrete, remote-friendly practices that actually help your team get work done.

A team I know moved to remote work by replicating every office ritual over Zoom—morning standups, afternoon check-ins, end-of-day summaries. Within a month, everyone was exhausted and nobody could get work done. They hadn't gone remote. They'd added commute-free surveillance.

Going remote isn't changing *where* you work—it's rethinking the assumptions baked into *how* you work. **The shift is behavioral, not geographic.** Most of those assumptions are so deeply embedded you don't notice them until they break.

Challenge your assumptions

Presence doesn't equal productivity

Most organizations assume `time + physical presence = results`. The office reinforces this illusion—if someone's in a meeting, they must be productive, right? The data says otherwise. As discussed in *Parallelization and Flow*, interruptions destroy focus[54] for far longer than the interruption itself, and open offices trigger dozens of these context switches daily—a compounding tax on deep work. Most meetings are seen as unproductive—Microsoft[55] found roughly two-thirds are considered a waste of time, Atlassian[56] found most workers believe theirs could be done in half the time, and the science of meetings[57] shows leaders consistently overrate how well their own meetings go.

Going remote strips away the presence theater and forces you to confront what's actually getting done.

Open up your codebase—and your culture

Your organization should practice **inner source**—applying open source principles like transparency and collaboration to internal software development—even in an in-person setting. If teams silo work and hoard information, going remote only amplifies the dysfunction.

54. https://doi.org/10.1145/1357054.1357072
55. https://www.microsoft.com/en-us/worklab/work-trend-index/
56. https://www.atlassian.com/blog/workplace-woes-meetings
57. https://en.wikipedia.org/wiki/Steven_Rogelberg

Make it safe to speak up

Teams need psychological safety—the belief that you won't be punished for speaking up with ideas, questions, concerns, or mistakes. Without it, remote teams suffocate: engineers sit on critical bugs rather than admit mistakes, junior developers fake understanding instead of asking questions, and everyone waits for someone else to point out the obvious flaw. **Distance amplifies silence.**

> **Pro-Tip:** I learned this the hard way at an early GitHub Pages mini-summit. We'd gathered the team in San Francisco—everyone in one room except a teammate in Asia-Pacific who couldn't make the trip. When the architecture discussion kicked off, we did what you do in a room with a whiteboard: we crowded around it. To include our remote colleague, we pointed a dedicated laptop camera at the board. It was a disaster. They got a glare-streaked view of someone's handwriting from across the room, narrated by half-audible side conversations, with no way to pick up a marker.
>
> A whiteboard isn't a shared tool—it's a tool for the people standing next to it. We gave up and moved the whole conversation into a Google Doc. Suddenly everyone was on equal footing: same surface, same edit access, same view, whether you were in

> the room or eight time zones away. The fix wasn't a better camera. It was ditching the office tool for one that worked for everyone.

> 🤔 **Common objection: "We tried remote work and it didn't work for us."** The diagnostic question is *how* you work, not *where*: did you refactor the workflow, or just relocate it? A "failed" remote experiment is almost always the old process running at a distance—the same standups, the same approval chains, the same presence checks, now with lag. Remote work done badly is worse than office work, but **remote work done well is better than both.** You didn't test remote-first; you ran your old playbook at a distance and called the friction a verdict. For a catalog of the most common failure modes and how to fix them, see *Why Open and Async Change Fails.*

So if presence, synchronous rituals, and surveillance don't hold up—what does?

Trust comes first

Once we stop assuming time and work correlate, we need a new foundation: trust. Remote work demands more trust than office work—think of it as the Transport Layer Security (TLS) layer for your organization. The answer to "how do you verify work is happening?" isn't surveillance—it's *impact over input*: colleagues set expectations for what they'll deliver, and everyone trusts they'll get it done. If someone isn't delivering, hold them accountable—but start from trust until evidence says otherwise.

> **For managers: Model trust before you expect it.** Be the first to share works-in-progress, admit mistakes publicly, and evaluate your team on deliverables rather than timestamps. For concrete guidance on replacing activity proxies with outcome metrics, see *Impact Over Input*.

> **For individual contributors: Build trust by delivering on commitments and making your work visible.** The beauty of trust-based work is that it scales to different levels of ambition. If you can deliver in a four-day week, great. If you want to take on extra scope or stretch projects, also great. For practical strategies on visibility, see *Work Loudly*.

Trust reshapes more than how you measure work—it changes who gets heard.

Stop routing work through the org chart

In a physical office, architecture enforces the org chart: who sits behind a closed door, whose desk is nearest the VP, whose calendar an assistant guards. Remote work strips those enforcement mechanisms away—and exposes how much of your old workflow quietly depended on them. Approvals waited on hallway access. Ideas needed a sponsor in the room. Refactoring for remote means rebuilding those paths to run on the work itself, not on who sits where.

> **Pro-Tip:** I see this as a positive—ideas circulate and bubble up from anywhere in the organization—but if you're making a case for distributed and remote-first work, expect some to see that as a threat to their power or authority. Open organizations can coexist with hierarchy and top-down decision-making, but they require a different kind of leadership. That means "showing your work" and being more transparent about decisions beyond the fiat of "because I said so." Leaders in open organizations have more authority—they can influence and inspire beyond their direct reports by showing not just the "what" but the "why." That authority is earned, not granted by title.

The mechanics change with the architecture. When there's no floor plan gating access, anyone can DM the CEO, comment on a VP's proposal, or open an issue that lands in front of whoever's watching the repo. Information flows more freely, roles blur at the edges, and collaboration crosses boundaries that used to be walls. Hierarchy doesn't disappear in distributed teams—it loosens, and the work decides who gets heard.

> **For individual contributors: Route around the old gatekeepers.** That executive you'd never get

> past an assistant to reach? They're one well-crafted issue comment away. Write a thoughtful proposal, tag the right people, and let the work make your case. You no longer need a sponsor with the right desk—you need an argument worth reading. Lean into it: it's a career accelerator.

You still need to see each other sometimes

Remote or distributed doesn't mean 100% virtual. You still need to meet in person. Think department-wide gatherings, smaller team offsites (or, more accurately, "onsites"), or self-organized regional meetups. That's where you build relationships, brainstorm, plan long-term, and work through difficult decisions—reinforcing the trust that makes everything else work.

Company policies should assume that meeting in real life (IRL) is valuable. GitHub's remote culture worked best when people met two to three times a year. As the company grew, we evolved from a single company-wide summit to department-level gatherings and self-organized Hubber offsites. If teams must write lengthy business justifications for meeting in person (or jump through political hoops), those meetings won't happen, and the social bonds won't form.

We also had a longstanding rule: if you met up with another Hubber you didn't usually see in person, you could expense a reasonable meal. A small thing, but it sparked serendipitous connections that screens can't replicate. We didn't track it formally, but I'd see issues or pull requests later tagged with "met [person] in Amsterdam" or "got idea for feature Y over lunch in Dublin." Maybe a dozen times per quarter a real collaboration emerged from someone deciding to buy a coworker lunch. Not enough to be a tool, but enough to matter.

Build culture on purpose

There's a lot that in-person organizations get for "free." Birthdays in the kitchen, posters on the wall, extracurricular sports teams, happy hours. These build culture—and they're hard to replicate remotely. You can host virtual get-togethers and create non-work channels for interpersonal connection, but culture goes deeper.

The internet has its own culture—and remote teams can tap into it. Emoji and animated GIFs convey emotion and tone that text alone can't—but the real glue is memes, inside jokes, and shared experiences unique to your team that reinforce who you are.

That glue is increasingly borrowed from the whole internet, not invented fresh by each team. Internet culture and remote culture are converging—both are, at heart, ways to forge connection across distance—and the playful, meme-driven vocabulary that grew up on the early web now does real social work inside distributed teams. The trend is industry-wide: custom emoji have become a standard fixture of workplace chat, with some teams amassing thousands of their own.

Take Bufo, a googly-eyed cartoon toad whose name comes from the scientific genus of true toads, though nearly everyone calls it a frog. Bufo spread from workspace to workspace like folk art, accumulating more than a thousand community-built variants as each team remixed the meme to make it its own. It colonized GitHub's Slack the same way: there was a Bufo for *everything*, and if there wasn't, you made one. (`:bufo-intensifies:`)

At GitHub, `.sparkles` was a ChatOp for expressing gratitude—part of our appreciation economy. `.nat me` generated an image of the then-CEO holding a sign with whatever text you typed—part of our culture of taking the work seriously, but not ourselves too seriously. Our internal meme culture even accidentally invented the "Shipit squirrel," which spread to the broader developer community as a sign of approval.

> **Pro-Tip:** Use ChatOps-style commands for more than deployments. Lightweight, visible chat commands that celebrate wins, appreciate teammates, or create shared jokes scale culture asynchronously as effectively as they scale your infrastructure.

> **For managers: Culture doesn't survive the transition by accident—design it.** Identify three rituals your team values, then find their async equivalent. If it's birthday celebrations, that's an automated bot and a team channel. If it's whiteboard brainstorming, that's a shared doc with a 48-hour comment window. The rituals that feel "organic" in an office were never organic—they had the office as

> scaffolding. Remote work needs you to build that scaffolding intentionally.

Culture and trust are the baseline—but even the strongest culture buckles when your tools work against it. The tools your team picks shape the work: word processors fight version control, opaque binary formats fight async review, and print-era mental models fight every habit you're trying to build. The next chapter, *Retool Your Documents*, makes the case for plain text, semantic markup, and version-controlled collaboration—the same workflow developers have used for years, applied to the rest of the organization's writing.

Retool your documents

> **TL;DR:** Until your documents live in open, reviewable formats—not locked behind proprietary software—your team will keep tripping over lost edits, version confusion, and slow reviews. Learn how to transition to web-friendly tools that actually support async work, or keep losing good ideas to version chaos.

You open `final_v3_revised_ACTUALLY_FINAL.docx` and can't tell what changed, who changed it, or whether it's the latest version. The problem isn't the people—it's the tool. The print-era mental model baked into your word processor actively fights how distributed teams need to collaborate. Culture and trust are the baseline, but they won't hold if every shared document is trapped in software designed to produce printouts.

We taught computers to make paper, then forgot to stop

For decades, knowledge workers learned one move: open a word processor. The tool mimics a sheet of paper —margins, page breaks, print-centric formatting. That made sense when the output was a printout. Today, content lives on screens, travels across time zones, and needs versioning, review, and search. The muscle memory is now a liability.

Most organizations still collaborate on documents like this:

1. Draft content in a desktop word processor (or its online equivalent)
2. Save to a shared folder or email it around for comments and changes
3. Manually (and opaquely) reconcile changes one by one
4. Repeat steps 2–3 until satisfied with the document
5. **Convert to a web-friendly format**
6. Publish

Going digital is the *last* step—everything before it still optimizes for paper. If the internet is how we consume content, why not how we create it?

Word processors had one purpose: make paper. Their core features took shape when WordPerfect and Microsoft Word competed to replace typewriters. The prominent buttons—alignment, margins, page breaks—assumed a physical printout. "Collaborate asynchronously with a distributed team" never made the original toolbar. Web-native features like hyperlinks arrived later, buried in submenus as afterthoughts.

> **Pro-Tip:** Modern word processors *do* have features like tracked changes and version history, but most people overlook them—and they're literally marginal. Hard-to-find comments crammed into a document margin are a world away from the full-screen experience of a pull request, which puts version history front and center. Not to mention, they lack automated CI (Continuous Integration—automated checks that run on each change), and automation like GitHub Actions.

These tools became the corporate standard, then lock-in kept them there. Organizations poured money into training, standardized on file formats, and built workflows around them. The switching costs became self-reinforcing—every new hire trained on one tool made the next format change harder to justify. Even as the web reshaped how we consume content, the tools for creating it didn't budge.

It's not just the filenames. "The latest version is on the share drive." "Are you out of the doc yet?" "Can two people edit at once?" "Where's the diff?" Without version control, every document is a snapshot with no context—no record of what changed, who changed it, or whether your edit survived. And most documents people create today never take physical form anyway—they're shared via email, viewed on phones, posted to intranets. They need mobile responsiveness, machine readability, and programmatic access. Word processors were not built for that.

Appearance is opinion; structure is fact

Here's the difference between print-first and digital-first tools: Word processors encourage you to describe what something *looks like,* while **modern markup encourages you to describe what something *is*.** When you want a heading in Word, you select text and make it big and bold. When you want a heading in Markdown, you use `##` to declare "this is a second-level heading." Same visual result, completely different meaning.

This distinction seems academic until you consider who —or what—needs to understand your document. A sighted human can infer that big, bold text is probably a heading. A screen reader can't. Neither can a search engine, a table-of-contents generator, or an export tool converting your document to another format. When you describe appearance instead of structure, you're writing for exactly one audience: people who can see your specific visual presentation. Everyone else has to guess. **Markup is a contract; formatting is a costume.**

Semantic structure isn't just about accessibility—though that alone should suffice. Properly marked-up headings drive automated navigation, search optimization, and format conversion. Lists declared as lists—not indented text with dashes—let tools reformat, reorder, and extract them. Links declared as hyperlinks—not blue underlined text—let tools validate, archive, and follow them programmatically. The shift from visual to semantic isn't optional. It's the foundation of everything we expect digital content to do.

Machine readability matters even more once AI enters your workflow. Tools like GitHub Copilot can read and generate Markdown directly because it's plain text with clear structure. LLMs can summarize, search, and reason about semantic markup natively—try that with a `.docx` file, a zipped XML bundle that AI can't read without conversion tools. Markdown isn't just machine-readable—it's AI-native in a way proprietary formats never will be.

Developers solved this decades ago

Software developers solved the collaboration problem with version control. Born out of early operating-system work and hardened through the open source movement, version control handles the `main` copy, tracks every change down to the character, and gives you a transparent forum to discuss changes in context. No more shuttling edits via email or decoding filenames. Take a look for yourself[58]—a blog post of mine tracked through Git for years, with every edit and its reasoning preserved as a diff.

Word processing documents, by contrast, are tiny jails for content—proprietary formats blend text with the commands the software needs to recreate it, in formats built for the application rather than the reader. We put

58. https://github.com/benbalter/benbalter.github.com/commits/master/posts/_posts/2012-10-19-we-ve-been-trained-to-make-paper.md

in text—one of the simplest things computers understand—and get back a mess that only specific software can open. It's like keeping every grocery list inside a screenshot of an Instagram post: the words are there, but only one tool can read them, and you can't edit so much as a typo without retaking the picture.

> 💻 **For individual contributors: You don't need permission to start.** None of this requires an org-wide mandate or a migration project. Draft your next proposal in Markdown, keep it somewhere with version history, and share a link instead of an attachment. When your reviews move faster and your edits stop getting lost, the people around you will ask how—and the tooling starts to change from the bottom up.

> 👔 **For managers: Your team writes for the format you reward.** If you ask for a linkable, reviewable doc and someone hands you a `.docx`, send it back. Better, publish your own strategy and decision docs in version-controlled Markdown first. Nobody retools because of a mandate; they retool because the person reviewing their work clearly prefers a link to an attachment.

Switching to async-first tools is only half the battle. If your documents remain open but your hiring sticks to old habits, you're still dragging legacy workflow into a remote world. Modern collaboration starts with the people you bring on—so your hiring process has to reflect the way you'll actually work, not just the jobs you're trying to fill.

Hiring for Remote-First Teams

> **TL;DR:** The fastest way to hire the wrong remote engineer is the four-panel onsite—same format as 2015, same bias toward people who think out loud. Replace one round with a paid two-hour async take-home and a written design review, and you'll see who can actually do the job before they sign the offer.

Your hiring process is your culture, compressed into a few weeks. Every person you bring onto a remote team either reinforces your open and async practices or dilutes them. Yet most hiring processes are built for a world of lobby handshakes, conference-table body language, and candidates imagining themselves at a specific desk every morning.

Remote hiring isn't traditional hiring conducted over video calls. It's evaluating candidates the way you'll actually work together—through written communication, asynchronous collaboration, and independent problem-solving. Do it well and it's a competitive advantage. Do it poorly and it's where your remote culture quietly dies.

It cuts both ways. You're designing a process that selects for remote-ready candidates. Candidates are evaluating whether your remote practices are real or paint on a surveillance-and-meetings culture. The best remote workers know their worth and pick employers whose practices match their expectations.

> **For individual contributors: Reading this chapter before your next interview is a cheat code.** Everything this book covers—async communication, working in the open, writing as a core skill, impact over input—is what remote-first companies are evaluating you on, whether they say so explicitly or not. The sections below reveal what hiring managers look for and how interview processes are designed, so you know exactly what to demonstrate. Treat the rest of this book as interview prep and a way to size up your potential future employer—prep that also happens to make you better at your job.

Writing remote-ready job descriptions

Your job description is often a candidate's first exposure to your team's culture. If it reads like every other posting—vague requirements and corporate jargon—you're already signaling that you haven't thought deeply about remote work.

State remote expectations explicitly

- Is this role fully remote, hybrid, or remote-optional? Say so clearly.
- What time zone overlap, if any, is required? Be specific so candidates can self-select.
- What does a typical async day look like? Give candidates a sense of the rhythm.
- What synchronous commitments exist? Weekly team calls, quarterly planning sessions, annual gatherings?

Describe your communication culture

- What tools does your team use? Issue trackers, chat, video, async video?
- How do decisions get made? Through written proposals? Synchronous discussion?
- What's your team's relationship with meetings? Async-first? Meeting-heavy?

Signal what you value

- "Strong written communication skills" is the baseline—explain what that means for your team.
- If you value working in the open, describe how candidates will be expected to share their work.
- If asynchronous collaboration is central, describe what successful async work looks like.

Avoid red flags

- "Must be available 9–5 Eastern Standard Time (EST)" for a "remote" role signals you don't understand async work.

- "Fast-paced environment" often means "we'll Slack you at midnight and expect a reply by 12:05."
- Listing thirty different technologies suggests you don't know what you need.

Review your postings with fresh eyes—would a strong remote candidate understand what working on your team actually feels like? Better yet, have someone who joined remotely review them for authenticity.

If you're on the other side of the table, read postings like code. A role that says "remote" but requires 9-to-5 availability in a single time zone isn't async—it's an office without walls. If the posting doesn't spell out tools, decision-making norms, and meeting load, ask in the first conversation. The answers—or the awkward silence—tell you everything.

> **For managers: Your job description is your team's first async artifact—treat it like one.** Write it collaboratively in an issue or pull request, get feedback from current team members (especially recent hires), and iterate. If the posting reads like boilerplate, candidates will assume the remote culture is boilerplate too. A well-written job description attracts candidates who value the same clarity you do.

Async-first interviewing

Traditional interview processes are heavily synchronous: phone screens, several rounds of video calls, onsite visits. Each stage requires coordinating schedules across time zones and assumes candidates perform best under real-time pressure.

Async-first interviewing drops that assumption and evaluates candidates the way remote work actually happens: through thoughtful written communication and work completed on their own schedule.

At GitHub, the interview loop leaned heavily on take-home projects—realistic, async-friendly exercises candidates completed on their own schedule—rather than whiteboard theater. We'd built internal tooling to automate parts of the take-home evaluation: the infrastructure to make async hiring work was itself a deliberate investment. Applications came in by the thousands, so the first-pass filter did most of the work. What we looked for in those submissions—and what separated the people who thrived from those who struggled—is covered in *Evaluating remote work readiness*.

Written communication samples

Ask candidates to respond to realistic scenarios in writing. This isn't a trick—it's how your team communicates daily.

- "Here's an issue describing a proposed feature change. Write the comment you would add if you had concerns about the approach."

- "Describe a technical decision you made recently and the tradeoffs you considered."
- "Write the pull request description you would create for [specific task relevant to the role]."

You learn more from a candidate's written tradeoff analysis than from watching them think aloud under a countdown clock.

Asynchronous technical exercises

Take-home projects have a bad reputation because most are poorly designed: too long, too vague, or disconnected from actual work. Good ones share a few traits:

- **Time-bounded**—Specify a maximum time investment (two to four hours is reasonable) and design the exercise accordingly.
- **Realistic**—The exercise should resemble work the candidate would actually do in the role.
- **Compensated**—Respect candidates' time by paying for substantial exercises. This also removes financial barriers for candidates who can't afford unpaid labor.
- **Reviewed consistently**—Use a rubric so different candidates are assessed against the same criteria.
- **Room to go deeper**—Design exercises that can be completed well in the stated time but have room for candidates to go deeper if they choose. This reveals intrinsic motivation without punishing candidates who stick to the time limit.

Async code review

For engineering roles, have candidates review a pull request asynchronously. Provide a realistic PR—an anonymized historical one works well—and ask for written feedback. This tests several skills at once:

- Technical judgment and attention to detail
- Written communication style
- Approach to constructive feedback
- Understanding of code quality tradeoffs

Recorded video responses

Some aspects of hiring benefit from seeing candidates speak, but that doesn't require synchronous calls. Async video tools let candidates record responses on their own time—useful for:

- Behavioral questions where you want to see how candidates communicate
- Culture fit questions where authentic responses matter more than polished answers
- Questions where candidates might want time to think before responding

The goal isn't to eliminate synchronous interaction—it's to stop defaulting to it. Use async for what async does best and save live time for conversations that genuinely need back-and-forth.

> **For individual contributors: If a company asks you to do an async exercise, that's a good sign—**

> **treat it like real work.** Write clear commit messages, explain your reasoning in comments, and document tradeoffs. If they *don't* offer any async component—if the entire process is synchronous video calls—ask yourself whether that reflects how the team works day-to-day.

Video interviews that work

Even async-first processes benefit from live conversation. But video interviews for remote roles need a different playbook.

Reduce bias in video interviews

- **Standardize the setup**—Candidates' home environments vary wildly. Don't penalize someone for interviewing from a small apartment or lacking professional lighting.
- **Use structured questions**—Every candidate should answer the same core questions so you're comparing like to like.
- **Take notes during, not after**—Memory distorts quickly. Write down what candidates actually said, not your impression of how they said it.
- **Avoid "culture fit" traps**—"Would I want to get a beer with this person?" is a bias vector, not a hiring criterion. Focus on collaboration fit: Can this person work effectively with the team?

Structure for remote-friendly evaluation

- **Shorter, focused sessions**—Video fatigue is real. Two forty-five-minute conversations beat one ninety-minute marathon.
- **Clear agenda shared in advance**—Candidates should know what to expect. Surprise questions don't reveal job performance; they reveal comfort with high-pressure social situations.
- **Panel interviews done thoughtfully**—Several interviewers can be efficient, but panels of four or more faces on screen create an interrogation atmosphere. Consider having candidates meet team members in separate conversations.

Create equitable candidate experiences

- **Accommodate time zones**—If you're asking a candidate in Asia to interview with a team in North America, offer times that don't require them to sacrifice sleep.
- **Test technology in advance**—Candidates shouldn't discover connection issues during the interview. Offer a tech check beforehand.
- **Provide backup options**—Have a phone number ready if video fails. What matters is the conversation, not the medium.

> 👔 **For managers: Audit your interview process for unconscious bias.** Are candidates from different backgrounds having equivalent experiences? Do your interviewers know what to look for—and what

> to ignore? Consider bias training specifically for remote interview contexts, where nonverbal cues can be even more easily misread.

> **For individual contributors: Your job as an interviewer is to see the candidate's best work, not to "stress test" them.** Create conditions where they can show what they're capable of. If someone seems nervous, acknowledge it—"Video interviews can feel weird. Take your time"—and move on. Accurate assessment beats artificial pressure.

Evaluating remote work readiness

Technical skills and experience matter, but remote work asks a harder question: Can this person thrive without the scaffolding of an office? The traits that make someone effective remotely—self-direction, strong written communication, proactive visibility, and comfort with async collaboration—don't appear on a résumé. You have to design your interview to surface them.

> **Pro-Tip:** The single strongest predictor I saw for success at GitHub wasn't technical skill or prior remote experience—it was willingness to learn. Anyone can open an issue or a pull request; the mechanics are shallow. What separates people who thrive in a developer-tools-first organization from those who struggle is whether they treat picking up unfamiliar tooling as their job or as someone else's.

> The archetype that never worked, regardless of role, was the new hire who announced on day one that they "only use Excel" or weren't a developer and shouldn't have to use GitHub.
>
> The best answer I ever got in an interview, from a non-engineering candidate asked how they'd approach an unfamiliar tool, was "I brew a cup of tea and I figure it out." That person went on to succeed in the role. Developer tools aren't a dev-only medium in an open and async organization; they're the shared operating system every function gets work done on. If a candidate frames engagement with those tools as someone else's problem, the rest of the interview is a formality. **Growth mindset is the only non-negotiable hiring signal in an org where the tools will keep changing.**

These questions cut through rehearsed answers and reveal how candidates actually work:

- "Tell me about a time you had to work on a project where you couldn't easily get answers from colleagues. How did you make progress?"
- "How do you decide when to send a message versus schedule a meeting?"
- "Describe how you'd onboard yourself to a new codebase when your teammates are asleep."
- "How do you stay connected to your team when you don't share physical space?"
- "Tell me about a misunderstanding that happened over text. What did you learn?"

- My personal favorite: "How would you craft the same status update for an engineering versus a business stakeholder?"

> **For individual contributors: The interview evaluates the company as much as it evaluates you.** Turn these questions around: How does the *team* handle ambiguity? How do *they* decide between async and sync? Ask to see a real issue thread or pull request discussion. Ask what onboarding looks like for someone in a different time zone. If the interviewer can't answer concretely, the "remote-first" label might be aspirational rather than operational.

> **Pro-Tip:** Watch for red flags: candidates who describe their ideal work environment with lots of in-person interaction, who seem uncomfortable with written communication, or who expect constant availability from teammates. These aren't bad candidates—they may just be bad fits for remote work.

Closing candidates without the office tour

Remote offers can't rely on the walkthrough of a gleaming office and an introduction to the espresso machine. You convey culture differently: share documentation about your team's rituals and norms, let candidates observe your actual work (a public repo, an open issue discussion), and walk them through a typical async week. Be transparent about challenges—every remote team has them, and pretending otherwise damages trust before day one. Address career growth head-on: how do people get promoted without hallway visibility? (Hint: impact over input.)

> **For managers: Represent your team honestly when closing candidates.** Don't oversell the remote experience—candidates who join with unrealistic expectations leave faster. Be honest about what's hard, specific about what's great. Offer to connect candidates with current team members for unfiltered perspectives—and coach those team members to share their genuine experience, including what took adjustment, not the edited version.

The hiring loop as culture demonstration

Candidates read your hiring process as a preview of the job. They're right to.

If your interviews are disorganized and last-minute, candidates learn that's how your team operates. If communication is sparse and unclear during hiring—when you're presumably at your most polished—imagine a random Tuesday. If the process respects their time and communicates clearly, that's what they'll expect from the job.

> **Pro-Tip:** After each hire, ask new team members what the interview process told them about the team. Their answer reveals whether your hiring

> process accurately represents your culture—or whether you're accidentally misleading candidates.

Remote hiring isn't harder than in-person hiring—it's different. Design interviews to mirror actual work and you'll select candidates who thrive in that environment while giving them an accurate preview of what they're joining.

Hiring the right people is only half the battle. Even well-assembled teams can stall if the rollout goes sideways—and it goes sideways in surprisingly predictable ways.

Why Open and Async Change Fails

> **TL;DR:** Open and async work fails when you copy old habits to new tools instead of rethinking how your team actually collaborates. The right fix depends on whether the blocker is cultural or structural—diagnose which, or you'll burn months treating symptoms instead of causes.

You launched the docs repo three months ago. It has two hundred pages—a hundred and ninety of them untouched since the first week. Chat volume is *up* forty percent. Your weekly "async update" meeting still happens every Monday at 10 AM, because nobody trusts the written updates. The tools are in place. The logic seems sound. But people quietly revert to old patterns.

"People won't use GitHub" and "nobody writes documentation" are symptoms, not the root cause. The practices are usually sound; the problem is how they were introduced. A handful of failure modes explain nearly every open and async stall, and each has a different fix. Solve a structural problem with persuasion and you'll exhaust yourself. Fix a vocal skeptic by adjusting incentive systems and you'll waste months while the objection festers.

Translation rather than transition

Most teams treat remote work like a translation problem rather than a transition problem. You're not converting French to English; you're learning to think in a different language entirely.

Recording a synchronous meeting and posting it afterward isn't async-first—it's sync-first with an archive. Moving your daily standup to a video call isn't a new pattern; it's the old pattern with more overhead. Real transition means rethinking workflows from first principles. Ask not "how do we do this meeting remotely?" but "what problem does this meeting solve, and what's the best async-first way to solve it?" **Don't lift-and-shift your office culture to Zoom.**

> **Common objection: "We tried async and it failed—it just doesn't work for our team."** Did you try async, or did you just stop having meetings? Most teams that say async failed experienced the absence of structure, not the presence of async—the same trap as calling a relocated office a failed remote experiment. That's like ripping out your test suite and concluding that software quality is impossible.

Leadership doesn't model the change

If leaders say "work async" but still schedule synchronous decision-making meetings, still judge people by responsiveness, and still share important context only with direct reports, the message is clear: async is for other people. Your team doesn't listen to what you say—they reverse-engineer what you do.

I've been on the wrong end of this. I once championed an engineering-culture initiative—clear documentation norms, decision records, async-first defaults. The ICs wanted it. The tooling was there. The only thing missing was visible executive commitment. Managers wouldn't stake political capital on adoption their leaders hadn't endorsed, and the initiative died the way most culture initiatives die—not from opposition, but from exhaustion. **A grassroots push without air cover has a ceiling, and that ceiling is lower than advocates want to admit.**

The most corrosive variant is one-way transparency: executives who mandate open practices for ICs while exempting themselves. When you're expected to document every technical decision in a public issue while your director sunsets your project in a calendar invite with three attendees, you're not learning async—you're learning where you stand. That signals transparency is surveillance for people without political capital. ICs respond by producing minimum viable documentation while making real decisions the way leadership does: in DMs.

> **For managers: Diagnose *your* calendar before diagnosing your team's.** Which of your decisions last week were made in public channels? How many "quick syncs" could have been written proposals? For the specific practices to model, see *Working in the Open* and *Core Practices for Async Communication.*

Insufficient psychological safety

Open work requires psychological safety. People won't share in-progress work if they fear judgment. They won't document decisions if documentation might be used against them. Without trust, transparency feels like surveillance. **Openness without safety is just exposure.**

A team I advised deployed a knowledge-sharing platform and encouraged everyone to "document what you learn." Within weeks, an engineer posted a candid postmortem about an outage she'd caused. Her skip-level manager pulled her aside and said it "made the team look bad." The platform went silent overnight. The tool was fine—the culture wasn't ready.

You can't mandate psychological safety any more than you can mandate trust. You build it through consistent behavior over time. Every time someone documents a failure and gets thanked rather than blamed, you reinforce the norm. It's slow work, but it's load-bearing. Skip it and everything above collapses.

> **For individual contributors: You can build safety from the bottom up.** Be the first to share a mistake publicly—a postmortem on a bug you introduced, a candid "here's what I got wrong" in a retrospective. When a teammate does the same, respond with curiosity, not judgment. You can't control the org's culture, but you can set the tone for your immediate team. This is especially true when you have tenure or other forms of privilege. And when someone *does* get punished for openness, name it—privately to your manager if not publicly. Silence signals consent.

> **Pro-Tip:** Test your team's psychological safety with one question: "When was the last time someone publicly changed their mind based on feedback?" If you can't point to a recent example, the silence isn't agreement—it's self-preservation.

New tools without new habits

Creating a GitHub account doesn't make you async-first. Rolling out Notion doesn't create a documentation culture. Organizations that focus on tooling while ignoring culture end up with fancy software nobody uses correctly—or worse, software that recreates old patterns with more overhead.

The tool is never the solution—it's how people use it, supported by norms and incentives. **Tools amplify culture; they don't create it.** A great tool in a terrible culture just automates the dysfunction.

> **Common objection: "We rolled out the tools and nothing changed."** Nine times out of ten, "we tried async" means "we bought a tool." They deployed Notion or Confluence, sent a training invite, and waited for a documentation culture to materialize. That's cargo cult adoption[59]—mimicking the visible artifacts without building the underlying habits.

The flip side is worth naming: some initiatives look like failures for months before they become load-bearing. I launched communication rituals at GitHub—an engineering "Roundup" and a "business changelog"—that had near-zero traction in their first quarter. People forgot to file them. Every reasonable person would have canceled. We didn't, because a new ritual's first-quarter job isn't to work; it's to survive. Both eventually became staples—the things new hires asked about in their first week. **A new ritual's first quarter isn't about working—it's about surviving long enough to work.**

> **Pro-Tip: Treat initiatives like product launches.** Lean on early adopters to prove "product-market fit," and polish the experience before rolling out to the whole org. Don't expect everyone to jump in on

59. https://en.wikipedia.org/wiki/Cargo_cult

> day one, and don't cancel an initiative just because it doesn't hit critical mass immediately.

Recognizing resistance: active, passive, and structural

Even when leadership models the change and the tools fit, resistance shows up as cultural antibodies—the organizational immune system rejecting an unfamiliar practice. Misdiagnose which kind you're facing and you'll burn months applying the wrong fix.

Active resistance

Someone directly challenges the approach: "This async stuff is slowing us down." Teams openly refuse to adopt new tools. Leadership explicitly reverses course.

Active resistance is—paradoxically—the easiest to address, because it gives you something to engage with. The person arguing against public channels is revealing their mental model. Maybe they fear judgment. Maybe they've survived a poorly implemented rollout before.

Respond with dialogue, not defense—treat resistance as data about what's not working. Lead with curiosity. The loudest critics often become your strongest advocates once you address their concerns—because they cared enough to say something and see that you care enough to listen.

Passive resistance

Far more insidious. People nod in meetings, agree that open work makes sense, then quietly continue old behaviors. They create issues nobody reads because the "real" discussion happened in a hallway. They join async threads but hold the actual decision-making in DMs. **The most dangerous resistance looks like agreement.**

Signs include performative participation (comments without engagement), shadow processes (official discussion exists, real decisions happen elsewhere), and symbolic adoption (new tools for low-stakes work, old patterns for anything important).

Respond with visibility—when a decision gets made in a side channel, post about it publicly: "For anyone who missed the hallway conversation, here's what we decided and why." Do it without snark. Propose experiments with clear success criteria. Data converts skeptics faster than arguments.

> **Common objection: "People aren't resisting—they're just too busy to change how they work."**
> "Too busy" *is* resistance—it's just wearing a socially acceptable disguise. When someone says they don't have time to document decisions, what they're really saying is they'd rather spend thirty minutes in a recurring meeting than ten minutes writing something down once.

Structural resistance

The organization's systems actively fight async patterns, regardless of individual intentions. Performance reviews reward "visibility"—usually a proxy for long hours or chat availability. Promotion criteria favor those "always available" or "in the room when it matters." Deployment processes require manual approval from someone in a specific time zone.

With structural resistance, the people aren't resisting—the *systems* are. An IC might embrace async work, but if their review depends on their manager's perception of their "presence," they'll optimize for visibility. Structural resistance is pernicious because it operates invisibly. People say "async just doesn't work for our team" without recognizing that the review template has a section for "office presence" worth twenty percent of their rating.

Respond with systemic change, not persuasion—you can't workshop your way out of broken incentives. Fix the incentives, not just the messaging.

> **For managers: Conduct an incentive audit.** List what behaviors your organization rewards—promotions, bonuses, recognition. Ensure metrics are not self-defeating (Goodhart's Law).[60] Compare that with the behaviors you say you want. The gaps are your structural resistance points.

60. https://en.wikipedia.org/wiki/Goodhart%27s_law

In practice, you'll encounter all three simultaneously: the vocal critic in meetings (active), whose team nods along but doesn't change behavior (passive), all operating within systems that reward the old way (structural). Name the pattern, pick the right fix, and stop wasting energy on the wrong one.

Responding to what's actually broken

These failure modes reinforce each other. Leaders who don't model async often compensate with mandatory tools rolled out too quickly, in an environment where people don't feel safe admitting the new system isn't working, while the actual workflows are just translated office processes.

Flex the how, never the why—the principle is "important decisions need written context." The implementation might be GitHub issues, Confluence, or architecture decision records (ADRs). If someone hates your chosen tool, suggest an alternative. But don't compromise on the principle. And don't try to transform the whole organization at once—start with one team, one practice, one visible win. For the playbook on making results so compelling that others can't help wanting them, see *Lead by Example: Make Others Jealous*.

> **For individual contributors:** If the initiative stalls or your org never fully buys in, don't abandon your own practices. The individual payoffs—clearer thinking, a visible work trail, a promotion-

> ready portfolio—persist whether the org follows or not. Focus on the practices that help *you* most, and let the results do the evangelizing.

Don't argue for change—outperform the status quo. The active resister who felt heard becomes your most credible advocate. The passive participant who sees the written record outlast another forgotten meeting starts contributing. The structural barrier, once named, becomes a fixable bug instead of an immovable fact. **Make what works so visible that skeptics can't help wanting it.**

Lead by Example: Make Others Jealous

> **TL;DR:** You don't need to sell async work—you need results so visible that other teams can't help asking how you do it. Envy drives adoption more sustainably than any mandate ever will.

Your team closes every sprint with shippable features while the team "next door" holds yet another "alignment meeting" to figure out who's supposed to do what. A new hire ships their first PR on day three—meanwhile, the team "down the hall" is still hand-holding theirs through week two. You leave at 5 PM; they're joining their fourth sync-up of the day. Eventually, someone asks: "How does your team actually get stuff done?"

That's the moment you've been building toward. Not with presentations or policy changes—with **results so obvious they create their own gravity.**

The jealousy principle

Here's what drives adoption: envy. When people see your team operating at a different level—clearer communication, faster shipping, fewer emergencies, better work-life balance—they don't need a pitch deck. They want what you have.

> **For individual contributors: You don't need to be a manager to create envy.** When your PR descriptions are thorough and your async proposals save the team a meeting, other engineers notice. Start a practice—weekly written updates, a decision log in your project repo—and do it well enough that a teammate asks "hey, can you show me how you set that up?" That's adoption without a mandate, driven by one IC.

This is the opposite of mandates. You're not pushing change—you're creating pull. And pull is sustainable in a way push never is.

Think about how you choose tools in your own work. Did you adopt version control because someone sent a memo? Or because you saw a colleague roll back a bad change while you manually maintained backup copies? Did you start using a linter because of company policy? Or because you joined a codebase where every PR was clean and consistent, and you wanted your code to match?

People emulate success they can see. Your job isn't to convince anyone that async work is theoretically superior—it's to make the practical benefits impossible to ignore.

Make your wins visible

Practicing async well isn't enough. You need to **make the results legible to outsiders**—to work loudly. Not bragging. Creating evidence.

When your team makes a good decision asynchronously, don't just ship it. Share the story. "We almost built feature X, but @Sarah's written analysis in the RFC showed it would conflict with the Q3 roadmap. Caught it before we wrote a line of code." Now people see the value of written thinking. They see documentation preventing costly mistakes, not creating busywork.

When async communication prevents a crisis, highlight it. "The on-call engineer left detailed context in the incident doc at 2 AM. The morning shift picked it up cold—no confused Slack DMs, no emergency calls, no interrupted sleep." Async stops being an abstract ideal and becomes the reason twelve people got to sleep through the night.

When your well-documented codebase makes onboarding trivial, show it off. "New hire made their first production commit on day two using the setup guide. No hand-holding required." That's a concrete benefit everyone understands, especially managers drowning in onboarding overhead.

The pattern is simple: take the invisible benefits of async work and **make them stories with protagonists and outcomes.** Stories spread where principles don't.

> **Common objection: "Won't I look like I'm bragging or grandstanding?"** You would if you made it about you. Make it about the *practice*. "Our team's documentation saved us hours" isn't bragging—it's evidence. "Look how smart I am for documenting things" would be. Frame wins as proof points for the approach, not personal victories. You want people thinking "I want my team to work that way"—not "Wow, they sure think highly of themselves."

When that curiosity arrives—and it will—you need something better than a one-off Slack reply.

Open source your playbook

When people ask how your team does something, the worst answer is "It's complicated" or "We can chat about it sometime." The best answer is a URL.

Document your practices the way you'd document an API. Write a team handbook. Create templates for common workflows. Build decision logs that show not just *what* you decided, but *how*. These artifacts make your team more effective *and* become reference implementations for others.

This is the open source model applied to operations. Good documentation doesn't just help your current teammates—it becomes a pattern others can fork and adapt. When someone asks "How do you run async standups?" send them a link to your template and a few examples. They see what works, try it, iterate.

Best of all: **you spread practices without spending time evangelizing.** The documentation does the work. You're not scheduling meetings to explain your process—you're creating resources people consume asynchronously. The medium is the message.

> **For managers:** Your team's success is your most persuasive argument for async work. When your team consistently ships on time, your engineers report high satisfaction, and your retention outpaces peer teams—leadership notices. You don't need to sell async in the abstract; point to concrete outcomes.
>
> Here's the key, though: **spell out the causal chain.** Don't assume others will figure out that your results stem from your practices. When you ship a complex project smoothly, mention in the retro or the status update: "Our investment in written RFCs meant everyone understood the architecture before we wrote code. That's why we hit our dates with no last-minute surprises." Make the link between practice and outcome obvious.

> Your team's success also gives you license to experiment. High-performing teams get latitude that struggling teams don't.

Those are team-level wins. The personal payoff is just as real: open work compounds into a portfolio of evidence —PR descriptions that show your thinking, design discussions that show your judgment, decisions you can point to at promotion time. (See *Why You Should Work in the Open* and *Work Loudly* for the full case.)

> **For individual contributors: Make them curious, not converted.** You can't mandate that a skeptical peer work in the open—but you can make your work so visibly better that they ask how. Ship while the next team is still aligning. When someone admires the result, hand them the issue or doc behind it, so copying you is easier than reinventing it. The teammate who adopts your approach because they're jealous of your results sticks with it; the one you argued into it doesn't.

But visible work doesn't stay individual for long—it leaks across team boundaries.

The viral spread of good practices

What makes leading by example powerful: **good practices spread through contact**. They're contagious in ways policy memos aren't.

An engineer joins a cross-functional project and brings their team's documentation habits. Suddenly the PM sees how much easier it is when teams write decisions down. The PM starts doing it on other projects. Those teams see the benefit. It spreads.

A manager from another org joins your sprint review and notices you don't spend fifteen minutes at the start catching everyone up—the pre-read did that. They try it with their team. It works. They tell their peers. It spreads.

Someone from another team gets paged into an incident and sees how your runbooks make the response straightforward instead of chaotic. They go back and create runbooks for their services. Their on-call rotation gets less stressful. Word spreads.

This is grassroots adoption. No change management program. No executive mandate. Just people seeing something that works and thinking "We should do that."

Your role is to **make your practices visible enough to copy and simple enough to adopt**. When someone wants to emulate your team, make it easy. Share your templates. Explain your reasoning. Show them the before and after.

> **Pro-Tip:** Many open source communities maintain an "awesome list"—a curated collection of resources, examples, and templates. Do the same internally for async and open work practices. It

> becomes the go-to reference for anyone adopting these practices, and signals that this is a valued way of working.

Success creates its own momentum

Once your async practices are visibly successful, the questions shift.

Early on, people ask: "Why do you write everything down?" or "Isn't all this documentation slow?" These are skeptical questions.

After your team ships consistently, handles incidents smoothly, and onboards new people effortlessly, the questions change: "How do you write good RFCs?" "Can I see your team handbook?" "What tools do you use for async standups?" These aren't skeptical—they're **implementation questions**. They've already decided there's value; now they want the playbook.

That shift—from "why" to "how"—is the inflection point. The burden of proof has flipped. People aren't questioning whether async work is valuable; they're figuring out how to get those results themselves.

And once you hit that point, adoption accelerates. Each team that succeeds becomes another example, another source of know-how, another node in the network.

Your early investment in visible work and documented practices compounds. Every neighboring team gets a blueprint to follow.

> **Common objection: "What if my team isn't ready to be a showcase yet?"** You're picturing the wrong showcase. It isn't a flawless team—it's one honest artifact other people can see. A messy project documented in the open teaches more than a polished one nobody can find. Pick the work you're least embarrassed to show, make its reasoning visible, and let people weigh the outcome against their own closed-door version. You're not proving you're perfect; you're proving the practice beats the alternative.

Even a single clear win creates an opening. The question is whether you have the patience to let it compound.

The long game

Leading by example is slower than mandating change. No executive decree, no company-wide rollout, no transformation initiative with a Gantt chart and a steering committee. Just steady, visible success that accumulates.

The difference is durability. When you make others jealous of your workflow, you're not creating compliance—you're creating adoption. Teams emulate your practices because they've seen the benefits. They're not following orders; they're solving their own problems with tools they watched you use successfully.

That's how cultural change happens. Not top-down. Not through policy. Through **proof of concept too obvious to dismiss.**

> **For managers: Play the long game, and protect your team while you do.** Cultural change through example takes quarters, not weeks. Shield your team from premature "we need to scale this now" pressure. Let the results accumulate, let other teams come to you, and resist the urge to turn your organic success into a company-wide initiative before it's ready. The moment it feels like a mandate, the jealousy effect dies.

The full adoption arc—where resistance comes from and how to handle it, why initiatives fail, how to sustain change, and how to make results so visible others can't help but emulate them—comes down to one principle: **proof beats persuasion.**

Knowing *what* to build is one thing. Getting an existing team to change how it works—while still shipping—is where most transformations quietly die. This section covered the four ways that happens and what to do about each: rethink your processes from first principles instead of bolting office habits onto Zoom, hire for the way you actually work, diagnose why change fails before prescribing more of the same, and—when all else fails—stop convincing skeptics and start making them jealous.

Key takeaways

- Don't just move your meetings online—overhaul your workflows to prioritize trust, accountability, and asynchronous collaboration, or your remote team will fail for the same reasons office habits did. By the end, you'll be able to spot and replace legacy "presence theater" with concrete, remote-friendly practices that actually help your team get work done.
- Until your documents live in open, reviewable formats—not locked behind proprietary software—your team will keep tripping over lost edits, version confusion, and slow reviews. Learn how to transition to web-friendly tools that actually support async work, or keep losing good ideas to version chaos.
- The fastest way to hire the wrong remote engineer is the four-panel onsite—same format as 2015, same bias toward people who think out loud. Replace one round with a paid two-hour async take-home and a written design review, and you'll see who can actually do the job before they sign the offer.
- Open and async work fails when you copy old habits to new tools instead of rethinking how your team actually collaborates. The right fix depends on whether the blocker is cultural or structural—diagnose which, or you'll burn months treating symptoms instead of causes.

- You don't need to sell async work—you need results so visible that other teams can't help asking how you do it. Envy drives adoption more sustainably than any mandate ever will.

Notice a theme? Every failure mode in this section traces back to the same root cause: leaders who won't go first. You can't refactor processes you won't use yourself, hire for async skills you haven't practiced, or expect transparency while making decisions behind closed doors. That's where the next section picks up—what leadership looks like when charm doesn't commit to the repo and your team can't see you being decisive in a conference room. Adopting these practices is the hard part. Sustaining them is a leadership problem.

Leading in Open and Async Environments

Whether you're a VP, an engineering manager (EM), or a senior IC leading through expertise, the question is the same: how do you lead when your team can't watch you look decisive? Leadership in open and async environments isn't about title or org chart position—it's about influence, modeling behavior, and clearing the path for others to ship their best work. For managers, this is your chance to build the leadership culture you wish you'd experienced earlier in your career.

Strip away the office and much of traditional leadership goes with it—the hallway presence, the read-the-room instincts, the authority that proximity used to confer. The replacement is what you write down. That changes who can lead. It also changes how. A senior IC who publishes a thoughtful RFC influences more decisions than a director whose authority lives in hallway conversations. Leadership in this section means both—the playbook for managers leading distributed teams *and* the playbook for ICs leading the work without direct reports.

> **Common objection: "Senior leadership needs to be in the office." If leaders need to be physically present to lead, they're not leading—they're supervising.** Async leadership means setting clear direction, documenting decisions, and creating systems that work without constant presence. The best test of leadership isn't whether the team functions when you're there; it's whether it functions when you're not. Physical presence becomes a crutch that keeps leaders from building the clarity, documentation, and culture a distributed team demands.

The chapters that follow break this into specifics. They cover what leadership actually looks like when artifacts replace presence, why leaders show their work and how to do it, how to engage with dissent instead of routing around it, and what it means to lead like an engineer. They also cover how to rethink management for distributed teams, how to run 1:1s and career conversations in writing, weekly reporting that doesn't suck, and the zen of open and async leadership as a principles-oriented capstone.

How does leadership actually show up in a world where nobody's hovering over your shoulder—just the breadcrumbs you leave behind?

What Leadership Looks Like in Open and Async

> **TL;DR:** In open and async teams, your leadership is measured by the clarity and usefulness of what you document—decisions, priorities, and expectations—not your title or charisma. If you don't make your thinking visible, you're not leading anyone who isn't in the room with you (and in remote work, there is no room).

You know the type: they command the conference room, always have the perfect hallway chat ready, and somehow make every meeting feel decisive just by showing up. Now scatter that team across four time zones and replace the conference room with a Slack channel. The corner office means nothing when nobody shares your postal code. That confident body language doesn't travel through a pull request comment. Every leadership signal that worked in person—presence, charisma, real-time availability—vanishes. What's left is what you *produce*: documented decisions, visible priorities, clear expectations. **Your artifacts speak when you can't.**

> **For individual contributors: You don't need direct reports to lead in async environments.** Lead through the artifacts you create: well-written RFCs, thorough code reviews, onboarding docs that save teammates weeks of ramp-up. When you document a decision or write a runbook the whole team references, you're leading—even if the org chart doesn't reflect it yet.

In place of those old power signals:

Model the behavior you expect

If you want your team to work in the open, you must work in the open first. If you want thoughtful written communication, yours must be thoughtful and written. The clearest example of this I ever saw at GitHub wasn't a document—it was a decision.

We'd run out of stickers in the first few hours of a major cloud conference, and the Revenue leader at the time made the call in chat. Chat was exactly what it was for: Issues were our default; Campfire-then-Slack was the escalation point. The call was to find a Hubber near HQ, put them in an Uber to the office, put them on the next flight out, pay for their hotel, get several thousand more stickers to the booth by the next exhibition session.

Total elapsed time from "we're out" to "new stickers are on their way to the booth" was about 30 minutes. Nobody asked for approval. Nobody wrote a memo. A senior leader modeled customer-obsession as a verb—at the cost of a plane ticket and a hotel night—and every person who watched that decision cascade through chat learned more about our actual values than any slide deck could have taught them. **Leadership in an async company is what you do when the conference runs out of stickers.**

Create clarity

When team members can't pop by your desk to ask a quick question, you have to make expectations, priorities, and decision criteria explicit and findable. Instead of "let's tighten up our PR review turnaround," an effective async leader writes: "All PRs should receive a first review within one business day. If you can't review in time, reassign or comment that you're blocked."

Build systems, not just relationships

Personal relationships matter, but written processes and shared docs scale better than one-on-one conversations. A team handbook that answers "how do we handle on-call rotations?" serves every future hire—a Slack DM to your favorite colleague serves exactly one person, once.

Trust by default

When you can't see people working, monitoring activity is a dead end. Stop asking "what did you do today?" Start asking "what shipped this week, and what's blocking you?" Outcomes are legible across time zones. Keystrokes aren't.

Trust-by-default shows up at the IC level too. The most-linked document on one of my teams wasn't a manager's strategy memo—it was a senior engineer's runbook for a common support edge case, written the night they got tired of re-explaining the same procedure in chat. No title change came with it. What came instead was better: every prioritization conversation for the next two months cited that write-up by name, every new hire was pointed at it their first week, and every cross-team conversation about that bug started with its URL. That engineer was leading the work. The org chart took a year to catch up. **Influence accrues to whoever wrote the document everyone keeps linking to.**

Trust-by-default shows up in unglamorous places at the executive level, too. Between my offer and my start date at GitHub, I attended a "Drinkup"—a customer meetup the company hosted in Washington, DC. I'd never seen so many people in suits talking about open source—contracting officers, policy wonks, lawyers from agencies whose open source policy wouldn't be written for years to come. One of GitHub's founders was told, mid-event, that non-developers were ordering on the GitHub tab.

The response wasn't to lock it down. It was to *double* the tab: "as long as they say the word 'GitHub,' they drink on us." That wasn't a bar budget line item. It was a policy choice—brand recognition purchased with trust, not audited with spreadsheets. The cost of a few extra rounds was trivial compared to the cost of a culture that assumed the worst about its own community. I hadn't started yet. I'd already learned how the company made decisions.

From charisma to artifacts

You can't coast on charisma when your influence lives in written artifacts anyone can examine. Every documented decision invites scrutiny. **Charm doesn't commit to the repo.** Harder, but more honest. Leaders who thrive in async environments embrace the trade: **judge me on my thinking, not my delivery.** That shift—from performing leadership to documenting it—is explored in depth in *Leaders Show Their Work*, and it plays out differently depending on your role:

> 👔 **For managers: Your leadership is visible through the systems you build, not the meetings you attend.** Every decision you make in private signals that opacity is acceptable—your team will copy what you do, not what you say in the all-hands. Audit your team's decision-making: if decisions happen in 1:1s or hallway conversations, move them to issues or decision records. Make your calendar, priorities, and reasoning public.

> Yes, this feels dangerous. What if you're not there to course-correct? What if someone misinterprets a decision and ships the wrong thing? I've watched both happen. The difference is that when decisions stay private, you catch the mistake *during* implementation—expensive course correction. When decisions are documented and visible, someone usually catches the problem *during* the discussion thread—before work even starts. The fastest way to model async leadership is to stop being the bottleneck in synchronous approval chains—replace yourself with documentation that works while you sleep. It's not removing your judgment. It's making your judgment visible early enough to actually help.

> **For individual contributors: Start building leadership artifacts this week.** Write the first RFC or design doc for a problem your team keeps discussing in Slack but never resolves. Volunteer to run the next postmortem and publish the write-up. Mentor a junior dev by pairing on an issue—then let them take the credit. These aren't résumé-building exercises; they're the exact behaviors that separate "senior" from "staff" in most leveling rubrics.

Make your thinking visible. The question isn't *whether* to show your reasoning—it's how to do it systematically, and what it costs when you don't.

Leaders Show Their Work

> **TL;DR:** If you document only what you decided, not why or how, you force others to repeat your work—or make costly mistakes—when context fades; by consistently showing your reasoning, you build trust, preserve knowledge, and make better leaders out of those who follow.

Every undocumented decision is a time bomb—context fades, people leave, and new hires inherit archaeology projects instead of explanations. Two years from now, someone will spend a week reverse-engineering a choice you could have explained in three sentences—and they'll probably get it wrong, because the chat thread where you worked it out was purged ninety days after you posted it. The decision didn't vanish. Just the reasoning behind it. And the reasoning is the only part that teaches anyone anything.

I've described the value of recording decisions through URLs as:

> *URLs provide a single, indisputable source of truth for the organization's intentions and, equally important, expose the reasoning behind the decision, reducing the tendency for top-down choices to be communicated as "because I said so."*

True, but a URL is necessary, not sufficient. To reap the benefits of transparency, leaders must share not just *what* they decided but *why* and *how* they got there. They can do this in two ways: adopt systems that naturally capture and expose process,[61] or hold each other to account for the extra effort of *showing their work*.

Yes, documentation takes more time up front—but it's short-term thinking to skip it. As the US Navy SEALs say, **"Slow is smooth, and smooth is fast."**

Decisions at scale get messy

As teams grow, the old ways of making decisions force a trade-off between transparency and speed:

When it's just you, there's no communication overhead —you know everything you know. Add a cofounder and decisions happen over lunch. Add ten engineers and that lunch conversation becomes a Slack thread. Add fifty and that Slack thread needs an all-hands, a project board, and a quarterly review cycle. The cost of keeping everyone informed grows faster than the team itself—communication overhead scales quadratically[62]

61. https://ben.balter.com/2015/11/18/tools-to-empower-open-collaboration/
62. https://en.wikipedia.org/wiki/Brooks%27s_law

whether you budget for it or not. **Collaboration doesn't have to be an O(n^2) problem**—but only if you show your work in systems that scale better than your headcount.

> **Pro-Tip:** The warning sign that you've outgrown informal decision-making: someone affected by a decision says "Wait, when did we decide that?" More meetings won't fix this—they're a linear patch on an exponential problem. Invest in documentation systems that let decisions reach people without requiring their presence.

To handle this, many organizations add a management layer, tasking managers with coordinating decisions across teams and business units. Managers make the calls, then relay what people need to know—visibility is a core part of the role. But each relay loses fidelity. Someone has to run a human extract-transform-load (ETL) operation[63] to shuttle context from one reporting structure to the next, and with each layer, the signal degrades.

> **Pro-Tip:** I use "management" here broadly. Yes, this could mean a people manager, but it applies just as well to product managers, program managers, and individual contributors in leadership roles. At GitHub, we called this the directly responsible individual (DRI).

63. https://www.ibm.com/think/topics/etl

Transparency is cheaper than you think

Most teams treat transparency as a tax on their real job. The right systems surface the *how* and *why* as a byproduct of daily work, not as homework after the fact.

At GitHub, we adopted workflows from the open source community, working transparently through GitHub issues and pull requests. Managers captured bugs and feature requests as clear problem statements and prioritized them in a public backlog.

> **Pro-Tip: If you want an org to accept a cut, let them watch it happen.** When GitHub's product organization was trying to narrow a sprawling list of in-flight projects, someone opened a single issue —the first issue in a new Product repo—and listed *everything* the company was currently building. Every team. Every project. Each one got a reaction emoji: 🚢 for ship it, ❄️ for put it on ice.
>
> What would have been a months-long off-site full of political landmines became a public, async, one-thread conversation that anyone in the company could watch, weigh in on, or link to later. The decision about what *not* to do is usually harder than the decision about what to do—and it lives or dies on how visible the reasoning is.

Developers pick issues off the top of that queue and open a pull request with their proposed fix—linking back to the issue and @mentioning the responsible team. Peers review, discuss, iterate, and merge. Anyone in the organization (or for open source, the world) can watch it happen. Six months later, someone can use file history, `git blame`, or issue search to find exactly who changed what and why—as if they'd been in the room.

That same transparent process extends beyond code. At GitHub, we used the same flow to propose, discuss, and ship changes to architecture, policy, process, and documentation—even how we work. Yes, working transparently takes more effort up front, but **transparency is an investment, not an expense.** And it breaks the false choice between transparency and speed that plagues top-down decision-making.

The hidden cost of skipping the write-up

As GitHub grew, I was guilty of starting a DM, collaborative doc, or video call, tempted by the siren song of working things through in private. One example that still haunts me: a Hubber-enablement (associate engagement) conversation that *should* have been an issue everyone could see and weigh in on. I pulled the two most invested people into a DM to "resolve it faster." We landed on a half-measure, I announced the outcome, and then spent months watching teams work around it—because the people who cared most never saw the reasoning, only the verdict.

The damage wasn't the decision. It was the quiet signal that the real conversation happened somewhere they weren't invited. Just as quick technical fixes saddle a team with technical debt, communication shortcuts create communication debt. **Near-term convenience**

creates long-term communication debt. And like technical debt, it compounds—the longer you wait to document those opaque decisions, the more expensive the cleanup gets as people stack assumptions on top of guesses.

Nothing's inherently wrong with chat, collaborative docs, or video calls—sometimes they're the best tool for the job.[64] But we routinely skip sharing outcomes with everyone who needs them.

> **Common objection: "Writing everything down is too formal and bureaucratic."** This confuses documentation with bureaucracy. Bureaucracy is process for its own sake—forms no one reads, approvals that add no value, meetings about meetings. Documentation is memory with purpose. The difference is intent: are you creating paperwork to feel busy, or capturing context so decisions outlive the meeting? Good documentation is often *less* formal than endless meetings—a quick note in an issue, not a 50-page spec. The most bureaucratic organizations I've seen run on hallway decisions and tribal knowledge, forcing newcomers to navigate invisible power structures.

Sharing a decision can be as simple as "We decided X" or "You must now do Y"—through email, chat, or a quick meeting update. But these efforts too often focus on the *what*, even when the *why* or *how* isn't clear to outsiders.

64. https://ben.balter.com/2020/08/14/tools-of-the-trade/

Over the long tail of history, the reasoning behind a decision matters more than the outcome. **The "why" outlasts the "what."** Sharing only the conclusion feels efficient now, but racks up context debt that compounds every time someone new encounters the decision.

Leaders hold the missing context, and sometimes they assume that sharing the change is enough. But humans aren't web servers—you can't deploy a diff of "what changed" and expect people to absorb it. Code goes live with a deployment; people need the full picture to grasp not just what changed but *why* they should care and how it affects their work. Smart people—especially engineers—want to understand the how and why, and to double-check their leaders' logic. Good engineers tease out edge cases. I use the phrase "being treated as an adult" to describe this culture—it's about respecting people enough to share the reasoning, not just the result.

> **Pro-Tip:** I've seen a number of non-engineers take on leadership roles within engineering organizations only to be surprised by the questions they receive in response to decisions. Think about it from the engineers' perspective. They are trained to poke holes in vague instructions to tease out and resolve the edge cases. They're not being critical. They're being thorough in their implementation.

Skipping the write-up is costly—but not every leader buys transparency. Some see openness as an invitation to second-guessing; others treat it as their single best decision-making tool. The divide says more about the leader than the practice.

Transparency is a competitive advantage

Ask leaders about transparency and you'll get one of two reactions:

When you see it as a risk

Seen as a liability, transparency exposes you to the risk of looking "wrong"—or at least the fear, uncertainty, and doubt (FUD) that someone might ask a well-meaning but hard-to-answer question. This mirrors the FUD around the insecurity of open source.[65] Yes, decisions have had poor rollouts, just as some open source projects have had bugs. But more eyes render all bugs shallow. Rejecting security-through-obscurity—or here, management-through-obscurity—produces better outcomes when you pair it with a healthy culture of collaboration.

That fear is real—but it's also backwards. The risk isn't that someone will question your decision. It's that no one will, and you'll ship a bad one unchecked.

When you see it as an advantage

Seen as an asset, transparency reflects the belief that making decisions together leads to the best outcomes. In theory, that unwanted criticism becomes early feed-

65. https://ben.balter.com/2014/09/22/open-source-is-not-insecure/

back that helps you course-correct. In practice, people appreciate the openness, but you'll often struggle to get engagement on non-controversial decisions.[66] I've owned or joined thousands of decisions at GitHub. I can't think of one where upfront transparency didn't produce better results—even with the short-term cost. **Secrecy doesn't protect decisions—it just hides the bad ones.**

How to actually show your work

The easiest way to show your work: default to async over real-time, even when it feels less convenient in the moment. Optimize for the reader, not the writer.

Naturally transparent tools do most of the work, but async isn't always the right call. When you need to add transparency after the fact, here's how to hold yourself and others to account:

- State the problem you're solving and why
- List your goals and the principles you followed
- Communicate not just what you decided but how and why
- Link to source materials or prior art you used
- Include what alternatives you evaluated and why you dismissed them
- If it's not clear, explain who contributed to the decision and their roles

66. https://ben.balter.com/2016/05/11/moderating-a-controversial-pull-request/

- Set expectations for feedback, improvement, or participation, if any
- Explain the state of the decision (for example, final or proposed) and when you'll revisit it, if ever
- Distill meeting recordings and chat transcripts into a concise record others can quickly scan
- Avoid using "best practice," "industry standard," or "parent company/former employer does X" as a justification
- Set clear timelines and share regular updates—silence looks like abandonment

Showing your work applies regardless of role:

> **For managers: Lead with transparency by sharing your reasoning publicly.** When you face a tough call, document your reasoning where your team can see it—building trust and teaching them how to think through similar choices. Hold yourself to the same standard—if you're asking your team to work in the open, show your work too.

> **For individual contributors: Post a weekly "what I'm working on" update in your team's public channel—three bullets, five minutes, done.** When you make a technical decision, drop a comment in the relevant issue explaining what you chose and *why* before moving on. Chose Redis over Memcached? Write it up in the PR description, not just in your head. Better still, create a dedicated

> "show and tell" discussion in your team's repo. The goal isn't to narrate your entire workday—it's to leave a trail that helps future-you (and your promotion packet) prove what you actually built.
>
> And if your leadership isn't showing *their* work? Ask for it. "Can you share the reasoning behind that decision in the issue?" isn't insubordination—it's the kind of question that signals you're thinking beyond your own tasks.

Individual transparency builds trust, but good intentions don't survive turnover. People leave, Slack threads expire, and the reasoning behind last quarter's reorg becomes organizational folklore—everyone has a version, none of them match. That's where decision records come in.

Decision records

If issues track what work is happening, management decision records (MDRs) capture the *how* and *why*—a permanent, searchable log of your organization's decision history that outlasts the people who made the calls.

> **Pro-Tip:** Call them ADRs, MDRs, business decision records (BDRs), or whatever fits your team's vocabulary—the acronym matters less than the habit. Start simple: a one-paragraph summary of the decision, the alternatives you considered, and why you chose this path. You can formalize the

> template later. What matters is capturing the *why* while it's fresh.

The simplest form is a decision log—borrowed from project management. Each time you make a decision, record it as a comment on an issue or as a pull request to a Markdown file. Every decision lives in a searchable, durable medium—context and rationale included. **If it's not written down, it wasn't decided.**

At GitHub, this extended well past engineering: the vacation policy, travel reimbursement rules, and other HR documents lived as Markdown files in internal repositories, with changes proposed and reviewed through pull requests like any other code. More than once, a reviewer caught a real issue in a policy PR before merge—the kind of edge case a closed-door drafting process would have shipped company-wide and then tried to unwind through exceptions. The decision trail *was* the diff—you could `git blame` a sentence in the benefits policy and land on the conversation that put it there. Every durable decision, not just the technical ones, deserves a commit message.

> **Common objection: "Documenting decisions slows things down—we need to move fast."** You're confusing speed of action with speed of outcomes. Quick decisions made in hallways get forgotten, relitigated, and reversed—that's slow. Documented decisions stick. They don't need to be re-explained,

> re-debated, or re-made when new stakeholders join. Think of it like skipping tests to ship faster—sure, you save ten minutes now, but you'll burn hours debugging when things break and you can't remember why that conditional exists. A five-minute decision record saves hours of "wait, what did we decide?" conversations. The fastest teams don't revisit the same decisions twice.

For quick decisions, a line in the issue thread is plenty. Bigger ones deserve more structure.

Steal the ADR format from engineering

For larger choices, engineering teams often use an architecture decision record (ADR).[67] ADRs capture not just the decision but its context and consequences—and invite stakeholders into the process. The person responsible writes their proposal in long-form prose and submits it for discussion and refinement before it's merged.

While ADRs target engineering decisions, the format adapts to any decision with lasting consequences—especially management decisions with broad reach. Management decision records don't democratize or crowdsource management. They make visible how you already make those decisions.

> **For managers: Use decision records for choices that will impact many teams or outlast a single**

> **quarter.** The act of writing forces clarity, and the review process surfaces perspectives you'd otherwise miss. Even when you have final authority, collaborative review leads to better decisions—and better buy-in from those affected.

> **For individual contributors: Decision records are how you show strategic thinking.** When you're leading technical initiatives or proposing process changes, use the format to build consensus and show leadership. A well-written decision record shows exactly what advancement requires: weighing tradeoffs, understanding who's affected, and communicating clearly.

Once the habit's in place, hand the routine work off to machines.

Let the robots handle the busywork

GitHub is extensible, so day-to-day issue management automation comes cheap with shared GitHub Actions. If an objective or key result (OKR) hadn't been updated, we used GitHub Actions to nudge the responsible person. When status updates came in as issue comments on a regular cadence, Actions updated the project board so we could see the health of all our OKRs in a single view. Automation can even summarize weekly activity for dif-

67. https://github.com/joelparkerhenderson/architecture-decision-record

ferent audiences. We used Actions to automate issue creation at planning kickoff and to create regular meeting and 1:1 agendas each week.

> **Pro-Tip:** Taking the metaphor to its logical extreme, there's no reason why a manager's workflow couldn't have its own "CI." Automated checks could set a high bar for decision-making—require the right reviewers on each proposal, give everyone time to weigh in before it merges. We used this lightly in some places to encourage inclusive language or improve the readability of documentation.

Automation's real value isn't efficiency—it's consistency. Automate the routine stuff and you free up headspace for the hard calls. Automated checks maintain standards long after the humans who wrote them have moved on.

Show your work, earn their trust

Without systems that capture process daily, transparency takes effort—but the payoff compounds. Hold one another to account for showing the work: not just what you decided, but *how* and *why*. Do it consistently and you capture institutional memory, model your team's values, and train the people who'll make decisions after you leave.

Transparency isn't an occasional virtue—it's a daily practice. Show your work, and trust stops being something you ask for. The record proves it.

Engaging with Dissent

> **TL;DR:** Shut down dissent and you don't end it; you just push it into DMs and side channels where it festers out of sight. Engage it in public, and the same pushback that felt like a threat becomes your best source of buy-in and better ideas.

You've done the work. Gathered input, weighed trade-offs, documented your reasoning, and made the call. You're confident and ready to move forward. Then the pushback arrives—questions, objections, frustration. In a remote team, it shows up as pointed comments in the announcement thread, skeptical questions in chat, or worse, conspicuous silence from people you expected to have opinions.

> **Pro-Tip:** Leadership once paid for not engaging dissent hard enough. A controversial, wide-reaching top-down engineering decision drew internal skeptics; over time, leaders wrote them off as merely negative and stopped engaging. The ignored concerns festered and grew in private,

> where they were hardest to address. Nothing tanked morale faster. The leadership instinct at the time was to read the pushback as resistance to change. It wasn't. They just wanted to be heard and understand the decision and how it affected them. Years later I can say it plainly: the dissenters were asking the right questions.

Every leader has faced this pull: shut it down, move on, "control the narrative." You have more context. The decision is final. Rehashing feels unproductive. Understandable—and almost always wrong.

Why "controlling the narrative" backfires

Suppressing dissent backfires in any organization, but in remote and async environments, the damage compounds. When your team is distributed, you can't gauge the mood, read body language, or pull someone aside. Written communication is the medium, and written silence—or written dismissal—speaks volumes.

It erodes psychological safety

When you shut down conversation, you signal that your team's concerns don't matter. Worse, you imply you have something to hide—or that your reasoning can't withstand scrutiny. In a remote team where psychological safety already bears load for open work, that's corrosive.

It drives dissent underground

Ignoring questions doesn't make them disappear—it pushes them into DMs, private channels, and side conversations where they fester without your context. People speculate, gossip, and grow resentful. The resistance you tried to sidestep becomes the resistance that's hardest to address because you can no longer see it. In an async environment where everything should have a URL, pushing discussion into private channels is the organizational equivalent of undocumented technical debt.

It stifles learning

Transparent decisions teach the next generation of leaders. When you explain your reasoning under scrutiny—not just when announcing the decision, but when defending it—you teach your team how to think about tradeoffs, weigh competing priorities, and make difficult calls. That's showing your work at its sharpest: not just documenting *what* you decided, but modeling *how* to lead through disagreement.

> **Common objection: "Engaging with pushback just invites more negativity."** What feels like "more negativity" is usually existing frustration becoming visible. The frustration was already there—in DMs, side conversations, and eye rolls you couldn't see. Public engagement gives you the chance to address misunderstandings and—crucially—show the rest of the team that pushback leads to dia-

> logue, not punishment. Teams that see leaders engage thoughtfully with criticism become more constructive over time, not less.

“Caremad” is a feature, not a bug

Your team’s pushback isn’t a problem to manage—it’s proof they care.

Think about the alternative. A team that greets a major decision with total silence isn’t a team that agrees—it’s a team that has disengaged, grown indifferent, or learned to fear speaking up. If they don’t care enough about *this* decision to voice concerns, there are almost certainly bigger issues they’re not raising either.

The people pushing back are what developers call “caremad”—frustrated precisely because they care about getting the right outcome. They’re not trying to undermine you. They’re processing. You’ve had weeks to sit with the decision; they just got the news. The gap between your readiness to move forward and their need to understand isn’t insubordination—it’s a timing mismatch.

Bridging that gap is the job. The *emotional labor* of helping your team process the decision, voice their concerns, and find a path forward—even when the decision itself isn't changing—is what leadership actually looks like after the announcement goes out.

> **For managers: Create explicit space for post-decision feedback.** When announcing a significant decision, don't just share the outcome and rationale. Add a section that invites response: "I know this will generate questions. Here's where to ask them, and I commit to responding to each." In async environments, a dedicated issue or discussion thread works well—it keeps the conversation visible and gives you time to craft thoughtful replies. At GitHub, the company's main synchronous ritual—a monthly all-hands called GitTogether—gave roughly a third of each session (the share varied over the years) to live Q&A. Leadership could have filled the hour with presentations, but choosing to spend it fielding unfiltered questions sent a clear signal: your questions matter more than our slides.

> **For individual contributors: Channel your frustration into constructive questions, not complaints.** When a decision frustrates you, resist the urge to vent in DMs. Instead, ask in the public thread: "Can you help me understand how X was weighed against Y?" or "What would need to

> change for us to revisit this?" These questions surface your concern *and* give leadership a concrete opening to provide context. You're more likely to influence future decisions by demonstrating thoughtful engagement than by broadcasting disagreement privately.

The playbook: transparent, open, accountable

The best leaders respond to dissent with the same principles that make async work effective: transparency, openness, and accountability.

Be transparent

Share the data, constraints, and context that informed your decision. Explain the criteria, tradeoffs, and implications—including the options you considered and rejected. Name what you don't know. Don't spin or sugarcoat. The same principle that makes decisions worth documenting makes them worth defending: future you—and future team members—will benefit from a written record of not just the decision, but the dialogue that followed.

Be open

Invite questions and genuinely engage with them. Approach concerns with curiosity, not defensiveness. Respond thoughtfully, even when the questions feel repetitive or adversarial. Don't dismiss, deflect, or rebut—sit with the discomfort and respond honestly. In async environments, this means actually replying to every substantive comment in the thread, not just the friendly ones.

Be accountable

Take responsibility for the decision and its outcomes—including the ones you didn't anticipate. If the decision turns out to be wrong, say so. Admit mistakes, correct course, and improve. A leader who can say "I got this wrong, here's what I've learned" earns more trust than one who was right all along but never acknowledged the possibility of error.

> **Pro-Tip:** The clearest worked example of this playbook I watched at GitHub was the response to "Dear GitHub"—an open letter from maintainers of major open source projects flagging long-standing gaps in the platform they used every day. The response wasn't a roadmap deck or a promise to do better in the next quarterly plan. It was a program of small, specific, visible fixes—Paper Cuts—shipped in public over a short window: the kind of concrete, user-facing improvements the letter had been asking for.
>
> The pattern mattered as much as the product work. A strategic deck would have reassured executives; it wouldn't have rebuilt anything. The accumulating evidence of merged pull requests did,

> because trust with a developer community is rebuilt at the pace of shipped fixes, not planning cycles.

Dissent in async environments

Remote and async work cuts both ways with dissent. You lose nonverbal cues that distinguish "frustrated but engaged" from "angry and disengaged." But writing forces both sides to articulate clearly—and that clarity has real advantages.

Written dissent creates a record

Unlike a heated exchange in a conference room—which five people will remember six different ways—async disagreement leaves a record. This is a feature: future team members can see not just what the team decided, but how they processed it. The discussion thread becomes institutional memory.

Async provides processing time

A critical comment in a thread means someone sat with the problem long enough to write it down. Your reply gets the same breathing room. This natural cooling-off period reduces the temperature of disagreements that might escalate in person. Use it intentionally—don't fire off reactive replies.

But text lacks tone

A genuine question can read as an accusation. A concise response can feel dismissive. Both leaders and team members need to write with intentional warmth during disagreements. Don't assume bad intent, acknowledge emotions explicitly ("I can see this frustrates you"), and err on the side of over-explaining your reasoning rather than under-explaining.

> **For managers: Model how to disagree well by responding thoughtfully to every substantive concern—especially the ones that challenge you most.** Your team watches how you handle criticism more closely than how you handle praise. If you engage respectfully with the hardest questions, you set the standard for how disagreement works on your team. If you dismiss them, so will everyone else.

> **For individual contributors: Dissent is most effective when it's specific, public, and solution-oriented.** "This decision is wrong" gives leadership nothing to work with. "I'm concerned that X will cause Y because of Z—have we considered an alternative?" gives them everything. Post your concerns in the public thread, not in DMs. If you've been heard and the decision stands, respect it—disagree and commit. Continuing to relitigate privately undermines the async culture that gives you a voice in the first place.

When disagreement hardens into conflict

Not every disagreement stays productive. Sometimes a thread gets personal, tone sharpens, and two people who used to collaborate start talking past each other. In an office, tension telegraphs itself through hallway body language, pointed silences, and who suddenly eats lunch alone. Remote strips those signals. You have to watch deliberately and step in when you spot it.

Create safe channels for surfacing tension

Regular one-on-ones are your early warning system. Ask directly: "Is there anyone on the team you're finding it hard to work with?" and "Are there any tensions I should know about?" People won't always volunteer this information, but if you ask consistently, they'll share when it matters.

Intervene early

When you see tension building in public channels—messages getting shorter, tone getting sharper, people talking past each other—don't wait for it to explode. A private note to one or both parties ("I noticed the thread got heated—is everything okay?") can prevent escalation.

Model constructive disagreement

Your team watches how you handle conflict. If you avoid hard conversations, they'll learn avoidance is acceptable. If you handle disagreements with directness and grace, they'll learn that conflict can be productive. When you disagree with a proposal in a public issue—"I see the appeal of microservices here, but our team size makes a modular monolith more practical right now. Here's my reasoning..."—your team learns that respectful dissent with evidence is how decisions get made.

Don't solve everything yourself

Your job isn't to resolve every conflict personally—it's to ensure conflicts get resolved. Sometimes that means facilitating a conversation. Sometimes it means coaching someone on how to have a difficult conversation themselves. Sometimes it means bringing in outside help. Know your role in each situation.

> **For managers: Write your team's conflict norms down—literally.** Something like: "If a thread gets heated, move to a call within 24 hours" or "Disagree with the idea, not the person." When you disagree publicly with a peer or manager, do it respectfully and with evidence—your team is watching to learn what's safe. If two reports are stuck in a loop, don't let the thread grow to 30 messages—step in, name the tension, and work toward a resolution.

When to revisit (and when to commit)

Not every dissenting voice should change the decision—but every dissenting voice deserves engagement. The distinction matters. You can fully hear someone's concern, take it seriously, and still conclude that the original decision stands. What you can't do is ignore the concern and expect commitment.

Healthy teams also know when a decision is final. "Disagree and commit"—where team members voice their objections, accept the decision, and execute fully—only works if the "disagree" part is genuine. If people never feel heard during disagreement, the "commit" part rings hollow.

> **For individual contributors: "Disagree and commit" only works if you genuinely commit.** Once you've raised your concerns and the decision stands, execute it fully—don't slow-walk the implementation or relitigate it in every standup. If results later prove you were right, bring data, not "I told you so." The leader who sees you execute well despite disagreement is the leader who seeks your input next time.

> **For managers: Be explicit about which decisions are open to revision and which are final.** "I'm genuinely seeking input" is different from "I've decided, and I'm explaining why." Conflating the two is how trust erodes. If you're seeking input, be open to changing course. If the decision is final, say so—and invest the emotional labor in helping your team understand and accept it.

The instinct to cover your ears when your team pushes back is human. But leadership isn't measured only by the quality of your decisions—it's measured by how you bring your team through the hard ones. Sit with the discomfort. Be transparent, be open, be accountable. The team that can disagree in public, process honestly, and still ship together is the team that sticks around to keep doing it.

Lead Like an Engineer

> **TL;DR:** Stop running parallel project spreadsheets—lead your team where they work by managing everything in issues, pull requests, and project boards. When you make decisions and progress visible in the same tools your engineers use, you save time, reduce confusion, and give your team the clarity they need to move faster without constant meetings.

The day I became a manager, I was handed a spreadsheet. "This is how we track projects," they said. I stared at it—dozens of tabs, color-coded cells, formulas that broke when you looked at them wrong. The timeline column was wishes. The "status" column was whatever I'd typed the last time someone asked, which was already stale. None of it auto-updated against the real state of the work. Worst of all: *it wasn't where my engineers were actually working*. They lived in issues and pull requests. I was maintaining a parallel fiction in a tab, and every Friday I was the bottleneck translating between the two.

Meanwhile, the engineering team I now led had a beautifully organized project board with clear priorities, documented decisions, and a searchable history of every choice they'd made. **Why were we using medieval tools to manage the team that built with modern ones?**

Most engineering leaders started as engineers. On a typical team, you capture work in issues, organize it in project backlogs, and review it in pull requests. These tools work. Why abandon them when you move into management?

> **Pro-Tip:** Whether your team uses Scrum (fixed-length work cycles with defined ceremonies), Kanban (continuous flow with visual boards), or something else entirely, the fundamentals are the same: track what needs doing, review proposed changes before they're merged, and make progress visible. If you're new to engineering leadership, start by observing how your team already works—then use those same patterns for your own tasks.

When engineers move into management, they adopt entirely different tools—more cumbersome, more opaque—because nobody ever got fired for choosing a spreadsheet. If issues, pull requests, and project boards are the best way to develop software, shouldn't they also be the best way to lead software development teams?

Management is just another codebase

Using engineering tools like GitHub to track management tasks isn't just an alternative to personal lists or collaborative docs—it forces you to work more *transparently* than traditional management does. **Make work visible. Write things down. Manage like an engineer.** I've written about the value of showing your work, and those benefits apply directly: capturing institutional knowledge, letting others learn through observation, reinforcing culture, driving engagement, and keeping the bar high. Tools that make work visible by default bake those benefits in—you don't have to remember to be transparent.

> **Common objection: "Engineering tools are for engineers—management requires different approaches."** Why? The principles that make engineering tools effective—transparency, version control, peer review, and documented history—are universal. Traditional management tools (spreadsheets, slide decks, email threads) obscure decision-making, lose context, and create information silos. Engineers designed these tools to manage complexity, track changes, and enable collaboration. Those challenges aren't unique to code—they're exactly what management needs. The resistance is usually about familiarity, not effectiveness.

Start with the simplest unit: the issue.

Open an issue for everything

This isn't a new idea. Long before the term "inner source" became popular, GitHub had co-opted open source workflows and communication patterns for internal development. While plenty has been written about "how GitHub used GitHub to build GitHub," the concept of using GitHub to *manage* GitHub fell out of favor as GitHub grew (and outgrew its tools). Once GitHub introduced native planning and tracking capabilities, the case for management use became hard to ignore.

Issues are the atomic unit of work across teams—how you plan, track, coordinate, and communicate it. Preparing a deck for a business review? Refreshing career ladders? Planning an offsite? Capture that work in an issue. Visibility and accountability come free.

> **Pro-Tip:** Track tasks and their progress in issues, cc relevant teams, and cross-reference related issues to naturally capture process. Issues bring the most value when the real work happens on and around them—not when the meaningful discussions happen in chat or over video and the issue becomes a glorified checkbox or a status broadcast (for which Discussions are better suited).

Link issues to each other and they form a hierarchy—department-wide goals break down into initiatives, epics, stories, and tasks. All the management "meta work" becomes visible, navigable, and connected to the strategy it supports.

> **For individual contributors: Open issues for your own work, even if nobody asked you to.** When you track a research spike, a refactoring effort, or a cross-team dependency in an issue, you're making invisible work visible. Your manager can see what you're spending time on without asking; other teams can discover related efforts without a meeting. It takes thirty seconds to open an issue, and the payoff compounds every time someone finds context they would otherwise have asked you for in a DM.

> **Common objection: "My non-engineering teammates won't adopt GitHub."** Start with what they already know: issues are structured to-do items with built-in discussion, and pull requests are tracked feedback on documents. If someone can comment on a Google Doc, they can review a pull request. At GitHub, marketing, legal, finance, and HR teams all used issues and pull requests for their own work—not because anyone forced them, but because the workflow beat email threads and status meetings. Start with one team and one project board, and let the results sell the approach.

Individual issues capture individual tasks—but teams need a way to see the full picture.

Project boards show who's doing what

Project boards organize, prioritize, and surface those issues—showing at a glance what's in progress, what's blocked, and what's coming next.

I've written about how we used issues and projects at GitHub for planning and tracking.[68] We used issues and a project board to track our department-wide objectives and key results (OKRs). Teams layered on labels, milestones, and assignees to slice the view by priority, timeline, or owner.

The department tracked its management tasks in issues, visible company-wide as a management backlog via a GitHub Project. Anyone curious about an initiative or administrative epic could click into the linked issue or subscribe for updates.

Document what should live longer than a task

While issues are ideal for tracking active work, Markdown files are where long-lived information belongs. Team charters, process documentation, runbooks, and architecture decision records (ADRs) all belong in version-controlled Markdown files rather than issues that will eventually close. (For more on ADRs, see decisions as documentation.)

68. https://github.blog/engineering/how-the-github-security-team-uses-projects-and-github-actions-for-planning-tracking-and-more/

Think of it like variables versus a database: issues hold temporary state that's useful while work is in flight, then they close and fade from view. Markdown files are persistent storage—the durable record you query months or years later when you need to understand how something works or why a decision was made.

Pull requests turn proposals into conversations

Pull requests are how teams review proposals and make decisions. Updating documentation? Proposing a process change? Refining a team charter? The pull request workflow gives reviewers a chance to weigh in before anything is finalized.

The discipline works beyond code. Any Markdown file—from onboarding guides to meeting agendas—benefits from the same pattern: propose a change, gather feedback, and merge when ready.

From theory to pull requests

Your tools shape your behavior—entropy favors opacity, so transparent tools make transparent leaders.

> **Pro-Tip:** Transparent and inclusive decision-making comes more naturally in tools built for collaboration, like GitHub, than in tools built for conveying information, like chat or email. You *can* do it in chat—but the tool will fight you every step of the way. Pick the tool that makes the right behavior the easy behavior.

Still, the tools alone won't do it. Leaders have to work deliberately for the team to benefit.

Engineer-inspired principles that effective remote leaders live by:

- **Make work visible**—Share as broadly as the subject allows. You'll often need to restrict HR and other personnel matters due to sensitivity, but you can share most management work with increasing circles of trust (peers, other managers, the team, the org, the company, etc.). I've even seen one team use Mermaid diagrams in Markdown files[69] to visualize their org chart. Reorg by PR? 🤨 Like any production system, observability is critical.
- **Write things down**—Especially the why and how. Ensure everything has a URL. Be generous with links.
- **Overcommunicate**—Use a durable, searchable, and discoverable medium. Let others opt in to context and subscribe to updates.
- **Bias for shipping**—Ship early, ship often. Whether decisions, processes, or "manager code," ship a minimum viable product (MVP) and iterate. Minimize batch size.
- **Streamline and automate**—Never force a human to do what a robot can. Prefer non-blocking over blocking operations—codify policy as code.

69. https://github.blog/developer-skills/github/include-diagrams-markdown-files-mermaid/

- **Embrace collaboration**—How we work is as important as what we work on. Software doesn't ship solo. Involve the team in setting goals and driving initiatives forward. Everyone sees how their work fits the larger strategy—and helps shape it.
- **Asynchronous first**—Reserve higher-fidelity media for conversations that require them.
- **Practicality beats purity**—These are guidelines, not rules. The process should drive outcomes.

For a concrete version of this, early at GitHub, we used the DRI (Directly Responsible Individual) model—originally called PRP (Primary Responsible Person)—to let one IC drive an initiative across a matrix of teams that didn't report to them. I took the DRI role for removing tracking cookies from GitHub.com, coordinating work across teams I had no authority over.

The authority wasn't positional; it came from the transparency of the work: a public project board, an issue per team, the plan written where anyone could read it, regular updates pushed to everyone whose cooperation the work required. When the DRI's work is legible, other teams pitch in without needing to be convinced in a meeting. **A DRI with a URL beats a committee with a mandate.**

The same engineer-brain applies to process itself. In my time working within Trust & Safety, I picked up a habit from security-minded peers: if you give people an opportunity to abuse a system, someone eventually will, so design assuming they will. That adversarial eye turns out to be surprisingly useful for the opposite job—legitimately *hacking* the bureaucracy.[70] Every process has a stated purpose and a figurative surface; when the two diverge, you can usually automate, simplify, or route around the surface without compromising the purpose. **Apply a security engineer's mindset to process, and the compliance surface shrinks without the compliance getting weaker.**

> **For managers: Make your own management backlog visible.** When you track your work in a public project board, you create accountability and model the transparency you expect from your team. It also answers the perennial question "what does my manager actually do all day?" Instead of tracking tasks in your head or a private doc, open issues for your management work and invite input before deciding.

> **For individual contributors: Apply engineering rigor to your non-code work—it's the fastest way to demonstrate strategic thinking.** Proposing a process change? Open an issue that frames the problem with data, outlines options, and recommends one. Driving a cross-team initiative? Track it on a project board where stakeholders can see progress without asking. Write decision documents as PRs so people can comment inline and your reasoning is permanently linked. This

70. https://www.hackyourbureaucracy.com/

> isn't busywork—it's how you build a searchable track record of impact that makes your case for you at promotion time.

These principles are tool-agnostic, but your workflow shapes how well they translate to async environments.

Why Kanban suits async better than Scrum

Whatever the tool, the moves are the same: make work visible, review changes before they merge, and ship incrementally. Kanban maps more naturally to async environments than Scrum does.

My own product-management style leans hard into this: I'd rather land a dozen small, boring, easily reversible ships—each one measurably doing the thing I claimed it would do—than bet the quarter on one big reveal. Then, when the time is right, I string the boring ships together and tell the thematic story of what's already quietly in place.

Customers don't buy the drill; they buy the quarter-inch hole. Ship the hole. The press release is a lagging indicator of a dozen unglamorous pull requests that have already been running in production. **Boring ships, strung together, tell a thematic story.** The alternative—the one big launch—is the version where you find out on launch day what you should have learned six months earlier, and it's already too expensive to change.

Scrum's time-boxed sprints create artificial urgency and require coordination ceremonies—sprint planning, daily standups, sprint reviews, retrospectives—all within fixed intervals. That works when a team can easily gather. It breaks down across a dozen time zones. Kanban's continuous flow model sidesteps the friction:

- **No sprint boundaries**—Work flows continuously without arbitrary start and end dates requiring synchronous ceremonies.
- **Work-in-progress (WIP) limits**—Constraints are encoded in the system (column limits on the board) rather than negotiated in meetings.
- **Pull-based work**—Team members pull the next item when ready rather than committing to fixed amounts in planning sessions.
- **Visual transparency**—The board always reflects current reality without requiring a meeting to update status.

> **Pro-Tip:** Scrum can still work for distributed teams—many pull it off. But if sprint ceremonies eat more time than the work they coordinate, Kanban's continuous model is worth a serious look.

Whichever model you pick, the harder coordination problem isn't within a team—it's between them.

Managing dependencies across teams

Tracking work within a single team is one thing. Coordinating across teams—program management—is another. Traditional approaches rely on program increment planning, Scrum of Scrums, and other synchronous rituals that falter in async environments.

Async program management relies on making cross-team connections explicit in the same tools you already use:

- **Dependency issues**—Cross-team dependencies tracked as issues with clear owners and due dates, not verbal commitments from a meeting.
- **Automated notifications**—When a dependency's status changes, the downstream team learns immediately rather than waiting for the next sync.
- **Liaison issues**—Issues that connect work across team boundaries, giving both teams visibility into the other's progress and blockers.
- **Visible roadmaps**—High-level roadmaps in a central project board or Markdown file showing what each team is working toward, updated asynchronously through pull requests or issue comments.

When dependencies surface in tracking systems before they become emergencies, you know the system is working. When they only surface in a Scrum of Scrums meeting the week before a deadline, your tools aren't doing their job.

> **For managers: Be explicit about what cross-team coordination is truly necessary.** Many synchronous ceremonies exist because "we've always done it that way." Challenge each one: What decision requires this meeting? Could a written proposal and review replace it? Reserve synchronous time for genuinely ambiguous situations.

You already know how to build systems that are transparent, auditable, and resilient. Your management practice deserves the same rigor. When the system is transparent, everyone can see what's in flight, what's blocked, and what's shipping—without scheduling a meeting to find out.

Rethinking Management for Remote Teams

> **TL;DR:** Most of what we call management is just relaying information that transparent systems now handle automatically. Strip out the message-passing and managers can do the work only a human can: coach, unblock, and lead.

I once worked at an organization with six management layers between the CEO and the engineers writing code. Every week, updates traveled up the chain: engineer to team lead to manager to director to VP to senior vice president (SVP) to C-suite. By the time information reached the top, it was a week stale and mangled by six games of telephone. Decisions traveled back down the same chain, taking another week and acquiring six layers of interpretation.

That's not management. That's an expensive relay race with no finish line.

> **For individual contributors: You can short-circuit the relay race from any seat.** Every time you post a status update in an issue instead of telling your manager over chat, you've removed one hop from the chain. When you document a decision where stakeholders can read it directly, you've cut a relay where each hop loses fidelity. You don't need to wait for a reorg—you can reduce management overhead right now by making your work legible to anyone who needs it, not just the person above you.

> **Common objection: "Teams need managers—you can't just remove them."** This conflates management overhead with leadership value. Nobody's arguing that teams don't need direction, support, or strategic guidance. The question is: How much of what we call "management" is actually coordination that transparent systems could handle automatically? When updates are posted in the open, when decisions are documented, and when status is visible by default, managers can stop being information routers and start being leaders. Fewer layers don't mean no leadership—they mean freeing leadership from administrative busywork.

Management as message passing

Traditional management exists to support work by:

- Shuttling information
- Coordinating across business units
- Aligning efforts with organizational priorities
- Ensuring people do good work
- Recruiting new team members

This role made sense historically. When conveying information was cumbersome, the only way for Adam to tell Becky what he was working on was to stop working, walk down the hall, and interrupt her. To streamline this, organizations hired Charlie to run meetings and shuttle information. Charlie became a human message broker. Indispensable when direct communication was expensive—but an increasingly expensive intermediary now that systems handle it automatically. An engineer posts a status update in a GitHub issue, and anyone who needs that context—their manager, the PM, the adjacent team—gets it simultaneously, without Charlie lifting a finger. **Stop being the router; start being the coach.**

> **Pro-Tip:** I use the word "management" here, which I distinguish from "leadership." Leadership —strategy, vision, direction—is about setting the course, and there's no reason a non-manager (individual contributor) can't be a leader. Management is about steering the ship day-to-day, which is what I'm referring to here.

What if Adam could email Becky, or better yet, post to a shared collaboration space? Would Charlie's role have been necessary? Would management have evolved the same way if sharing information cost nothing?

The open source community already ran this experiment: same coordination challenges, no traditional hierarchy. It coordinates through transparent, persistent communication—everything from code to decisions happens in the open, archived for all to see—and contribution that stands on its substance, not its source. Contributors propose, discuss, and refine ideas through opt-in participation, shipping the best ones. Take Kubernetes, which powers much of the world's cloud infrastructure. Thousands of contributors across hundreds of companies coordinate without a traditional management hierarchy—decisions happen in public GitHub issues and pull requests, and contributors earn maintainer status through their work, not their title. **Influence earned beats authority assigned.**

This model won't fit every workplace, but shipping gets measurably faster when you strip out the managerial overhead. A product decision that requires a team lead to brief a manager, who briefs a director, who approves it and sends it back down? Two-week round-trip. The same decision as an issue tagged with the relevant stakeholders, resolved in the comments? Two days. Status updates belong in issues and project boards, not meetings—and reserve your 1:1s for conversations that actually need a human on the other end. **Those who show up to do the work should make the decisions.**

Organizational friction is no longer a sunk cost—and neither is management. Every "quick sync" that just relays information between two people who could read the same issue thread is a tax on everyone's calendar. Reducing layers doesn't mean removing leadership. It means rethinking *how* you lead—and specifically, knowing when to tighten control and when to let go. **Hierarchy is a cost; make sure it's worth paying.**

Cathedral vs. bazaar: knowing when to direct and when to facilitate

If management overhead is the problem, the answer isn't just "fewer managers"—it's knowing which *kind* of management the moment requires. I once watched two managers on the same team take opposite approaches with identical results: frustrated engineers. One prescribed every detail—what to work on, how to structure the code, when to ship. The other gave almost no direction at all, trusting the team to figure it out. Both meant well. Both failed. The first team felt suffocated; the second felt abandoned.

Eric S. Raymond's *The Cathedral and the Bazaar*[71] contrasts closed-source and open source development: the cathedral, where a central authority designs and builds top-down, versus the bazaar, where a decentralized community collaborates within a modular framework. The same tension plays out in people management—and getting the balance wrong costs you.

71. https://en.wikipedia.org/wiki/The_Cathedral_and_the_Bazaar

The cathedral manager is an architect with a blueprint. They plan meticulously, assign roles, establish standards—and monitor closely enough to give precise instructions at every step. Decisions flow one way: down. Predictable results in stable environments, clear expectations, a sense of order. But the cathedral style stifles creativity and speed—especially when the work demands experimentation. Worse, the close monitoring it relies on doesn't scale when your team is scattered across six time zones and you can't walk by someone's desk to check their progress. **Control doesn't scale; trust does.**

The bazaar manager is an organizer, not an architect. They set a broad vision and a flexible plan, with a flat network of roles across the team. Instead of dictating tasks, they define goals, provide guidelines and resources, and let the team determine how the work gets done. A bazaar manager might open a GitHub issue that says "We need to cut page load time by 40%" and let the team self-organize to decide whether that means caching, lazy loading, or a complete rewrite.

The bazaar handles ambiguity well—when the problem isn't well-understood upfront, decentralized teams adapt faster than ones waiting for instructions—and gives team members genuine ownership over their work. Leaders create space to explore and contribute toward shared goals, building trust in the process. People learn from and challenge one another. It's a natural fit for async workflows across time zones. You can't micromanage someone eight hours ahead of you, but transparent, open work lets you trust without constant check-ins.

GitHub's flat-org experiment

GitHub ran this experiment at scale. Until April 2014, the company had no managers at all—roughly 200 Hubbers coordinating through issues, pull requests, and chat. The flat era had real problems. The most honest way to describe it is that we were building roughly ten startups in parallel under one logo—every team pulling toward whatever its members found interesting, with little mechanism for coordinating bets across the company.

What finally broke the flat model wasn't a single crisis—it was Dunbar's number.[72] Past roughly 200 Hubbers, it stopped being feasible for any one person to have a working relationship with everyone else, and the flat org's coordination model had quietly been running on exactly that assumption. **The flat org was always running on Dunbar's number; it just didn't know it.**

Even once we hired people to do the coordinating, the title "manager" was controversial enough that the first cohort was called "Leaders." Their job was explicitly strategy and direction, not people management. Formal performance reviews didn't exist yet, and bonuses were broadly standardized. But one lesson stuck: when the default is bazaar, the organization learns to route around missing hierarchy instead of waiting for it. Even

72. https://en.wikipedia.org/wiki/Dunbar%27s_number

after managers arrived, assigning work top-down was explicitly off the table—engineers still pulled from the backlog and self-routed between teams.

> **For managers: Your goal is to become less necessary, not more.** The flat-org experiment taught us that good management builds systems that work without the manager in the room. If your team can't function when you're on vacation, you're a bottleneck, not a leader. Design workflows where information flows without you, decisions happen at the lowest reasonable level, and your 1:1s are for coaching—not status updates you could have read yourself.

When managers were finally formalized, the role came with explicit guardrails: 1:1s were for coaching and career growth, not status updates—the written record *was* the status update. The point wasn't to graft the middle layer of corporate America onto a company that had worked without one—it was to add coaching, career support, and clearer escalation paths *without* re-introducing the message-passing tax the flat era had already eliminated. Once a team knows it can operate without a cathedral, adding one becomes a deliberate choice rather than a reflex. **The measure of good leadership isn't that you automated yourself out of a job—it's that you fostered a culture that made the job obsolete.**

Cathedral and bazaar aren't ideologies—they're management operating systems. For distributed teams, the default should lean bazaar (autonomy plus transparency), but knowing when to shift toward cathedral matters just as much. Get the balance right, and your team ships better work with less friction.

> **For managers: Distributed teams generally thrive with bazaar-style leadership because it emphasizes autonomy and trust**—exactly what you need when you can't see people working. But be ready to shift toward the cathedral when onboarding new team members, during crises requiring rapid coordination, or when establishing standards everyone must follow. The point isn't ideological purity; it's flexibility. Question which management layers exist primarily to shuttle information, and spend the freed-up time on work that actually needs you: strategy, coaching, and clearing systemic blockers.

> **For individual contributors: Knowing your manager's style helps you meet them where they are.** If they lean cathedral, proactively share progress and ask clarifying questions before proceeding. If they lean bazaar, take initiative and document your decisions. Senior ICs often operate bazaar-style regardless of their manager—defining problems, proposing solutions, and bringing others along through influence rather than authority. For more on what IC leadership looks like, see *What Leadership Looks Like in Open and Async*.

If you're standing up a new team, the order matters

Over a decade at GitHub, I helped stand up more than half a dozen teams, and the single biggest lesson wasn't any one practice—it was the *sequence*.

> **Pro-Tip: The order for standing up a team:** build trust, ship something small, write the charter, sketch a roadmap, decide operating norms, pick metrics, and build the dashboard. Reverse any two and something breaks later.

A charter written before the team trusts each other is a document nobody believes in. Metrics picked before anything ships are dashboards of zeros. Ceremonies imposed before the first win get quietly skipped. Each step earns the right to the next one.

Two tactical moves worth calling out. **Create the public infrastructure on day one**—a Slack channel, a repo, a team @-handle, all with the same descriptive name and a one-line purpose. Not because you need the tools immediately, but because *where* a team's early conversations happen becomes permanent. The conversations you have in a public channel in week one are the conversations future colleagues can learn from; the ones you have in a group DM are gone forever.

And **ship *something* before you write the charter**, even if it's tiny. A long-standing bug. A small feature you can finish in a day. A policy doc that needs updating.

Momentum is the cheapest form of alignment, and a team that has shipped together writes a different charter than one that has only talked about shipping.

If you're inheriting a team rather than building one from scratch, resist the urge to prove yourself on day one. I've written separately about how I approach joining a new team:[73] listen first, ask questions in the open, document what you're learning as you go, and don't re-org your way out of ambiguity. **The fastest way to lose a team's trust is to change things before you understand why they're the way they are.**

Free managers from playing telephone, and the most valuable thing they can do is have the conversations that actually need a human—starting with their 1:1s.

73. https://ben.balter.com/2019/06/28/joining-a-new-team/

How to One-on-One

> **TL;DR:** If your 1:1s are status updates, you're wasting your team's only protected real-time slot for coaching, hard feedback, and the conversations too risky to put in writing. Status belongs in issues; 1:1s are for everything else.

It's Thursday afternoon. You (or your direct report) sit down and read from a list: "Closed three bugs, reviewed two PRs, started the migration doc." You nod. They nod. Thirty minutes pass without either of you saying anything that couldn't have been a comment on an issue. I know the shape of this meeting because I was on the receiving end of it before I ever ran one. A previous manager of mine spent the entire thirty minutes asking me to recite what I'd shipped that week—information he could've pulled from my issues in under a minute.

When I became a people manager myself in February 2016, I almost defaulted to the same pattern, because it was the pattern I'd been trained into. The only reason I didn't is because I'd just spent years resenting it.

That recited-status meeting is the loud, obvious way 1:1s fail. The second is softer and more insidious: sugarcoating. Early in my management career, I softened hard feedback because I thought I was being kind. I'd wrap a real concern in three compliments and an escape hatch, and the person on the other end would walk out of the room reassured when they needed to walk out *clear*. It took one direct report telling me, plainly, "please just tell me the actual thing" for the lesson to land.

People prefer the truth—even when it's uncomfortable, especially when it's actionable—over the fog of good intentions. Sugarcoating isn't kindness; it's conflict-avoidance wearing kindness as a costume, and the cost of that costume is paid by the person who walks away unclear on what they actually need to do. 1:1s are where you pay that debt down, in real-time, with enough time and presence to sit with the discomfort together. **Say the actual thing.** And for high-stakes feedback—performance reviews, scope changes, anything career-shaping—send the written version a day ahead.

> **Pro-Tip:** Asking someone to absorb, process, and respond to a career-affecting conversation live is unreasonable. Twenty-four hours to read it, sit with it, and come back with their own thoughts is just respect.

If you're spending your 1:1s telling your manager what you worked on last week (or your report is telling you), you're doing it wrong—and your manager is failing you by not redirecting the conversation. Status belongs in issues, project boards, and weekly snippets. 1:1s are for everything else: coaching, feedback, career growth, clearing the air, and the kind of honest dialogue that feels risky to put in writing.

> **Common objection: "We already talk asynchronously. Do we really need 1:1s?"** Yes. Async excels at transferring information, documenting decisions, and coordinating across time zones. But some things need real-time, high-bandwidth conversation: working through ambiguity, processing hard feedback, building trust, having dialogue that's too nuanced for text. 1:1s aren't a failure of your async practices—they're a complement to them.

The meeting that's actually about you

Great 1:1s focus on topics that only work synchronously: career growth, coaching, feedback, and clearing the air. These are the conversations where tone matters, where nuance gets lost in text, and where real-time back-and-forth lets you pick up on what's left unsaid. In remote work, 1:1s also carry a load that offices handle passively—human connection. There's no hallway where you bump into each other, no lunch where you catch up as people rather than roles. 1:1s are often the only space where that happens.

What doesn't belong in a 1:1

Protecting 1:1s means guarding them from topics that belong in writing—and in async-first organizations, that's most of them.

- **Status updates.** Doubly wasteful when your team has a written trail of async updates in issues, PRs, and project boards. Use 1:1 time for what text can't convey.
- **Information transfer.** Write it down and share it beforehand. Save synchronous time for discussing implications, not conveying facts.
- **Approval requests.** Don't save up yes/no questions for your 1:1. That creates bottlenecks. Ask async.

Do the prep work async

Great 1:1s start before the meeting does—and in async-first teams, the prep work is what makes the synchronous time worth protecting.

Keep a **running shared agenda**—a Google Doc, a GitHub issue, whatever works—where both parties add topics throughout the week. Add context to each item: don't just write "career growth"—write "I've been thinking about whether to pursue the tech lead path or people management, and I'd like to talk through the tradeoffs."

The more context upfront, the less synchronous time you spend on setup and the more you spend on the conversation itself.

> **Pro-Tip:** A good test of your 1:1 preparation: could you cancel the meeting without losing anything? If yes, you either don't have enough prepared or you're covering topics better handled async. If no, you've identified conversations that genuinely need synchronous time.

Less agenda, more conversation

Start with the human, not the agenda. In remote work, this isn't small talk—it's the relationship maintenance that hallways and lunch lines handle automatically in an office. If someone is stressed about something outside work, that context matters—and you won't pick it up from a Slack status.

A later manager in my career—one whose 1:1s I actually looked forward to—gave me a structure I've carried ever since.

- Spend roughly a third of the time on whatever the report came in wanting to talk about.
- Spend another third on whatever the manager came in wanting to talk about.
- Spend the final third on the future—career, trajectory, where the work is heading, what's going to matter six months from now that isn't urgent today.

The only thing you can't batch or write down is the conversation that needs two humans and thirty uninterrupted minutes. If the future-third gets squeezed out every single week because the present keeps eating into it, you're not running management—you're running crisis triage, and it's worth naming that out loud rather than letting it quietly become the pattern.

Remote 1:1s need extra care

Keep video on when you can. Facial expressions and body language matter in these conversations—if someone seems hesitant, you won't catch it in text. Respect camera fatigue, though; some days a phone call while walking works better than yet another video call.

One exec I worked for at GitHub actively encouraged walking 1:1s—turn off Zoom, pick up an old-fashioned phone, and go for a walk. The first time he suggested it, I thought it was a step backward: no shared doc, no screen to glance at, no bulleted agenda to steer by. It was the opposite. Without the screen demanding attention, the conversation loosened up. Thinking got deeper, not shallower—the kind of reflection that doesn't fit between two tiles on a video grid.

Not every 1:1 is right for that format; the ones that lean on a shared doc or a demo still need pixels. But for that particular relationship, on a nice-weather day, an audio-only walk beat any meeting room we could have booked. I carried the practice forward. **Sometimes the**

richest channel is the quietest one. If your calendar is back-to-back video calls, one audio walk a week is a remarkably cheap upgrade to your thinking.

Be explicit about wanting honest feedback and show—repeatedly—that you can receive it without flinching. Trust takes time to build, especially across screens.

> **For managers: The awkward silences are the point.** In remote 1:1s, resist the urge to fill every pause. When you ask "what's really on your mind?" and get silence, wait. Count to ten. The discomfort you're feeling is the cost of building trust—and what comes after the silence is usually the thing they actually needed to say. If you fill every gap, you'll only ever hear the safe answers.

> **Pro-Tip:** Never schedule a "quick sync" with a direct report without context. A vague calendar invite—no agenda, just your name and "15 min sync"—triggers immediate anxiety: "Am I being fired? Did I mess up?" Even if your intent is harmless, the ambiguity activates worst-case thinking. Always include a brief note: "Want to discuss the Q3 roadmap" or "Checking in on the new project." Two seconds of context from you saves hours of anxiety for them.

After the 1:1, capture key decisions, action items, and follow-ups in the shared agenda. Without notes, the same topics resurface weekly and action items quietly die.

Protect the time. It's tempting to cancel when calendars get crowded or there's "nothing urgent." Resist. Regular, predictable connection matters more in remote work, not less. A thin agenda beats no agenda—consistency matters more than content.

Cadence matters more than duration

For most remote relationships, **weekly 1:1s of 30 to 45 minutes** are the right rhythm—frequent enough to catch issues that would otherwise fester without hallway check-ins. If you consistently have more to discuss, handle some topics asynchronously. Adjust for the relationship: new team members or people navigating challenges may need more frequent check-ins; highly autonomous senior ICs may do fine with less.

> **For individual contributors:** **Advocate for the cadence that works for you.** If weekly feels too frequent and you're running out of things to discuss, propose biweekly with a standing offer to add ad-hoc sessions when needed. If weekly isn't enough—you're new, the project is complex, or you're navigating a career transition—ask for more. Your manager isn't a mind-reader, and the right cadence changes over time. Own the adjustment.

Leaders and ICs have different jobs

> **For managers: Prepare for every 1:1 like it matters—because it does.** Spend five minutes beforehand reviewing your direct's recent work, open PRs, and any flags from last week. Bring one question you don't already know the answer to —"What's frustrating you right now?" beats "How's it going?" If your directs aren't finding 1:1s valuable, ask them directly and change your approach based on what they say.

> **For individual contributors: Your 1:1 is your time—own it.** Come prepared with topics, questions, and challenges you want to think through. Don't wait for your manager to set the agenda—propose a shared doc where both of you add items throughout the week. If your 1:1s are still status updates, redirect them: "I've started posting weekly updates in the team channel—can we use this time for coaching and growth instead?" If you're not getting what you need, say so directly. Your manager can't read your mind, and most will welcome the clarity. In short, make your manager work *for you* during *your* 1:1s. It should be the one time, at minimum, that the roles are reversed.

Watch out for these traps

- **The manager monologue.** The manager talks the whole time, sharing information, giving advice, or thinking out loud. I once had a manager who would talk at me for twenty-seven of our thirty minutes, notice the time, and then ask if I had anything I wanted to discuss. 1:1s should be conversations, not presentations—and the clock is not a cue; it's an indictment.
- **The reverse 1:1.** The manager lacks the domain context to coach, so the entire meeting becomes the report briefing them on the work. It's a sign the reporting line is wrong, or that the meeting should be in writing—either way, it's not coaching. **If your report is educating you for thirty minutes, you owe them a different format, not a recurring appointment.**
- **The therapy session.** Frustrations are legitimate topics, but 1:1s that become extended venting without action items don't serve either party. Acknowledge feelings, then focus on what to do.
- **The ghost meeting.** Neither party prepares, there's no agenda, and you spend thirty minutes in a conversational holding pattern. In remote work, this is worse than in an office—you can't even salvage it with a walk to the coffee machine.
- **The cancellation cascade.** 1:1s keep getting canceled because "something came up." In distributed teams, where there's no hallway to catch up informally, a canceled 1:1 is a missed connection with no substitute.

One of the best managers I had ended every 1:1 with the same question: "So when are you taking your next time off?" It took me a while to notice what it was doing. The question normalized rest as a planned, expected, operational thing—not a reward for finishing, not a confession of weakness, just part of the work. **The managers who protect your time off are the ones you'll still be working for in five years.**

1:1s reflect how you lead

Your 1:1s are a microcosm of how you lead. Shared agendas, documented outcomes, async preparation—every practice that makes a 1:1 great is the same practice that makes a distributed team work. Get the 1:1 right and the rest follows.

Career Conversations

> **TL;DR:** The conversations that actually shape a career—growth, coaching, honest feedback—are the easiest to skip when this week's bug is louder. Have them on purpose, and you'll surface burnout or a flight risk long before the annual review would. Here's how to start them—and keep them going.

"Where do you want to be in a year?" The question hangs in the air. The IC shrugs: "I don't know, I haven't really thought about it." The manager nods and moves on to the next agenda item. Nobody restarts the conversation, because next week's 1:1 has its own bug to triage and its own status to check. The growth plan you would have built—if either of you had actually had the conversation—stays unbuilt until someone else builds it for them. *Whether you run the 1:1 or attend it, this chapter is for you*: someone has to start the career conversation, or it never happens.

Career conversations are the highest-impact use of a 1:1, and the easiest to skip. This week's bug is concrete; next year's trajectory is fuzzy. So the tactical work wins—until someone quits, gets passed over, or burns out doing work that was never going to get them where they wanted. The topics that demand synchronous dialogue—career growth, coaching, feedback, human connection, clearing the air—are the same ones that make 1:1s worth protecting. The hard part isn't making space for these conversations—it's knowing what to *do* with that time.

Make growth a recurring topic, not an annual event

If career growth only shows up at annual review time, you've already lost. The runway is gone: someone else got the stretch project, the skill gap calcified, the promotion cycle closed. **Annual review season is too late to start the conversation.**

Growth belongs in the rotation. Not every week—weekly career conversations get repetitive and performative—but frequently enough that the topic doesn't feel like a special event. Monthly is a reasonable floor. Put it on the shared agenda so neither of you has to work up the nerve to raise it.

The questions worth returning to:

- What do you want to be doing that you aren't doing now?
- What's a skill you'd like to develop this quarter?
- What kind of work energizes you? What drains you?

- If you could change one thing about your role, what would it be?
- What's getting in the way of the growth you want?

None of these have a "right" answer. The value is in the conversation, not the conclusion.

Talk about promotion before it's a promotion conversation

By the time someone asks "What will it take to get promoted?" the conversation is already awkward. Make the expectations visible earlier and more often.

> **For managers:** Know the criteria for the next level cold, and be specific about where your report stands against each one. "You consistently operate at senior; the gap to staff is scope of influence and cross-team technical leadership" is useful. "Keep up the good work" is not. If a promotion isn't on the table this cycle, say so—and say why—long before the cycle closes. Surprises at review time are management failures.

> **For individual contributors:** Ask directly: "What would it take for me to be operating at the next level?" Then ask for concrete examples of what that looks like in practice. If the answer is vague, push. "Be more strategic" is not actionable; "lead the design for the billing migration end-to-end" is.

> Write down what you hear, revisit it quarterly, and track your progress against it in the open.

Feedback is a two-way exchange

Feedback that only flows downward is a sign the relationship isn't working.

For managers giving feedback: be specific, be timely, and separate observation from interpretation. "In yesterday's design review, you interrupted Priya twice before she finished her point" is observable. "You're dismissive of your peers" is an interpretation masquerading as fact. Give the observation, share the impact, and leave space for the other person to respond.

For ICs giving feedback up: your manager needs it more than you think, and gets it less than you assume. Start small—"It would help me if the agenda for staff meetings went out a day earlier"—and build from there. If your manager gets defensive, that's useful information. If they engage, you've just made the relationship stronger.

Receiving feedback is its own skill. Resist the urge to explain or defend in the moment. Say thank you, ask a clarifying question, and give yourself time to process.

The feedback you get in a 1:1 is often just the tip—what's underneath surfaces later, if you've shown you can hear it.

> **Pro-Tip:** End career conversations with written next steps, not just good vibes. "You're going to scope the onboarding revamp by end of month; I'm going to introduce you to the platform team lead this week" is a plan. "We had a great chat about growth" is a memory that evaporates by Friday. Capture commitments in the same durable place you track action items from any other 1:1.

Find the overlap

Before GitHub formalized people management, we described where to spend your energy as the overlap of two circles: what *you* care about, and what the *company* cares about. Live in that sweet spot and your work compounds—you're doing something you'd pick voluntarily *and* something someone will pay you for. Drift outside either circle and something breaks: all-you with no company alignment becomes a passion project nobody funds; all-company with no personal investment becomes a grind that ends in burnout or attrition.

As orgs grow and roles specialize, a third circle shows up: what your *role* is for. Engineers care about technical craft. PMs care about strategy and user research. Designers care about interaction and systems. Managers care about people and throughput. The highest-impact work sits at the intersection of all three: something you want to do, something the company needs done, and something your role is uniquely positioned to deliver. Career conversations are about finding and expanding that overlap—and being honest when one of the circles isn't where you thought it was.

Your career is your job, not your manager's

Managers can sponsor, coach, and create opportunities. **They can't want it for you.**

> **For individual contributors:** Treat career conversations as tools for your development, not obligations to perform for your manager. Come in with a point of view—even a tentative one. "I think I want to move toward staff IC work, but I'm not sure if the trade-off on people leadership is right for me" gives your manager something to engage with. "I dunno, whatever you think" gives them nothing. The ICs who grow fastest aren't the ones with the best managers; they're the ones who drive the conversation.

> **For managers:** Your job is to create the conditions, not dictate the direction. Ask what they want, tell them honestly whether it's available here, and help them build a plan—even if that plan eventually takes them off your team. **The managers people stay with longest are the ones who'd help them leave.**

The conversation compounds

One good career conversation won't change anyone's trajectory. A hundred will. The growth, the trust, the candor—none of it shows up in a single meeting. It shows up in the pattern: that this is where the real stuff gets talked about, not deflected to "let's discuss later."

Protect that. It's the thing that makes the rest of the job worth doing.

These conversations give synchronous time its purpose—but the rest of your team's work needs visibility too. How do you keep leadership informed without turning every Friday into a status-deck assembly line? The trick is making visibility a byproduct of the work, not a tax on top of it.

Weekly Reporting That Doesn't Suck

> **TL;DR:** Stop assembling Friday status decks from scratch—if your daily work already lives in issues and project boards, reporting is just a query you run, not a document you write. Automate the highlights, and your boss never has to ask, "What's everyone working on?"

It's 4 PM on Friday. You've spent the week shipping real work, and now you're staring at a blank status report, trying to reconstruct what you did from memory, Slack threads, and the archaeological record of your browser tabs. Across the hall—or the ocean—your manager is doing the same thing in reverse, assembling everyone's updates into a deck that leadership will skim for thirty seconds. Both of you are doing unnecessary work—the IC writing it, the manager rolling it up, the leader skimming the result, all reconstructing by hand what the tools already captured.

During an annual review, I received surprising (and humorous) feedback: "Your team **loves** your reporting process. I've never seen a team say anything positive about reporting before." I was working in tools that made progress visible as a byproduct of doing the work —no manual updates or status meetings layered on top. **Good reporting is a side effect of good work.** Here's what I tell my teams:

What actually works

- **If it takes less than ~1 hour, do it**—no need to add overhead. Track work in the most relevant repository and share information as broadly as possible. Usually that means issues and ongoing comments.
- **All programmatic work should have an associated issue** on the team project board. When your team works across time zones, tracking work in issues means no one has to wait for a meeting to know what's happening.
- If work doesn't fit neatly into an issue, **share it in the team chat** by end of day Friday so it lands in Snippets—the brief, informal weekly updates the team posts to a private team repository for internal visibility, which then roll up the org chart to leadership.

> **Pro-Tip:** GitHub project boards respect issue visibility. If a viewer can't access an issue, they'll see a placeholder that doesn't reveal the issue's content.

Capturing work in issues gets you halfway—but someone still has to surface the highlights.

Give leadership the headline, not the novel

The team lead typically reviews team activity across GitHub issues and authors team Snippets each week, publishing them by end of day Friday. But ICs shouldn't wait for their manager to tell their story. Post your own brief weekly update in the team channel or your initiative's tracking issue, using the situation-action-result format with links to your PRs and closed issues. Your manager gets your actual voice rather than their interpretation; other teams see your work without a managerial filter; and you build the evidence trail that's invaluable come performance review season.

Quick, informal updates build awareness

Snippets were a Friday-afternoon ritual, and nothing enforced them—no bot threatening escalation, no manager dunking on you in 1:1s—but your teammates noticed when yours was missing, and the social pressure of a visible gap was enough. The format stuck because it mirrored how Hubbers already worked—write in the open, let others read on their own schedule—rather than bolting a reporting process on top.

Your daily work is the source

Throughout the week, work on GitHub issues and post updates when you hit milestones, make decisions, or get blocked. If activity happens outside issues, capture it in an issue. These updates are the raw material for team Snippets.

> **Pro-Tip:** If working regularly on GitHub issues is new to you, that's okay. To ease into things, post a weekly update by end of day Friday so it's captured in the team's Snippets.

Not everything needs reporting

Progress updates aren't a comprehensive list of everything the team did, or proof you're working. By default, your employer trusts you're doing great work, even if you don't say so. There's often "Keep the Lights On" work, papercuts, and so on that the team prioritizes but that don't make the update. Some weeks you'll have a lot to share; some weeks you won't. Expected and intended. When in doubt, focus on business impact.

> **Common objection: "If I don't report everything I did, my manager will think I'm not working."** If your manager needs a comprehensive task list to believe you're contributing, that's a trust problem—not a reporting problem. Good reporting highlights impact, not hours. A single line about a shipped

> feature says more than a dozen bullet points about meetings attended.

So if you're not cataloging every task, what *should* you write?

How to write updates worth reading

Frame updates as situation, action, and result (business impact, or "why should the organization care"). That structure forces concreteness.

Be specific about what you shipped

Accomplishments should include specific ships, achievements, critical decisions, and business results from the week. Brag about the impact your work is having. For example:

> *Shipped v1 of the contractor onboarding policy*[74] *to reduce time-to-first-day from 14 days to 7.*

Or:

> *Selected and executed our contract with the new water-resistant manufacturer to kick off Project Basketweaver.*[75]

Or:

74. *https://github.com/acme/handbook/pull/482*
75. *https://github.com/acme/basketweaver*

> *Merged a change to WidgetMe[76] that cuts Hubbers' self-service widget request time from minutes to seconds.*

Skip the filler

Avoid phrases like "made progress on," "continued to," and "met with"—the status update equivalent of a loading spinner. **Report impact, not activity.** Reread one of your own updates a month later—if you can't tell what shipped, rewrite it. Updates like these are better suited for a broader `Insight` or a status update on a team initiative issue. For example:

> *Project `abc` continues to progress nicely.*

Or:

> *Continued to think about how we will monetize our new underwater-woven baskets.*

Or:

> *I met with the revenue team to discuss how they are using the Abc widget.*

> **Pro-Tip:** Keep a running "brag doc" throughout the week—a simple list where you jot down accomplishments as they happen. By Friday, your weekly update is just editing, not remembering. Bonus: this same document becomes invaluable during performance review season.

76. *https://github.com/acme/widgetme/pull/901*

Write for someone who doesn't know your project

Include enough context and references that someone unfamiliar with your project can follow along:

- Link to issues, pull requests, and collaborative docs so readers can click through for more context. Most accomplishments should include a link.
- Check that your links are accessible to most readers. Linking to repos some readers can't access is fine, but favor more broadly accessible links when you can.
- Spell out **all** acronyms, internal and external, even if they seem obvious to you.
- When referencing a "codenamed" project, explain in a few words what the project is and link to its home repository.

> **For individual contributors: Your weekly update is your career narrative in miniature.** Every update is a chance to center your narrative on impact, not activity. Write for your future self during performance review season—when you look back at six months of updates, you should see a clear story of problems solved, decisions made, and value created. If your updates don't tell that story, rewrite them until they do.

Writing good updates is a skill—but it shouldn't eat your Friday afternoons.

Automate the boring parts

When your systems already capture what happened, treat activity as data and automate reporting up and across the org.

> **Pro-Tip:** While you'll capture most activity in issues, some may happen elsewhere. One trick is to post an automated reminder to your team chat weekly, prompting any further updates from the team.

The management equivalent of automated telemetry—you're instrumenting your work so reporting becomes observation, not construction. **The best status reports write themselves.**

> **For managers: If you're asking your team to write status reports, you should be writing one too.** Publish your own weekly update—what you worked on, what decisions you made, what's coming next—in the same channel your team posts theirs. It models the behavior, gives your team visibility into what you do all day, and builds trust. The manager who reports alongside the team earns more credibility than the one who only reads reports.

Query for what happened

For years, I kept a set of saved search queries that I'd paste into GitHub each week to surface my team's recent activity. I might search for all the issues a team member touched in the past week (`org:github involves:@monalisa is:issue updated:>=XXXX-XX-XX`), or all the issues on the team project board that received a comment in the past week (`project:github/1234 is:issue updated:>=XXXX-XX-XX`). Those queries gave me a comprehensive view of the team's activity, and I'd pull the most critical updates into our team Snippets. (You can also automate these queries using the GitHub API.)

Let AI write the first draft

I've experimented with AI to draft weekly highlights—imperfect, but it beats staring at a blank page. Think of it as a robot intern for your first draft. As discussed further in AI as a thought partner, gathering the activities can be automated, but reviewing and synthesizing *is* the uniquely human work. Don't outsource it.

> **Pro-Tip:** Set a recurring Friday calendar reminder that includes your saved GitHub search queries as clickable links. One click to see your team's activity, another to draft the summary. The best reporting workflow is the one that's already halfway done when you sit down.

See the appendix for an example prompt you can adapt for your own team's reporting needs.

Share your updates with your team, too

I post my updates as discussions in a private repository that the team and my leadership can access. Notifications stream into the team chat channel, so the team sees what everyone else is working on, what I'm highlighting for leadership, and can chime in when something piques their interest. Teammates in different time zones catch up on their own schedule—no synchronous overlap required. Bonus: seeing what gets highlighted sharpens their sense of team priorities.

> **For managers: Read the updates. Respond to them. Use them.** Nothing kills a reporting habit faster than writing into the void. When someone shares a win, acknowledge it. When you spot a theme across updates, share the insight. Your team's updates are ammunition for advocating on their behalf to leadership—use them to tell the story of your team's impact in places your reports can't reach. But keep the system lightweight: if your team spends more than an hour per week on reporting, something's broken.

Reporting doesn't have to be a chore. When your tools make work visible as a byproduct, automate the highlights and spend Friday afternoons on actual work. Your team stays in the loop, leadership gets what they need, and nobody has to ask, "What's everyone working on?"

Reporting doesn't exist in isolation. The practices throughout this section—showing your work, leading like an engineer, tracking work in the open, documenting decisions—reinforce each other. Get one right and the others get easier.

Practices are tools, though, and tools eventually hit edge cases. When the playbook doesn't quite fit—when transparency feels like surveillance, or async stalls instead of accelerating—you need something deeper: principles that guide your judgment when the specific technique breaks down.

The Zen of Open and Async Work for Leaders

> **TL;DR:** Your team won't be braver than you are. Every open and async practice eventually breaks at the edge—and when it does, you don't reach for a better tool, you reach for four principles: psychological safety, explicit expectations, visible work, and the openness you model before you ask anyone else for it.

A decision record sparks a flame war instead of alignment. A transparency initiative feels like surveillance. A skip-level asks why nobody told them about a shipping delay, even though someone posted it in a public issue three weeks ago. Every practice eventually breaks at the edge. Practices are tools. Principles are what you reach for when the tools don't fit.

These principles aren't just for people with "manager" in their title. They apply to anyone who influences how work gets done—start now, even if you never want the title.

Four principles that compound

Open and async leadership rests on four reinforcing principles:

- **Psychological safety** makes it safe to work visibly, even when work is imperfect.
- **Explicit expectations** clarify what information is worth sharing and how the team should make decisions.
- **Visible work** creates the raw material for informed decisions.
- **Modeled transparency** gives visible work its audience—your team's ceiling for openness is whatever ceiling you set for yourself.

None of these is revolutionary alone. Together they compound: safety unlocks visibility, expectations turn visibility into signal, signal creates the artifacts modeling has to point at, and modeling resets what feels safe to share. The rest of this chapter is a brief tour of each, and a diagnostic for when the loop breaks down.

Psychological safety

Start here. If there's *one* principle to get right first, this is it—transparency without trust collapses into surveillance, and the internet is an intimidating place to feel watched. *Why Open and Async Change Fails* makes the broader case for organizational trust; this section is about what *you* do to build it. **Be open to feedback, admit your mistakes, and show vulnerability.**

Leader vulnerability sets the ceiling, not the floor. **Your team won't be braver than you are.** If you never post "I got this architecture decision wrong—here's what I learned" in a public channel, your team won't either. They're watching to see what's actually safe, not what the handbook says is safe. ICs build psychological safety too—often faster than managers—by being the first to admit mistakes publicly, ask "naive" questions in open channels, and share work before it's polished.

Concretely: be open about your strengths and weaknesses (a Human User Guide[77] linked in your chat profile gives this a permanent address); respond constructively to feedback even when it stings; let team members drive 1:1s; and say "I don't know" out loud rather than performing certainty you don't have. Every time you reach for confidence-as-armor, you raise the floor your team has to clear before being honest with you.

> **Common objection: "Being vulnerable as a leader will make my team lose confidence in me."** Think about the worst managers you've had. Were they the ones who admitted mistakes, or the ones who never did? Leaders who project infallibility don't inspire confidence—they inspire fear. Their teams learn to hide problems, avoid risks, and never surface bad news until it's a full-blown cri-

77. https://github.com/matthewmccullough/human-interaction-templates/blob/master/human-user-guide.md

> sis. When you say "I was wrong about this approach—here's what I learned," your team doesn't hear weakness. They hear permission to be honest. Google's Project Aristotle[78] found that psychological safety—the belief that you won't be punished for making mistakes—was the single strongest predictor of high-performing teams. You can't build that while pretending you never screw up.

Explicit expectations

Write a set of agreements as a team and capture them as Markdown files in your team's repository. Cover working and communication styles, response times, and preferred channels. Spell out what is expected of team members, what they can expect from each other, and what they can expect from leaders. **Unwritten expectations are just assumptions.** New teams and reorgs make this urgent—without written agreements, everyone imports assumptions from their last job. Revisit quarterly so they reflect how the team actually works.

In practice: be explicit about which standing meetings require live attendance and which can be caught up on async, and give each one back to the team if you can't justify it. Honor protected focus time—Days of Learning, No-Meeting First Fridays, whatever the local equivalent

78. https://rework.withgoogle.com/intl/en/guides/understand-team-effectiveness

is—by rescheduling around it instead of through it. Maintain a single source of truth for team decisions that someone can find without a search party.

> **For individual contributors: Don't wait for your manager—propose a team agreement yourself, or document your own working preferences in your profile.** Setting expectations is a leadership act, regardless of title. Write your own user manual: working hours, preferred communication channels, how you handle interruptions, and what "urgent" means to you. Share it in your team channel or chat profile. You'll answer a dozen recurring questions before they're asked—and you'll signal that you take async norms seriously enough to codify them.

> **Pro-Tip:** Draft your team's working agreements as a pull request in your team repo and ask everyone to review it. You'll surface misaligned expectations before they become conflicts—and the PR itself becomes a permanent artifact of how the team agreed to work together.

Visible work

Clear expectations mean nothing if the work itself stays hidden. Make priorities, decisions, and progress visible by default—not just when someone asks.

In practice: keep a leadership team project board so people can see what's in flight without asking (ICs, run a personal or squad-level board for the same reason). Seek feedback *before* you decide, not after, and document how you incorporated it—silent adoption looks identical to ignoring people. Automate as much status reporting as your tools allow; if someone already noted progress in an issue, don't make them retype it in chat. When a weekly report has a sensitive section, mark it private and share the rest openly rather than locking the whole thing down.

> **Pro-Tip:** Spend 15 minutes this week setting up a single project board that shows your team's current priorities. A simple "To Do / In Progress / Done" board eliminates half the "what's everyone working on?" questions that currently require meetings or DMs.

Modeled transparency

The fourth principle isn't a separate practice—it's how you do the other three. Whatever standard you set for safety, expectations, and visibility, your team will quietly adjust to a slightly lower one. So set it deliberately, and set it high.

Post your own work-in-progress before asking anyone else to. Share decisions you're still uncertain about, not just the polished after-action versions. When you escalate something to a meeting, narrate why async didn't work this time, so the exception teaches the rule. Modeling isn't about performing transparency for an audience —it's about being the first person willing to do the thing you're asking everyone else to do.

When the loop breaks: a diagnostic

When something feels off, don't blame the tooling. Diagnose which principle is weakest:

- **People hoarding information?** Usually a psychological safety problem, not a tooling problem.
- **Constant "what should I do?" questions?** Your expectations aren't explicit enough.
- **Recurring "I didn't know that was happening" surprises?** Work is happening but staying hidden—a visibility problem.
- **The handbook says one thing but the team does another?** Modeling. Look at what leadership actually does, not what the docs say.

Fix the weakest link first. The other three won't stick without it.

> 👔 **For managers: Run a quarterly "principle health check."** In a retro or async survey, ask four questions. "Do you feel safe sharing mistakes?" covers safety. "Are expectations clear enough to act on?" covers expectations. "Can you find what you need without asking someone?" covers visibility. "Does leadership do what it asks of others?" covers mod-

> eling. Score each 1–5 and invest where the number is lowest.

> **For individual contributors: Look for these principles in your own environment.** Do you feel safe taking smart risks? Are expectations clear? Is work visible? Can you find what you need without asking someone? These four things make the difference between remote work that thrives and remote work that exhausts you. If they're missing, you can help build them—you don't need a title to model psychological safety or make your own work visible.

Async and distributed work isn't just an IC skill. Leaders shape the environment where these practices take root. Teams that get it right build institutional knowledge that compounds, keep the people who value autonomy, and create cultures where the best ideas win—regardless of who had them or what time zone they came from.

Leadership in open and async environments is less about authority and more about removing friction so other people can ship. The ten chapters in this section divide into three movements. First, what leadership looks like when nobody can watch you look decisive—and why the loss of that performance is itself the upgrade. Then the recurring rituals that hold a distributed team together when they no longer happen by accident: 1:1s, career conversations, weekly reports, engaging with dissent before it goes underground. And finally the principles that hold all of it up when the playbook doesn't quite fit. Whether you have direct reports or you lead through technical influence, the same operating principles apply—because in async environments, leadership is what you produce, not where you sit.

Key takeaways

- In open and async teams, your leadership is measured by the clarity and usefulness of what you document—decisions, priorities, and expectations—not your title or charisma. If you don't make your thinking visible, you're not leading anyone who isn't in the room with you (and in remote work, there is no room).
- If you document only what you decided, not why or how, you force others to repeat your work—or make costly mistakes—when context fades; by consistently showing your reasoning, you build trust, preserve knowledge, and make better leaders out of those who follow.
- Shut down dissent and you don't end it; you just push it into DMs and side channels where it festers out of sight. Engage it in public, and the same pushback that felt like a threat becomes your best source of buy-in and better ideas.
- Stop running parallel project spreadsheets—lead your team where they work by managing everything in issues, pull requests, and project boards. When you make decisions and progress visible in the same tools your engineers use, you save time, reduce confusion, and give your team the clarity they need to move faster without constant meetings.

- Most of what we call management is just relaying information that transparent systems now handle automatically. Strip out the message-passing and managers can do the work only a human can: coach, unblock, and lead.
- If your 1:1s are status updates, you're wasting your team's only protected real-time slot for coaching, hard feedback, and the conversations too risky to put in writing. Status belongs in issues; 1:1s are for everything else.
- The conversations that actually shape a career—growth, coaching, honest feedback—are the easiest to skip when this week's bug is louder. Have them on purpose, and you'll surface burnout or a flight risk long before the annual review would. Here's how to start them—and keep them going.
- Stop assembling Friday status decks from scratch—if your daily work already lives in issues and project boards, reporting is just a query you run, not a document you write. Automate the highlights, and your boss never has to ask, "What's everyone working on?"
- Your team won't be braver than you are. Every open and async practice eventually breaks at the edge—and when it does, you don't reach for a better tool, you reach for four principles: psychological safety, explicit expectations, visible work, and the openness you model before you ask anyone else for it.

Team Health, Culture, and Sustainability

Team health isn't a soft topic—it's a hard competitive advantage. Companies that invest in it attract better talent, keep experienced employees longer, and get better work from people who want to be there. Workers increasingly *demand* sustainable, enjoyable work, not just tolerate it—and unlike offices that can mask dysfunction with perks or proximity, remote teams live or die on their culture and practices.

Here's a question nobody asks in sprint planning: how many of your best engineers are quietly updating their résumés? Not because of the tech stack or compensation—because nobody noticed them. Because a three-day Slack argument went unresolved. Because "we'll fix the culture later" has been the plan for eighteen months.

Walk into any office and you'll absorb culture without trying—who gets recognized, how leaders react to bad news, how colleagues treat each other. Remote teams can't rely on those passive signals.

You make values visible through documentation, celebrate wins in shared channels, and create deliberate space for connection. **Intentional culture beats accidental culture.**

> **Pro-Tip:** **"You can't build culture remotely"** is an excuse, not an observation. What skeptics mean is "we don't know how to build culture without co-location." That's a skills gap, not a fundamental limitation. If you've ever felt genuine community in an online gaming guild or open source project, you already know distributed culture works.

Think of team health like technical debt. Ignore it long enough, and everything grinds to a halt—not with a crash, but with a slow accumulation of friction that makes every project take longer, every decision harder, every hire less likely to stick. None of this is warm and fuzzy. It's operational efficiency dressed in human language. **Culture is whatever you tolerate twice.**[79]

> **Common objection:** **"Remote work leads to burnout."** This conflates "remote" with "always-on." Office work had built-in boundaries: the

79. The phrasing echoes Steve Gruenert and Todd Whitaker's *School Culture Rewired* (ASCD, 2015): the culture of any organization is shaped by the worst behavior its leaders are willing to tolerate.

commute, leaving the building at 6 PM, physical separation between work and home. Remote work requires deliberate boundaries, but it also offers *more* flexibility—take a walk at 2 PM, start late after a doctor's appointment, stop when you're done instead of waiting for others to leave. The real burnout risk comes from poor remote practices (constant video calls, no asynchronous options, surveillance culture), not from working remotely.

For managers: Your team's culture is whatever you consistently do, not whatever you say you value. If you celebrate shipping but ignore burnout, that's your culture. If you praise overtime but talk about "balance," your team hears the praise. Audit your own behavior first: what did you recognize this week? Whose boundaries did you protect—or accidentally bulldoze?

For individual contributors: Make your contributions visible through artifacts, not announcements. Post weekly updates focused on what you *shipped* and what's next, not what kept you busy. When you close a tricky issue, write a brief comment explaining your approach so others (and future-you) can find it. Link your work in standups

> **and 1:1 docs so your manager doesn't have to guess what you've been delivering.**

Healthy teams need healthy individuals—and the shift from office to remote surfaces personal challenges that no team process can solve for you.

Remote work puts the responsibility for boundaries—and visibility—squarely on your shoulders. That shift can catch even seasoned pros off guard, especially in the early weeks. Nobody hands you a roadmap for thriving remotely; you're left to piece it together as you go.

What I Wish I Knew Before Going Remote

> **TL;DR:** Nobody tells you this before you go remote: your success hinges on owning your own onboarding, shipping something—anything—within your first two weeks, and surviving the month-one firehose of async communication without panicking. And if you're the manager, your job is to design the experience so none of that depends on luck.

Your first month remote will feel like joining a codebase with no README. Nobody hands you a checklist—you're writing your own. Slack moves faster than you can follow. You ship something small and hear... nothing. Not criticism—just silence. Around week four, you'll wonder whether you're thriving or slowly becoming invisible.

I went through this myself going from government bureaucracy—where my job description ran 30 pages and specified the heaviest box I might have to lift—to GitHub's async-first culture. Here's what I wish someone had told me.

Own your onboarding from day one

For my first three or four days at GitHub, I'd bump into a colleague at HQ; they'd welcome me and ask what I was working on. I'd respond, "I have no idea." I was waiting for someone to tell me what to do. In a distributed organization, onboarding requires more initiative—especially now that remote onboarding is the norm.

> **Pro-Tip:** I liked to joke that URLs were a Hubber's love language. If you asked a question and someone shared a URL in response, they weren't being dismissive—they were giving you the gift of information. It was your job to unwrap that gift and learn from it.

You might receive a handful of links to documents and recorded talks. Getting up to speed and setting your own pace falls to you. If the reading pile feels impossible, balance it with 1:1 connections and spread the rest across your first few weeks. You're not "on your own," but without a buddy checking in over coffee, you'll need to seek out connections deliberately.

> **For managers: Your new hire's first week is a test of your async culture—act like it.** If onboarding requires a dozen DMs to find the right docs, your documentation has gaps. Assign an onboarding buddy, create a "first week" checklist in a public issue, and check in by day three—not to micromanage, but to make sure they're not stuck in

> silence. The speed at which a new hire ships their first contribution tells you how good your team's documentation actually is.

Later in my first week, I started mentioning "government-y things" in conversations with colleagues. Most Hubbers replied with genuine curiosity—and sometimes surprise—at how much that perspective was needed. Those conversations sparked ideas that wouldn't have surfaced if someone had handed me the 30-page job description I'd come to expect.

Ship something in your first two weeks

Find something small and inconsequential to ship in your first two weeks, whether you're starting an internship, an entry-level role, or a leadership position. The first ship is always the hardest, and clearing that hurdle makes everything else easier. It's far better to learn the unspoken rules on something low-stakes than to misstep on your first major project. Call it a "training-wheel ship"—it helps you find your balance.

It could be a single character, a word, a sentence, code, or prose—it doesn't matter. What matters is learning the workflow by actually using it. **Your first ship just needs to exist.** If it's day 15 and you haven't shipped anything, don't panic—but set the goal from day one and push past the jitters. The slack your peers give you is inversely proportional to your time on the job, so use the "new person" card while you can. Think of it as your first commit to a new codebase—the goal isn't perfection; it's getting comfortable with the development environment and merge process.

> **Pro-Tip:** My own first ship at GitHub started as a coffee-machine conversation (ironic, I know) with a colleague I barely knew. We were talking about government agencies that technically had to publish data publicly but refused to use modern tools—too unfamiliar, too risky, too "not how we do things." Idly, we wondered: what if GitHub rendered GEOJSON (Geographic JSON) files automatically? An agency uploading an already-public map dataset would see it turn into an interactive map with zero extra work. The hook was psychological more than technical. The data was already public. The platform was free. But getting an agency to put *anything* on GitHub was the whole game—once they'd done it once, they'd do it again.
>
> The feature shipped a few weeks later. A hallway conversation became production code in weeks, without a steering committee or a roadmap review. That's the tempo you want to calibrate to.

If you're looking for something to ship during onboarding, critically review internal and user-facing docs. Is something outdated? Did the author skip a step? Could you clarify something? Even correcting a typo has value, whether in the knowledge base, team processes, or customer-facing docs. It's also a great way to learn how the organization operates.

Learn how your team actually works

The corporate world, the technology industry, and startups each speak their own dialect. With any luck, your new team communicates more asynchronously and more transparently than you're used to, so it may not be as easy (or appropriate) to virtually walk up to a coworker's desk or send a quick email when you have a question. Good. It means the information is available to everyone, not just those in the right place at the right time.

If your first ship is something small like documentation, your second ship should be learning how the organization works and, more importantly, learning how to learn. If you don't know something, what do you do? Where do you look? Who should you ask? Over time, you'll build the mental model to find the information yourself (and do the same for others).

About one month in (or six), you'll get overwhelmed

Just as you're getting the hang of things—about one month in—you'll become overwhelmed. You'll stare at your inbox, notifications, or to-do list and not know where to start or what to do. You'll be sure that your employer made a grave error in hiring you (or that you made one in accepting the offer).

> **Pro-Tip:** Anyone who tells you they didn't hit this point is a dirty, stinking liar. Please don't believe a word they say.

That's okay. It happened to all of us. Async workflows produce a firehose of information, endless opportunities to chase, and so much to do that you won't know where to start. You'll get frustrated. You'll probably experience impostor syndrome[80]—the feeling that you don't deserve your role or that peers will expose you as a fraud. You might even want to quit. Stick with it. The feeling will pass.

Whether you feel overwhelmed in your first month or your 101st, communicate with your team and take a mental health day (or a week—or even just a morning or afternoon). Go for a walk, assemble that new bookcase, or run errands—anything offline. You'll come back with fresh eyes and a shorter to-do list in your head.

> **For individual contributors: The firehose is by design—learn to filter it.** You don't need to read every issue, every Slack channel, every notification. Start by subscribing only to your team's core channels and the repos you work in directly.

80. https://en.wikipedia.org/wiki/Impostor_syndrome

> Expand from there as you learn what's signal and what's noise. The engineers who burn out fastest are the ones who treat every notification as urgent. The ones who thrive build filters aggressively and protect their focus.

Professional, not formal

Communicating in a modern workforce should be professional, not formal. Respond with emojis, animated GIFs, and a human tone—not the sanitized corporate voice you might default to. For more on writing like a human in async environments, see *Core practices for async communication* and *Chat Responsibly*.

> **Pro-Tip:** If your internal post is titled "Update on X" or "Changes to Y," make it more descriptive. If two posts can have the same title, neither is useful. If you're trying to obscure the content of the post, rethink your decision.

Time management is on you

Modern employers treat knowledge workers like adults, trusting social norms over technical or administrative controls. That freedom is real—and so is the responsibility.

If it's your first time working from home (or with unlimited vacation), you may be tempted to take a four-hour lunch every day, make every weekend a four-day weekend, or stay out late every weeknight—and chances are, nobody will notice *for a while*. The opposite risk is real too: without the physical distinction between work and life, you may find yourself working late or logging extra hours. Either way, it's on you to get your work done and communicate your availability—without letting the job quietly expand to fill every hour.

> **Pro-Tip:** Create a commute. Mine has taken different shapes over the years—walking the dog, a school pickup loop, or just the ritual of changing into comfy clothes at the end of the day. Whatever the form, it has to be something that physically marks the boundary your office building used to mark for you. Without that mental separation, work and life bleed together. I also keep a separate personal device for non-work reading, messaging, and scrolling—even when company policy allows *de minimis* personal use on a work laptop. My brain reads the device as a mode indicator: work machine means work brain, personal machine means the day is done. **Your brain treats rituals as mode switches—give it something to switch on.**

Share your experiences, but be prepared to unlearn things

Almost every new team member brings something the existing team can't see—a different industry, a different workflow, a different set of assumptions about what "normal" looks like. As one former colleague put it, you're the world's foremost subject matter expert on being a newcomer. If you see something that doesn't seem right, have a "duh, why aren't we doing X?" idea, or have seen a challenge that your last job solved differently, speak up. Working on the same problem with the same group long enough leads to tunnel vision—you may be the fresh eyes your team needs.

Prepare to unlearn some prior habits, though. Many modern tech companies work and think differently, and "this is how we did things at X" rarely persuades without a strong reason *why* it's better than what's already in place. Approach your organization's workflows and culture with an open mind. Give it a few months before you write it off—once you get the hang of it, chances are you'll prefer it.

Your employer wants you to grow and learn

Don't wait until you feel fully qualified to raise your hand—especially when you're new. Volunteer for the task that makes you a little nervous, whether that's your first open source contribution, a cross-functional project, or a domain you've only read about. Your team expects new hires to stretch and will help fill the gaps. I've often referred to these as "extracurricular activities," borrowing the concept from school where they're not required, but they help you stand out.

Calibrating how far to stretch, investing in learning, and making that growth visible are career-long skills—and *Corporate Self-Care* covers them in depth.

> **For managers:** Remote onboarding doesn't happen by osmosis. Build a structured first-week path with clear milestones, pair new hires with a go-to teammate for questions they think are too basic to ask, and check in more often than feels necessary—what took thirty seconds at the next desk over can take days when someone's unsure who to ping or whether it's okay to interrupt.

> **For individual contributors: Start building career-ownership habits from day one.** Document what you ship while it's fresh, track the impact of your onboarding contributions, and don't assume your manager sees everything you do. The habits you form during onboarding compound over time—and they're easiest to build when everything is new and worth recording. (For a complete system for tracking and sharing your wins, see *Corporate Self-Care*.)

The habits you build during onboarding—owning your schedule, shipping early, asking for help—stick around long after you stop feeling new. But this chapter covered *your* side of the equation. How teams design onboarding systems, documentation, and structure that turn disoriented newcomers into effective contributors matters just as much. *Remote Onboarding Done Right* tackles that half.

Remote Onboarding Done Right

> **TL;DR:** Remote onboarding can't coast on proximity the way the office did—every unwritten rule a new hire used to absorb by osmosis now has to be written down on purpose. Do it deliberately and it's more equitable and consistent than in-person ever was.

Remote onboarding is a system you design, or a lottery you run. Without deliberate design, a new hire is parachuting into a country where they don't speak the language, don't know the customs, and nobody mentioned the currency. In an office, they'd absorb a thousand small things by accident—who sits near whom, which meetings matter, how people actually talk to each other when the slide deck is off. At home, they see a laptop, a Slack sidebar full of strangers, and whatever you deliberately put in front of them. Everything that used to happen through proximity now has to happen on purpose.

That sounds like a problem. It's an upgrade. Office onboarding is a lottery—your experience depends on whether the person next to you happens to be chatty and competent. Remote onboarding forces you to write things down, schedule the conversations, and name the unspoken rules. Done well, it's more equitable, more consistent, and scales further than any "come grab coffee with me" tradition.

The job splits neatly between two people. Managers own the system: documented, repeatable, and resilient enough that a new hire who starts the week you're on vacation still has a productive first week. When onboarding goes sideways, that's a process failure, not a person to blame. New hires own their side too: ask questions freely, flag broken documentation, and treat every gap you find as the welcome issue for the person behind you.

Why remote onboarding is different

A new hire sitting in their home office has no peripheral vision into the organization. They can't overhear decisions, notice which meetings matter, or absorb cultural norms by watching colleagues. This creates two related risks:

Knowledge gaps

Without osmotic learning, new hires miss context that "everyone knows" but nobody thought to explain. How do you get help when you're stuck? What's the unwritten process for proposing a new idea? Who are the informal power brokers? That tacit knowledge separates struggling newcomers from effective contributors.

Isolation

The social fabric of an organization is invisible in remote work. New hires don't encounter colleagues accidentally—every interaction requires intention. Left alone, they spend their first weeks talking to documentation and async messages from faceless strangers.

Organizations that master async communication and working in the open have already laid the groundwork. Documented processes, transparent decisions, and written norms give new hires exactly the explicit context they need.

> 🤔 **Common objection: "Remote onboarding can't replace the in-person experience."** It doesn't have to replicate in-person—it can be *better*. The best remote onboarding programs outperform in-person ones precisely because they can't coast on proximity: everything the office left to osmosis, they make explicit.

Three phases matter: what happens before day one, what happens in the first week, and what happens over the first ninety days. Treat them as distinct problems with distinct goals.

Before day one

Onboarding starts the moment the offer is signed, not the moment the laptop boots. The gap between "yes" and "start date" is when a new hire decides whether they made a good choice—and whether your team has its act together.

Ship the laptop, ship the access, ship the welcome

Nothing says "we weren't ready for you" like a new hire who can't log in on day one. Ship equipment early, pre-configure accounts, and have someone test the login before the box arrives. The IT ticket filed on the new hire's first morning is the ticket that defines their first week.

While you're at it, time the swag to arrive with the laptop. A hoodie, a notebook, a decent mug next to the machine turns a package delivery into a welcome moment. Skip the cheap junk—quality matters because remote employees have no office photos, no branded kitchen mugs, no shared wall of stickers to reinforce belonging. A well-made hoodie that becomes someone's favorite work-from-home layer does more cultural work than any all-hands slide.

A few days before the start date, the hiring manager should send a short, personal note. Not an HR form letter—a real message: what to expect on day one, who they'll meet, what tools they'll use, and critically, what you *don't* expect of them in the first week. Tell them plainly: "Your job for the first week is to learn, connect, and ask questions. You are not expected to produce anything. Success looks like understanding how we work, not shipping output." New hires will show up terrified of looking slow. Take that fear off the table explicitly.

Assign a buddy, not just a manager

Managers have performance conversations. Buddies answer the questions you're too embarrassed to ask your manager. Pair every new hire with someone on the team—ideally not their manager, ideally someone who joined in the last six to twelve months. Recent enough to remember what was confusing. Settled enough to know where things actually live.

The buddy's job is explicit: daily async check-ins during week one, answering the "dumb" questions, and being the first line of defense against the silent spiral where a new hire gets stuck on something small and says nothing for three days.

Curate the reading list, and the welcome issue

Dump every document that matters into a single welcome issue in your tracker—links to key documentation, scheduled meetings, the buddy's handle, team introductions, and a short ordered reading list. Tier it ruthlessly: what they need this week, what they'll need eventually, what to explore later. Nobody absorbs your full internal wiki in five days, and asking them to try is a way to fail them before they start.

> **Pro-Tip:** Treat the welcome issue as a living document. Ask new hires to check off completed

> items, log confusing bits, and fix the documentation as they go. The person most qualified to improve your onboarding is the one currently suffering through it.

> 🤔 **Common objection: "You can't mentor junior employees remotely."** Mentorship is structured guidance, not proximity. Remote mentorship is often *better* because it forces explicit communication, creates documented context the mentee can revisit, and removes the crutch of "just swing by my desk." Pairing sessions, async code reviews with detailed feedback, and written coaching notes scale further than an open-door policy ever could. A written review keeps teaching every junior who reads it later, not just the one in front of you today.

The first week

The first week has two jobs: orient the new hire to the organization (whether you or someone you're onboarding), and connect them to actual humans. Everything else can wait.

Introductions, not a firehose

Resist the temptation to stuff week one with a giant "meet the team" meeting where twelve people take turns saying their title. Nobody remembers any of it. Schedule short 1:1s with the people the new hire will actually work with—five or six of them, spaced across the week, each a real conversation about what that person does and how they'll collaborate.

Balance async with sync. Self-paced reading, recorded talks, and documentation let new hires absorb context on their own clock (especially across time zones). Synchronous meetings answer the questions the documentation didn't anticipate and provide the human connection that async can't. Too much async feels like solitary confinement with homework. Too much sync is Zoom fatigue by Wednesday.

The power of cohorts

If you're hiring more than one person at a time, start them together. A cohort of five asking the same "dumb" question out loud is collective learning. A solo new hire asking the same question feels like a personal confession.

Cohort bonds tend to persist—people who joined the same week often remain each other's peer support network years later. Spin up a dedicated chat channel for each cohort and let it outlive onboarding. Shared lunches, group Q&As with leadership, and collaborative first projects turn "group of strangers" into "people who have each other's backs."

> **For managers: Batch your hiring timelines when you can.** Even two people starting the same week is better than two starting a month apart.

> They'll normalize each other's learning curve and reduce the load on mentors and buddies.

Ship something tiny

By the end of week one, the new hire should have merged something. Anything. A typo fix, a one-line config change, a documentation patch. The *content* is beside the point—the value is running the full workflow end to end: branch, commit, open a pull request, get reviewed, merge, deploy. Reading about your deployment pipeline for a month won't teach you what shipping a one-line change teaches in an hour.

Maintain a curated backlog of "good first issues"—the open source practice ports perfectly to onboarding. Small scope, clear success criteria, low blast radius. If nobody hands a new hire a starter task, a good new hire should find one themselves. That initiative is exactly the signal remote teams are reading for.

> **For individual contributors: Ship something real in your first week, even if it's trivial.** You're not proving productivity—you're demystifying the workflow and buying yourself a concrete win when everything else still feels foreign. And when you find the inevitable broken link, outdated README, or missing step in the setup guide, fix it. That's your first real contribution, and it's worth more than it looks.

The first ninety days

Ninety days is the traditional evaluation milestone for a reason: it's roughly how long it takes for a new hire to stop being new. The first month is about context; the second is about contribution; the third is about fit. By the end, someone should be genuinely integrated—technically competent, culturally fluent enough to know how decisions get made, and connected enough that they're not working in isolation.

The first meaningful ship

Somewhere in the first month, the new hire should complete something that matters—a real project with real stakes, not a training exercise. Not a heroic launch; just a piece of work with their name on it that the team genuinely needed. This marks the transition from "new person doing starter tasks" to "team member with a track record."

Pair it with an expanding network. Introduce them to stakeholders, collaborators in other groups, and the people whose work intersects with theirs. Remote teams have to manufacture the hallway collisions that offices produce by accident. **If you don't put those introductions on a calendar, they don't happen.**

The overwhelm wall

Everyone hits a wall somewhere between weeks three and six—universal, temporary, and rarely flagged in advance. (For the new hire's perspective on this, see *What I Wish I Knew Before Going Remote*.)

As a manager, name it out loud before it happens: "Around week four, most people feel underwater. That's the pattern, not a problem." Then build a real safety net. Weekly 1:1s during onboarding should go beyond status updates—ask specific questions ("What's the biggest thing confusing you right now?") instead of generic ones ("How's it going?"). In remote settings, people hide their struggles because they can't see anyone else struggling. Make it safe to say "I'm drowning."

Signs of success, signs of struggle

By ninety days, you should see specific signals. Healthy onboarding looks like: the new hire is driving their own work instead of waiting for assignment, asking better questions (more specific, less foundational), building relationships beyond their manager and buddy, pushing back on things they disagree with, and fixing documentation as they encounter it. They've had at least one substantive feedback conversation—not a formal review, but a clear sense of where they stand.

Struggling onboarding looks like: weeks of "going well!" with no specifics, no visible output, no relationships outside the immediate team, no questions, and no opinions. Silence from a new hire at ninety days is almost never a good sign. It usually means they're stuck, isolated, or quietly deciding to leave.

> **For managers: Make the ninety-day conversation explicit, not implied.** Don't let the milestone pass without a dedicated check-in. Share concrete

> feedback on what's working and where they need to grow, then ask directly: "Is this role what you expected? What would make this better?" A candid ninety-day conversation surfaces small misalignments before they harden into resentment—or resignations.

> **For individual contributors: Audit your own fit at ninety days as honestly as you'd audit a codebase.** Does the day-to-day match what you were promised in the interview? Are you growing in directions that matter to you? If something is off, raise it now—course-correcting at three months is enormously easier than at twelve. And if the role is what you hoped, say that too. Managers need positive signal as much as the constructive kind.

The habits you build in the first ninety days—how you communicate, how you ship, how you ask for help—compound for years. Make them count.

Corporate Self-Care

> **TL;DR:** In a remote world, your growth and well-being won't manage themselves—learn how to set boundaries, document your wins, and run regular "career retros" so your work stays visible and your career stays in your hands. If you don't, burnout and missed opportunities become the default—not the exception.

I watched a colleague—brilliant, driven, beloved by her team—burn out spectacularly. She'd been the go-to person for everything, never said no, worked nights and weekends for months. When she finally crashed, the company lost not just her productivity but her entire accumulated expertise. She left. The institutional knowledge she'd never documented? Gone.

> **For managers: If someone on your team looks like this, don't admire their dedication—intervene.** The "always-on, never says no" pattern reads as commitment until the day it reads as a resignation letter. By then it's too late. Notice the signs early:

> weekend commits, thanking-them-for-grinding patterns in standup, the colleague everyone routes around because they "always say yes." Then have the conversation *before* the burnout, not after.

Here's the uncomfortable truth: no one is going to protect your well-being at work. Not your manager, not HR, not the company wellness program. If you don't build habits that sustain your energy and career, you'll join the ranks of people who gave everything to jobs that didn't reciprocate.

Ship before it's perfect

In a co-located office, people see you working—furiously typing, filling whiteboards, huddling over a prototype. Remote work strips all of that away. The only evidence of your work is what you share. **Unshipped work is invisible work.**

That's why the most effective remote workers share a trait: they ship. Not perfectly, not completely, but consistently. Progress visible to others is worth more than perfection hidden on their local machine. Regular shipping creates visible momentum, answering "What have they been working on?" before anyone asks. Set a personal rule: if you've been working on something for more than a day or two without sharing any progress, you're probably holding on too long.

> **For managers: Create environments where shipping early is safe.** Celebrate work-in-progress and never punish someone for sharing something imperfect. When someone shares rough work, respond to the substance, not the polish. Your reaction to the first imperfect draft determines whether you'll ever see another one.

> **For individual contributors: Frame your early ships appropriately.** "Here's a rough draft for feedback" sets different expectations than "Here's my final recommendation." You can ship early and still manage expectations—just be explicit about what you're looking for. (For more on making your work tangible and sharing early, see *Work Loudly*.)

Shipping keeps you visible, but visibility without growth is a treadmill.

Stay curious or fall behind

Remote work creates learning opportunities that offices can't match. Switching from a standup to a book chapter feels natural when you're already at home. Tell your team and manager you're blocking time to learn, then use async workflows to protect it.

Open work adds another dimension. When decisions happen in public issues and code lives in visible pull requests, you can read others' work, follow design discussions, and watch how senior engineers approach problems—without interrupting anyone. That ambient learning doesn't exist in conference rooms or private Slack threads.

Stretch 10% beyond your comfort zone. Pair with a developer to ship a change and pick up a new skill or domain along the way, or ask to join a product launch outside your usual domain. When you learn something useful, share the highlights with your team so the investment compounds.

Keep a running record of your wins

Staying sharp matters, but staying sharp *and invisible* gets you nowhere. Working in the open creates a natural paper trail—public pull requests, documented decisions, visible contributions—but that trail only matters if you curate it. Maintain a "ship log"—call it a "brag doc," "hype doc," "smile file," whatever gets you to actually use it. Each time you hit a milestone, record it with its impact and any relevant metrics. Async work hands you a head start: your contributions are already timestamped and linkable.

Your ship log combats impostor syndrome, makes annual self-assessments easy to write, and keeps your professional profiles—résumé, LinkedIn—current. **If you didn't log it, it didn't happen.** When promotion conversations come around, you'll have months of evidence instead of a frantic scramble to remember last quarter. Every Friday, spend five minutes adding bullets: what you shipped, what you unblocked, what decisions you influenced.

> **Common objection: "Self-care is selfish—I should be focused on the team's needs, not my own."** This gets causality backwards. Running on fumes doesn't make you a hero—it makes you less effective, more prone to mistakes, and eventually pushes you out the door. Sustainable high performance requires maintenance. Elite athletes don't train through injuries; they invest in recovery as seriously as practice. Corporate self-care isn't about choosing yourself over the team—it's how you keep contributing your best long-term. Teams that burn out don't outperform anyone. Put another way, capitalism is a transaction. You exchange your time and skills for compensation. If you don't take care of yourself, you're shortchanging your most valuable asset: you.

That's the philosophical case. Here's the practical one: in a remote organization, nobody's compiling your stats for you. Your manager has their own deliverables, their own manager to impress, and a dozen other direct reports. They aren't maintaining a highlight reel of your career—and they can't observe your contributions through office proximity. That's your job. Share highlights with your manager regularly. The best time to make your case for promotion is months before the conversation happens.

Build relationships, even at a distance

Office networking happens naturally: you eat lunch with colleagues, chat in the elevator, grab coffee with people from other teams. Remote work demands intention—but the effort pays back disproportionately.

Trust is what holds remote teams together. When you can't see what someone is doing or read their body language, you have to trust the work and the words. Small acts of reliability—responding when you say you will, delivering what you promised, flagging problems early—build a reputation that opens doors. Broken promises destroy trust faster than kept ones build it.

> **Common objection: "You can't build real trust without meeting in person."** Trust isn't built through proximity—it's built through reliability, vulnerability, and shared experience. Some of the strongest professional relationships form through years of consistent collaboration without ever meeting face-to-face. Think about open source maintainers who've worked together for a decade across continents. The trust that matters—"Will they deliver what they promised? Will they have my back when things go wrong?"—shows through actions, not handshakes. In-person meetings can

> accelerate trust, but they're not required to build it.

Distributed networking isn't about collecting contacts or maintaining a sprawling LinkedIn network. It's about building genuine relationships with people whose work intersects with yours, whose perspectives differ, and whose advice you'll value. Open and async practices create networking opportunities that don't exist in closed environments—contributing to someone's pull request introduces you to their work, public channels let people discover your expertise, and documented decisions showcase your thinking to people you've never met.

Effective distributed networking looks like:

- **Contributing to public discussions.** When you add value to a thread in a public channel—answering a question, sharing a resource, offering a thoughtful perspective—you're making yourself known beyond your immediate team.
- **Collaborating generously.** Help others even when it's not your job. In remote environments, generosity is visible and remembered.
- **Participating in communities.** Internal communities of practice, guilds, or interest groups connect you across offices, time zones, and org charts—people you'd never bump into in an office you don't share.
- **Maintaining weak ties.** A brief "How's that project going?" message every few months keeps relationships alive without eating your calendar. In a distributed org, these lightweight check-ins replace the hallway encounters that keep connections warm.

Flexibility is a feature—use it

Remote work gives you flexibility. Yes, there are obvious uses—going for a walk when you're stuck on a problem or avoiding a heated message until you've cooled down —but the less obvious ones are just as good. I can't count the times I've listened to company all-hands from the dog park (which I called an "all-paws") or put in a load of laundry when a meeting ended early. Whatever your remote work "hack," don't think of it as "cheating" your employer. A breakthrough while washing dishes is infinitely more valuable than staring at a blank screen for an hour.

The strangest remote day I ever had was the day the Microsoft acquisition of GitHub was announced. I closed my laptop and then just sat there thinking, *okay, now what?* No reception to walk to, no office to drift through, no hallway where I could read the vibe off a colleague's face. The news was enormous and the physical context was completely unchanged.

But distance cuts both ways. On the rough days—the bad review, the failed launch, the meeting that went sideways—you can also close the laptop and walk away without anyone watching you process it. You're not performing composure for a room. **Distance denies you the room's reaction, and grants you the room's**

permission to leave. Take the permission, especially on the hard days. The quiet after a bad day is a feature of remote work, not a flaw.

> **For managers: Model boundaries publicly—don't just permit them.** If you tell your team to disconnect but you're sending Slack messages at 10 PM, they'll follow your behavior, not your words. Block off your own recovery time, protect your team's calendars from meeting creep, and normalize logging off by doing it yourself. The manager who says "I'm stepping away for the afternoon" gives everyone else permission to do the same.

> **For individual contributors: Define your working hours in your calendar and chat profile, then defend them.** Set Slack's notification schedule to auto-mute outside those hours—don't rely on willpower to ignore the red badge. When a teammate messages you after hours, respond the next morning without apology; the async contract means they shouldn't expect an instant reply either. The goal isn't to work less—it's to make your on-hours sharp by making your off-hours real.

No one else will manage your career

In remote organizations, career visibility requires deliberate effort. There's no hallway reputation, no casual office face time, no lunch with the VP where you happen to mention your project. If people don't see your work in pull requests, issues, or public discussions, they don't know you exist. Early in my career, I stayed quiet and did good work, assuming the right people would notice. Spoiler: they didn't—not because the work wasn't good, but because nobody else was tracking it.

Nobody else will manage your career, which means you have to ask for what you want. Interested in a new role? Talk to your manager. Want to join a new project? Ask. Don't rely on loyalty from companies that may not reciprocate—your skills are portable and your career belongs to you. Your 1:1s are the highest-impact thirty minutes on your calendar for this kind of advocacy—if you use them well.

Small talk isn't a waste of time

For my first few years at GitHub, I scoffed at colleagues who filled their day with social meetings. "Don't they have work to do?" I'd think. I was spectacularly wrong—and it cost me. When I finally needed cross-team support for a project, I had no relationships to draw on. The colleagues who'd been "wasting time" chatting had built networks that made them more effective, more resilient, and frankly, happier.

Remotely, that small talk doesn't happen by accident—you have to manufacture it. But those casual connections become the people who vouch for you during promotions, warn you about reorgs, and keep you grounded during crunch periods. (*Work Should Be Fun* covers how teams build this social infrastructure intentionally.)

Check these against your own work life. If you're not learning, not building relationships, and not celebrating wins—something needs to change. If you are, you'll outlast the people who aren't.

> **For managers: Budget for growth the way you budget for infrastructure—and make it async-friendly.** Learning stipends, book clubs, recorded conference talks—these matter more for remote teams who can't absorb knowledge through office osmosis. When your team has space for learning and renewal without feeling guilty about "not shipping," they stay sharper and stay longer.

> **For individual contributors: Schedule a monthly "career retro" with yourself—30 minutes, non-negotiable.** Review your ship log, ask whether your current work aligns with where you want to be in two years, and identify one skill gap to close next month. Without the ambient career signals of an office—overhearing who got promoted, sensing which projects get executive attention—you have to actively seek that information. Your company manages your role. You manage your trajectory.

Protecting your well-being and career is your job—but sustainable teams need care flowing in both directions. You're responsible for managing your energy and growth. Your organization and colleagues are responsible for showing that your contributions matter.

Showing Colleagues They're Valued

> **TL;DR:** Replacing an employee costs six to nine months' salary—and the exit interview rarely mentions the real reason: nobody noticed them. Recognition isn't a management perk; it's everyone's job, and the smallest gestures cost nothing while compounding into the kind of loyalty no retention bonus can buy.

I once had a teammate mention—offhandedly, in a chat thread about something else entirely—that it was her daughter's first day of kindergarten. I sent a quick message: "That's huge! Hope the drop-off went okay." She told me months later that it was the moment she knew our team was different. Not the onboarding. Not the sprint planning. A two-sentence message about kindergarten.

On a distributed team, these small gestures are the async version of the hallway high-five. Without them, the moments don't happen. **Caring, remotely, is a deliberate act**—and it's everyone's job, not just a manager's. The best recognition cultures run on peer-to-peer appreciation as much as top-down acknowledgment: a teammate who notices your thorough code review, a colleague who remembers your dog's surgery, an engineer on another team who thanks you for documentation that saved them hours. Even if you know nothing about a coworker beyond what's on a standard HR form, here are a few ways to show appreciation:

> **Pro-Tip:** Early GitHub was an "appreciation economy." We went out of our way to recognize each other's work. It showed up in three distinct layers, and each one did different work. First, the CEO personally called out individuals during weekly "beer:30" all-hands—"shout-outs"—for going above and beyond. Hubbers would email the CEO ahead of the all-hands to nominate someone, and the best ones got read aloud. Top-down recognition from the top of the company, in front of the whole company, is a signal money can't replicate. The practice didn't scale as the company grew—too many people, too many good nominations, too few minutes in the all-hands—which is how the second layer was born.
>
> `.sparkles` ChatOps decentralized the same intent: any Hubber could publicly thank any other Hubber in chat, which then piped into a channel everyone read. Same appreciation economy, distributed rather than centralized.

> Third, and easiest to dismiss as frivolous, was our heavy GIF and meme culture—we wrote like we were on the early internet because we *were* the early internet, and that vocabulary of celebration (the animated high-fives, the "ship it" squirrels, the inside-joke reaction images) made appreciation feel native rather than corporate. The principle's identical across all three: when recognition is baked into how your team runs—at the top, between peers, and in the medium you already type in—appreciation stops feeling awkward.

None of this requires a company-wide program. It starts with the small stuff.

> **For managers: Build recognition into your rhythm, not your to-do list.** Mention specific contributions in team channels, not just in private 1:1s. When recognition happens publicly and regularly, it becomes contagious—your team starts doing it for each other without being asked. The goal isn't one big annual award; it's a steady drumbeat of "I saw what you did, and it mattered."

Words of affirmation

Recognize what your colleagues actually did. A quick "great job on that presentation" is fine; "the way you structured that proposal made it really easy to follow" is better, because specificity proves you actually paid attention. Onsite, you drop those notes as you pass someone's desk. Remote, you have to be deliberate about it—and at younger companies, where formal recognition systems don't yet exist, your initiative matters even more.

> 💡 **Pro-Tip:** At GitHub, weekly reporting took the form of Snippets. Each week, I included "shout-outs" to colleagues who went above and beyond. Adding them to a weekly report makes recognition part of your team's regular rhythm—and puts wins in front of leadership.

> 🤔 **Common objection: "Sending a 'great job' message feels forced when I barely know the person."** It does feel awkward at first—especially if your team doesn't have a recognition habit yet. Point to the specific thing instead of the person: "That edge case you flagged in the review would've corrupted production data—nice catch" lands better than "Great job!" Specificity kills awkwardness because you're reacting to the work, not performing a compliment.

Some milestones come with a built-in calendar reminder—use them.

Remember their birthday

Most people have birthdays. Not everyone wants candles, singing, or mass attention—but a simple "Happy Birthday! 🎂 I hope you have something fun planned this weekend" costs nothing and lands every time. Most HR systems track birthdays; if yours doesn't, ask for the month and day with minimal awkwardness and add it as a recurring calendar event. In remote settings you miss the subtle cues onsite culture provides—flower deliveries, cake in the break room—so the deliberate ping is what's left.

Celebrate the milestones

Work anniversaries deserve a moment. At GitHub we called these Hubberversaries—your one-, two-, five-, or ten-year mark is worth a note, even if most organizations can't be bothered. Tell them why you're glad they're there, or call out what they shipped over the past year. The effect compounds at younger companies: three years into a five-year startup, given typical growth, you've likely been there longer than most of your coworkers. Internal social tools or the public blog are usually faster than relying on LinkedIn notifications.

Notice the big moments

Major lifecycle events—adopting a pet, buying a first home, getting married, becoming a parent—are exactly the things you'd notice at the water cooler and easy to miss without one. Are they going out to celebrate? Would a friend get them something to acknowledge it? Chances are you should, too.

As a manager, you'll hear about these obliquely: a report asking how to update their address with HR (they bought a house), or asking about health insurance and time off (they're getting married). As a peer, it's smaller—canceling a weekly meeting because they're taking their daughter to visit schools, sending a candle, a book, or even some company-branded baby swag. Whatever it is, the small something says more than you'd think.

> **Pro-Tip:** Create a shared "team milestones" calendar and invite the whole team. When someone mentions a birthday, anniversary, or life event, add it immediately. A shared calendar turns recognition from "one person remembers" into "the team celebrates together"—and it survives manager transitions.

That shared calendar should cover more than personal milestones.

Acknowledge what they celebrate

Holidays count too—from ones unique to someone's culture or heritage to a simple year-end "happy holidays." In an office, "Happy Thanksgiving!" happens in passing; without a shared hallway, you have to be purposeful about it. At minimum, just say it. Going further: a handwritten card, a donation to a relevant charity in their name, an expensed meal during a team social hour, or some custom swag for the team.

Recognize the effort behind the launch

Time recognition to the launch—when the site goes live or the feature ships, especially with physical goods. A quick "congrats on shipping!" message naming the contributors works; so does an expensed pizza party, credit to your company store, or a charitable giving platform.

For bigger ships, customized swag tied to the launch goes further. Major accomplishments require real sacrifice, or at least serious effort, and even a small token reminds people the effort wasn't invisible. The goal is surprise and delight, so this is one of the few places I encourage secrecy.

> **Common objection: "We don't have the budget for gifts or swag."** Recognition that costs nothing often means more than recognition that costs money. A specific, public message explaining exactly what someone's contribution made possible—posted where leadership can see it—is worth more than a gift card. The most expensive recognition is the kind you never give.

> **For individual contributors: Don't wait for a formal program—start a `#kudos` channel or weekly shout-out thread yourself.** When a teammate's code review catches a subtle bug or their documentation saves you an hour, say so publicly with specifics: "@alex, your migration guide saved me from a data loss edge case—thank you."
>
> This isn't just about being nice. Peer recognition builds the kind of culture where *your* contributions get noticed too, and a trail of public kudos gives your manager concrete examples to cite during performance reviews.

Two caveats. If someone went out of their way to help you ship a project, send them a box, bag, or bottle of their favorite beverage to show you noticed and appreciate it—this list barely scratches the surface. And be careful when giving even token gifts to superiors, as you may run afoul of written and unspoken rules.

No amount of birthday GIFs or housewarming gifts substitutes for genuinely caring about someone and building a real relationship. **Genuine interest can't be automated.** But when the logistics of remote work make it hard to show you care, small gestures mark the everyday moments—and make the workplace feel human.

> **For individual contributors: You don't need a title to be the person who makes someone's day.** The teammate who consistently notices others' work and says so publicly—even briefly—becomes the connective tissue of the team. It costs you thirty seconds to post "your RFC was really well-structured, thanks for making the decision easy" in a shared channel. That thirty seconds builds the kind of reputation that follows you across teams and roles.

> **For managers: Block 15 minutes every Monday to scan for recognition opportunities.** Check who shipped something notable, who hit a work anniversary, who mentioned a life event in chat. Put it on your calendar like any other recurring

> task—because if recognition depends on you remembering in the moment, it won't happen consistently. The managers whose teams feel most valued aren't more naturally thoughtful; they've systematized the habit.

That friendliness isn't just nice to have—when work is genuinely fun, it builds the trust, creativity, and psychological safety remote teams run on. **Nobody quietly quits a team that remembers their birthday.**

Work Should Be Fun

> **TL;DR:** Fun isn't a perk—it's infrastructure. A 15-minute Among Us session or a meme channel replaces the office water-cooler moments that build trust and psychological safety, and without them, async threads turn sour and top performers quietly slip away.

Early at GitHub, I was in a sprint planning meeting when someone said, "Hey, who's up for Among Us after this?"—the online social-deduction game where a crew works a spaceship while a hidden impostor sabotages them from the inside, and everyone argues over whom to vote out. Half the team dropped into a voice channel, and suddenly I was watching my new director accuse my manager of being the impostor—with compelling evidence. Everyone was laughing, scheming, and genuinely having fun—*during work hours.*

Coming from government, where even casual Friday felt radical, I thought I'd landed on another planet. But that Among Us session made me feel more like part of the team than any "mandatory fun" corporate event I'd ever attended. The specific game was incidental—a round of Jackbox Games, the party-game bundle where players use their phones as controllers to draw, bluff, and answer trivia prompts, would have done the same work. What mattered was the fifteen minutes of unscripted play.

Optimize for Developer Happiness made the case: happy developers ship better software, and the business results follow. But *how* do you make that happen day-to-day, especially when your team is distributed? Not through perks or platitudes. Through intentional, sometimes ridiculous, fun.

Pool tables in the office weren't the point

Visiting GitHub's office, you'd see pool tables, DJ booths, and video game rooms. After years in government, I found this deeply suspicious. Wouldn't an employer want its employees to be *productive*? Turns out, the opposite was true.

> 👔 **For managers: Make fun a line item, not an afterthought.** If your team can expense conference tickets but not a $50 game for a team social, your priorities are backwards. Allocate a small, recurring "team social" budget—even $25 per person per quarter—and make it easy to spend without three levels of approval. The ROI isn't measurable in sprints; it's measurable in retention.

The specifics evolved as GitHub grew, but the core held. As a distributed team, we made fun intentional. The little things added up—heavy emoji use (🎉, 🙌, 😂), memes, and animated GIFs in everything from chat to documents prepared for executives. Then the bigger things—dozens of social chat rooms dedicated to dogs, home automation, cooking, and whatever else people cared about, with a cultural norm that *encouraged* spending time in them. If your manager "caught" you posting about your bike during "work hours," they'd be more likely to join in than reprimand you.

Even the weirdly over-engineered internal tools had a thesis. The app we built to allocate baseball tickets to Hubbers—easily the most over-engineered piece of software I've ever seen relative to the problem it solved—wasn't really about the tickets. It was about making sure a remote Hubber flying in for the week had the same odds as someone who lived in San Francisco. You could feel the design intent in every line: the office is a shared resource, not an advantage for whoever lives nearby. **Beautiful internal tooling is a trust signal—it's what a company builds when it takes its own people seriously.**

> **Pro-Tip:** GitHub had a small policy with an outsized payoff: if you traveled to a conference to speak on the company's behalf, you could add a day on either end—the "+1 day." It cost the company one extra night in a hotel, a rounding error against the flight and the conference badge.

> What it bought was real. International travelers got a day to shake off jet lag before they had to be sharp on stage, and everyone got a few unscheduled hours to wander a city they'd otherwise only ever see from a conference hall and an airport. A negligible line item that quietly fought burnout and reminded people the company saw them as humans, not badges staffing a booth.

Whimsy worked on the boring work too. Early on, GitHub ran a weekly rotating role we called King—or Queen—of Developers: any engineer could sign up to spend a week clearing the support escalations that would otherwise rot in a backlog. On paper, thankless triage. In practice, an internal app stuck a crown on your avatar for the week, people addressed you as "your highness" in chat and issues, and at headquarters there was a decked-out battle station reserved for whoever held the crown. The work didn't change—still grinding through escalations—but the costume did. **Dress up the grunt work and people line up to do it.**

I set the expectation with every new team member: work when you're productive, don't work when you're not. Colleagues regularly took midday breaks to go for a run, take a nap, or play video games. The only expectation was that you got your work done and communicated your availability to your team.

> 🤔 **Common objection: "You can't have fun or build relationships remotely."** This assumes fun requires physical proximity—ping pong tables and office happy hours that feel performative anyway. Remote teams are often *more* intentional about fun and connection. Dedicated social channels, emoji-heavy communication, shared playlists, team gaming sessions, and the flexibility to integrate life into work create authentic relationships. If you've ever made genuine friendships in online gaming communities, you already know remote connections can run deeper than office small talk—because they require effort rather than geographic accident.

Why fun actually matters

For distributed teams, fun isn't an input to developer happiness—it's *how* you produce it. Happy developers stay longer and ship better work, and without an office doing the social work for you, fun is the mechanism left. When serendipity disappears, you engineer it.

Norway's Winter Olympics program proves it at national scale. Decades ago, Norway overhauled youth sports around a single principle they call "joy for all"[81]—no competitive scorekeeping for young children, affordable

81. https://www.idrettsforbundet.no/tema/barneidrett/

access to multiple sports, and an explicit goal of fun over winning. As a result, a country of 5.5 million people now consistently leads the medal count,[82] powered by athletes who kept training because they genuinely loved it, not because someone was tracking their stats in elementary school. American youth sports optimized for early competition and college scholarships instead. **We get burnout. They get gold.** The same dynamic plays out on engineering teams every day.

Talent chooses culture

The stereotypical "cool" tech company has a ping pong table in the break room, virtual or physical. It's not about the ping pong table—it's about the signal: *we trust you to manage your own time*. When talented engineers weigh competing offers with comparable salaries and interesting technical problems, that signal tips the scale. **Top talent chooses culture over compensation.**

Breakthroughs happen away from the keyboard

How many times have you struggled with a problem, only to have the solution come to you the moment you step away? A shower, a walk, a ten-minute round of Mario Kart—your subconscious keeps working when your conscious mind lets go. Punishing breaks punishes breakthroughs.

Trust compounds, then crystallizes

Taking care of your life without asking for permission requires trust from management and colleagues. Trust in small things—"I trust they'll respond when they're back"—scales into trust in big ones: "I trust their judgment on this issue." That trust is the precursor to psychological safety—the confidence that speaking up won't get you punished. When your team has shared laughs over Jackbox and bonded over dog photos, admitting "I broke the build" feels less terrifying. And rapport built over hobby channels and post-standup gaming carries into the moments that matter: when your team's primary interaction is async text, social capital is the buffer that prevents misunderstandings from escalating. **Social capital is conflict insurance.**

Cross-cutting connections flatten the org chart

You've argued about LEGO sets in a social channel with someone two levels above you. Now pitching a contrarian technical opinion to them feels a lot less scary. Shared interests cut across org charts. Social scientists call this "cross-cutting cleavages"—meaningful connections that span different groups.

> **For individual contributors: Start the fun—don't wait for permission.** Create the `#gaming`, `#pets`, or `#cooking` channel yourself. Propose a Friday afternoon Factorio (lean manufacturing as a video game) session. Post the first meme. The engineer who starts a social channel does more for team cohesion than a dozen "culture initiative" slide decks. If it feels awkward at first, good—someone

82. https://en.wikipedia.org/wiki/Norway_at_the_Winter_Olympics

> has to go first, and the person who does earns outsized social capital.

Create your own water-cooler moments

Without a physical water cooler or break room, remote teams manufacture serendipity. Social channels, emoji reactions, memes, and shared-interest rooms (gaming, pets, music, anime—whatever your team is into) spark cross-team connections that lead to new ideas and genuine friendships.

None of these are nice-to-haves. Every emoji reaction, every pet photo, every post-standup gaming session is load-bearing infrastructure for a distributed team. Remove it, and async collaboration slowly corrodes.

> **Pro-Tip:** An office gives you shared music overhead—remote doesn't. Recreate it asynchronously. I set up a bot to post the same prompt to our team channel every week: "What are you listening to?" People would thread their replies with links to playlists and albums. It cost nothing to run, surfaced how different everyone's tastes were, and turned into a steady drip of new artists to discover. A recurring prompt—music, weekend plans, the best thing you ate this week—does the social work of a shared physical space without anyone having

> to be in the same room, or even online at the same time.

> **For managers: Create space for joy, not surveillance.** Social channels, emoji reactions, gaming sessions, and flexibility to handle life—these aren't distractions from work. They build trust and keep communication human. Teams that have fun together handle conflict better, communicate better, and stay longer.

> **For individual contributors: Don't separate your work self from your human self.** Share your interests in social channels. Celebrate teammates' wins enthusiastically. Take breaks without guilt. The connection you build through casual interaction becomes the goodwill that carries your team through tough deadlines and difficult conversations.

The trust and psychological safety you build through fun become essential when things get hard. That same goodwill makes teammates read an async message charitably when it lands wrong—and async strips out tone and body language, so that default charity keeps text-based conversations from going sideways. Here's how to handle conflict when you can't resolve it face-to-face—because the best teams don't avoid hard conversations; they've earned enough goodwill to have them honestly.

Handling Conflict Remotely

> **TL;DR:** Remote conflict doesn't fade—it ferments. Catch the warning signs early (circular threads, escalating tone, withdrawal) and switch from async to a real-time call before a minor misread hardens into a lasting divide.

Early on at GitHub, I got into a three-day argument in a pull request thread over an API naming convention. By the end, there were dozens of comments, neither side had moved an inch, and a junior engineer told me weeks later she'd been too intimidated to post on any PR for a month. The fight wasn't really about the API—it was two people who cared deeply about their work, talking past each other in a medium that stripped away every cue that would have resolved things in ten minutes over coffee. Nobody picked up the phone. **Unresolved async conflict doesn't fade—it ferments.**

Disagreements are inevitable—they're a sign of engagement. **Conflict means people care enough to disagree.** The question isn't whether your team will have conflict, but whether it strengthens relationships or erodes them.

Text strips out the nonverbal cues

Text gives you time to think and a permanent record, but strips away the nonverbal cues we rely on to interpret intent. A terse message that would sound neutral in person can read as hostile in text. Sarcasm that would land with a smile can cut without the accompanying grin.

> **Pro-Tip:** "Care-mad" (when you care deeply about something being "wrong") is real. Notice when an "injustice" *isn't* in your area of responsibility—or as a former colleague put it, "not your circus, not your monkeys."

Without body language and tone, readers fill in the gaps with their own assumptions—and when tensions are high, those assumptions skew negative. A colleague having a rough day might interpret your neutral "Thanks for the update" as passive-aggressive dismissal. The delay between messages creates space for anxiety: "Why haven't they responded? Are they angry?"

Remote work makes it easier to avoid difficult conversations entirely. Without shared physical space, you can sidestep someone for weeks. Issues that an awkward-but-necessary hallway chat might have resolved fester in silence. The short-term comfort of avoidance becomes long-term damage.

> **Common objection: "You can't resolve conflict without being in the same room."** Actually, the room can make things *worse*. In-person confrontations create pressure to respond immediately, escalate emotional intensity, and reward whoever's most comfortable with confrontation—which isn't always the person with the best perspective. Async conflict resolution flips those dynamics: a carefully written message gives both sides time to process emotions, choose words deliberately, and respond to the argument instead of reacting to tone of voice. That's not a limitation—it's a feature. The trick isn't avoiding synchronous conversation entirely (sometimes you need to hop on a call), but starting with writing to clarify the real disagreement before adding real-time complexity.

Async gives you better tools to *resolve* conflict—but the bigger win is preventing it altogether.

Stop problems before they start

The best conflict resolution happens before conflict starts. Most workplace disagreements aren't about incompatible values—they're about unspoken expectations, unclear processes, and ungenerous interpretations.

Establish explicit norms

What's the expected response time for async messages? How do people signal urgency versus routine? What does "available" mean on your team? When norms are implicit, people operate on different assumptions, and those mismatches create friction. Make the implicit explicit, and you eliminate entire categories of conflict. A team README that says "Respond to async messages within 24 hours; use @urgent in Slack only for production incidents" prevents the friction of one person expecting instant replies while another batches responses twice a day.

Don't jump to malice

When you receive a message that could mean different things, choose the generous reading. The colleague who wrote "That's not what I meant" probably isn't attacking you—they're clarifying. The person who didn't respond isn't ignoring you—they might be deep in focus work. Doubly so in text, where tone is always ambiguous. **Assume no malice. When in doubt, reach out.**

> **For managers: Make "don't jump to malice" a documented team norm.** Add it to your working agreement: "If a message frustrates you, re-read it assuming the best possible intent. If it still bothers you after a walk, ask the person directly—privately." Model this consistently and name violations when you see them. That's how it becomes culture.

But there's a limit. If you're doing this repeatedly with the same person and nothing changes—if they respond with hostility, if they misread you on purpose, if apologies never come—that's different data. That's a sign to involve someone else or reset boundaries.

> **Pro-Tip:** When you catch yourself feeling frustrated by a written message, try reading it aloud in the most charitable tone possible. Often, the hostility you perceived disappears when you strip away the assumptions you added.

Separate the work from the person

Critique the code, not the coder. Question the approach, not the judgment of the person who proposed it. When feedback feels personal, defensiveness kicks in and productive discussion dies. Instead of "You didn't think this through," try "This approach might hit scaling issues past 10k requests—what if we added a caching layer?" Same concern, zero accusation.

How to tell when async isn't working

Async conflict doesn't blow up—it decays. The warning signs are easy to miss when you're in the middle of it.

The conversation is going in circles

You're making the same points in different ways. Each reply feels less like progress and more like repetition. People respond to what they *think* was said, not what was actually written, and context bleeds away across messages. When you catch yourself saying "As I mentioned earlier" for the third time, async isn't working.

Tone is escalating despite careful word choice

You're spending more time editing for tone than content. The other person's messages feel terse, even when the words are neutral. You see a notification from this person and your stomach tightens. When the gap between intent and interpretation keeps widening—and you're dreading the next message—text has become the problem.

The delays make it worse

In synchronous conversation, you clear up a misunderstanding in seconds. In async, each clarification takes hours or days, during which both parties fill the silence with assumptions. The latency itself becomes a source of tension.

Withdrawal replaces engagement

One party stops responding, or their responses become minimal. "Noted" and "Thanks" replace substantive engagement. **Silence isn't agreement—it's abandonment.** In async conflict, it usually signals someone has given up on being heard, not that they've accepted your position.

> **Pro-Tip:** Keep a mental checklist of these warning signs. When you notice three or more, change

> your approach. Don't wait until things are irreparable.

Those warning signs don't just stack—they feed each other.

The async doom loop

I call it the async doom loop: each message intended to clarify introduces new ambiguities. It's a runaway process where each iteration consumes more resources instead of converging—except the resource you're burning is goodwill, and there's no `kill -9` for goodwill.

Person A writes something that's 90% clear but leaves 10% open to interpretation. Person B interprets that 10% uncharitably and responds accordingly. Person A, seeing the misinterpretation, writes a clarification—but that clarification has its own 10% ambiguity. Misunderstandings compound with each exchange, spiraling further from resolution.

In practice: a tech lead writes "We should prioritize the API refactor before adding new features." A teammate reads this as "stop all feature work immediately" and pushes back. The tech lead clarifies, but *prioritize* parses as "the only thing that matters." By the fourth exchange, they're arguing about priorities, commitments, and communication style—none of which was the original point.

The emotional signs matter just as much. When you find yourself:

- Rehearsing arguments in your head during other activities
- Writing and rewriting messages before sending
- Checking for responses more frequently than normal
- Interpreting neutral messages negatively by default
- Feeling relieved when the other person is offline

...the async format is taking an emotional toll that outweighs its benefits. These aren't signs of weakness—they're signs the medium has become part of the problem.

> **For individual contributors: Recognize the doom loop—in yourself, not just in others.** If you're rehearsing arguments in the shower or dreading a notification badge, the medium has won. You don't need permission to propose a call—"I think we'd resolve this faster synchronously, would you be up for a quick video chat?" is always appropriate. Name the pattern and break it; that earns trust far beyond the conversation.

When to switch from async to sync

Not every disagreement needs a video call, but some definitely do. Think of communication channels as a ladder: start with async in public (transparency and a record), move to private channels if things get personal, escalate to a video call when async is going in circles, and bring in a neutral third party if direct conversation fails. Escalate because the medium isn't serving the conversation, not because you're frustrated—and don't skip levels.

> **Pro-Tip:** The draft folder is your friend. When you feel the urge to escalate, write the message you *want* to send, then save it as a draft and walk away. Come back in an hour. Half the time, you'll rewrite it entirely; the other half, you'll realize the conversation doesn't need escalating at all.

Pause before you escalate emotionally

When you read a message that spikes your frustration, close the tab. Don't draft a response. Walk away from your computer. The goal isn't to suppress your feelings—it's to create space between feeling and action. Go for a walk, work on something else, talk to someone uninvolved. Return when you can respond to what was said, not to what you feared they meant.

This pause is critical in async, where your words persist. In a heated face-to-face conversation, people forget the exact words. In async, your angry message lives forever in the thread—and someone will quote it back to you. **Angry words never expire.** The pause protects more than your immediate state; it's insurance against permanent damage.

> 🤔 **Common objection: "Suggesting a call feels like admitting defeat or escalating the conflict."** This fear keeps people stuck in unproductive async patterns. But proposing a synchronous conversation isn't an admission that async failed—it's recognition that the situation needs higher bandwidth. Frame it as "this deserves a richer conversation" rather than "we're failing at async." More often than not, the other person is relieved—they were thinking the same thing.

Gracefully transition from async to sync

The framing matters as much as the suggestion. "We need to get on a call because this isn't working" sounds like an ultimatum. Try:

- "I think we might be talking past each other here. Would you be open to a quick call to talk this through?"
- "This conversation deserves more bandwidth than async provides. When could you talk synchronously?"

Each one names the medium as the problem, not the person.

If they resist, don't force it

Sometimes the other person declines. They might prefer async, feel uncomfortable on video, or want to avoid real-time intensity. Don't take it personally.

Ask instead: "I hear you'd prefer to keep this async. What would make this conversation more productive in writing?" If they're willing, propose structure: "I'll write up where we disagree, you correct any misunderstandings, and then we each write our perspective on the path forward." Structure breaks the circular pattern.

If they won't engage constructively in any format, involve a third party.

When to bring in a third party

Not every conflict resolves between the two people involved. Involve a third party when:

- **Direct conversation has failed repeatedly.** You've tried async, you've tried sync, and you're still stuck. Fresh perspective breaks deadlocks.
- **Power dynamics are preventing honest conversation.** If one person has authority over the other, or if there's a significant seniority gap, direct resolution might not be possible without mediation.
- **Behavior crosses into harassment or discrimination.** If the conflict involves behavior that violates company policy or creates a hostile environment, involve HR immediately. Don't try to resolve these directly.

When you involve a third party, be clear about what you're asking for: mediation, coaching, decision-making authority, or a witness.

Provide context without relitigating the entire conflict: "Sarah and I disagree about the project timeline; we've discussed it async and had a call, but we're stuck." Then be specific about what you need: "I'm hoping you can help us find common ground" or "I need guidance on how to move forward when we can't agree."

Document the resolution

After a synchronous conversation resolves a conflict—or moves it forward meaningfully—document the agreements in writing.

First, both parties confirm they heard the same things. "Here's what I understood we agreed to" gives the other person a chance to correct misunderstandings before they become new sources of conflict. Second, it creates a record others can reference. Third, it signals closure—the thread that started with tension ends with agreement, or at least mutual understanding.

Use this format: "Thanks for taking the time to talk this through. Here's my understanding of what we agreed: [list key points]. Did I capture that right?" Keep it brief, focus on forward-looking agreements rather than rehashing the conflict, and give the other person an easy way to confirm or clarify.

Repairing trust after a blow-up

Sometimes conflict causes real damage. Trust erodes. Collaboration curdles. The easy path is avoidance—and in remote environments, avoidance is disturbingly easy. You can go weeks without interacting with someone you've worked alongside for years. **Avoidance isn't peace—it's compound interest on damage.**

Acknowledge the rupture

Before you can repair, you have to name what happened. "I think our last exchange got heated, and I'd like to make sure we're okay" opens the door for repair. Pretending nothing happened just teaches both parties to ignore conflict.

Choose the right moment

Don't ambush someone with a repair conversation during a standup or in the middle of a work discussion. Schedule dedicated time, signal what you want to talk about, and give them space to prepare emotionally.

Lead with ownership

Even if you think the other person was mostly at fault, start with your own contribution to the conflict. "I should have been clearer about my concerns earlier instead of letting frustration build up" demonstrates good faith and makes it safer for the other person to acknowledge their part.

Rebuild gradually

Trust isn't restored in a single conversation. After the initial repair, look for chances to collaborate successfully. Small positive interactions rebuild the foundation that conflict eroded.

> **Pro-Tip:** If you can't grab coffee, suggest a virtual version: a 15-minute video call with no agenda except catching up. Sometimes the repair work happens not through explicit conversation about the conflict, but through rediscovering that you actually like each other.

Your manager has their own role to play when conflict surfaces on the team—see *Engaging with Dissent* for how leaders mediate, model, and set norms around disagreement.

> **For managers: Don't let conflicts fester in async channels.** Watch for the doom loop—clarifications that introduce new ambiguities, tone escalating despite careful word choice, and silence replacing engagement. When you spot these warning signs, intervene before the situation becomes irreparable. Sometimes that means asking privately if someone needs help; sometimes it's suggesting a mediated conversation. Create a team culture where moving from async to sync isn't failure—it's choosing the right tool for the situation. Your willingness to address conflict directly prevents small

> disagreements from becoming team dysfunction. After you resolve conflicts, do a brief retrospective: What could we have done earlier to prevent this escalation? What did we learn about our team's conflict resolution process?

> **For individual contributors: When you find yourself writing and rewriting a message, stop and escalate.** Don't wait for permission to suggest a synchronous conversation—you can propose moving to a call regardless of seniority or role. "Would you be open to a quick call?" is always acceptable. Close the tab and step away before you start typing —don't respond until the emotional spike passes. Owning your part in a conflict, even a small part, resolves things faster than defending your position.
>
> And if you're watching someone else's thread spiral, it's okay to privately message one or both parties: "I noticed that thread seemed to be getting heated—are you okay? Do you want to talk it through?" Sometimes the person in the conflict is too deep in it to recognize they need help.

Healthy conflict doesn't arrive with the team—you build it, one awkward thread at a time. The deliberate norms you build to replace office social lubricant often work *better* than what they're replacing.

Every conflict skill in this chapter—pausing before you react, escalating wisely, repairing trust—depends on genuine relationships. You can build those entirely through async work, but there's a powerful accelerant most remote teams underuse: getting in the same room.

Making the Most of In-Person Time

> **TL;DR:** Onsites exist to build the trust that makes the next six months of async collaboration actually work—not to cram status updates into a conference room. Treat in-person time as a scarce, expensive resource and spend it on what only co-location can deliver.

You're three days into your team's annual onsite when someone schedules a two-hour status update meeting. Everyone sits in a conference room, laptops open, giving progress reports they could've posted to Slack last week. Meanwhile, the engineer who just relocated from Stockholm and the designer who's been remote since day one are having their first real conversation in the hallway—about their kids, their hobbies, the ridiculous commute to this hotel. That hallway conversation will do more for your team's collaboration over the next six months than any status meeting ever could.

In-person time for a remote team is precious, expensive, and shockingly easy to waste. Most teams treat onsites like conferences—pack the agenda, maximize "productivity," justify every hour to Finance. They're optimizing for the wrong thing. **The real ROI of gathering in person isn't the work you do together that week; it's the trust that makes the work you do apart easier for the six months after.**

Why you can't skip this

Remote work skeptics point at onsites as proof that distributed teams "still need offices." They've got it backwards. In-person gatherings don't compensate for remote work's weaknesses—they amplify its strengths.

When you work remotely, you're asking people to read terse Slack messages generously, to extend grace when pull request comments feel curt, to trust that silence means "I'm thinking" rather than "I'm ignoring you." That takes a kind of trust you don't get from text alone.

Face time builds that trust

A week together means you learn that Sarah's actually hilarious, that Marcus is thoughtful but takes time to process, that Alex's blunt code review style comes from genuine care about quality. You've seen them as whole humans—they have kids, hobbies, bad jokes, strong opinions about coffee. When you're back to async and Sarah's pull request comment seems snippy, you remember her actual voice, her sense of humor. You read it more generously.

At GitHub, teams that met in person twice a year collaborated more smoothly, resolved conflicts faster, and shipped better work than teams that stayed purely virtual. Not because they did magic work during those weeks —because they built relationships that made the other 50 weeks more effective.

> 🤔 **Common objection: "We can't afford to fly everyone together regularly."** Compare the cost to office leases. If you've closed physical offices, you've freed up budget that paid for real estate, utilities, furniture, snacks, and other building costs. A week-long team gathering twice a year—even with international travel—costs a fraction of what you'd spend keeping an office open year-round. It's not an expense; it's a reallocation.

The money question isn't *whether* to gather—it's what to do once you're there.

Return-to-office mandates are an operating-model failure, not a real-estate decision

When a company announces "everyone back three days a week" after years of remote work, it's almost never sold as what it actually is: an admission that leadership doesn't know how to run the company without proximity. The press release talks about "collaboration," "culture," and "innovation"—words doing a lot of work to avoid saying *"we never built the systems async-first companies built, and now we'd rather move the people than fix the systems."* Call it what it is: a return-to-office (RTO) mandate.

If the only way your culture functions is when everyone is in the same building, your culture depends on proximity, not trust. If the only way your managers know who's working is by looking across the room, you have a management problem, not a location problem. If the only way decisions get made is by ambushing people at the coffee machine, your decision-making isn't a process —it's a habit that scales with rent. **An RTO mandate is an operating-model bailout.**

The teams quietly building career-defining work right now aren't waiting in line for badge readers. They're shipping from twelve time zones, writing things down, and hiring the people who used to drive ninety minutes to sit in a conference room. The "great return" is a one-time productivity tax companies are paying to avoid the harder, longer-term work of redesigning how they operate. Don't be the team paying it.

What to do in person (and what not to)

The worst onsites I've attended tried to replicate normal work—just with everyone in the same room. Status updates. Sprint planning. What a waste.

You've got a limited number of hours when your entire team is together. Every minute you spend on something you could do asynchronously is a minute stolen from something you can *only* do in person.

Use face time for high-bandwidth, real-time interaction

RELATIONSHIP BUILDING AND TRUST

This is the primary purpose. Full stop. People need to see each other as humans, not Slack avatars. Schedule meals together. Go on a group activity—hiking, escape rooms, cooking class, whatever fits your team. Leave space for organic conversation. The best onsite moments happen in the margins: the late-night hotel lobby conversation, the impromptu working session over coffee, the ridiculous inside joke that becomes part of your team's culture.

> **For individual contributors: Use onsites to build relationships you can't build async.** The senior engineer on another team whose code you've reviewed for months but never met? The PM whose roadmap you've only read? These are the people to seek out at onsites. A twenty-minute conversation over coffee creates more trust than six months of Slack messages. Come with a short list of people you want to connect with—don't leave relationship-building to chance.

STRATEGIC PLANNING AND BRAINSTORMING

When you're setting quarterly goals, designing a new system architecture, or figuring out your product roadmap, real-time collaboration pays off. You can iterate quickly, gauge the mood, and build on each other's ideas without async latency. But these sessions need pre-work. Non-negotiable. Send background docs ahead of time. Use in-person time for synthesis and decision-making, not information sharing.

DIFFICULT CONVERSATIONS

Performance issues, organizational changes, interpersonal conflicts—these need face-to-face nuance. Tone, body language, and real-time dialogue make hard topics less likely to spiral. You can resolve tension in 30 minutes of honest conversation rather than weeks of careful Slack messages.

CELEBRATING WINS

Retrospectives, team awards, shipping milestones—mark the big moments together. Async celebration is fine for small wins, but major achievements deserve shared experience. Cheer the win. Take a team photo. Make a memory.

What not to do

Don't schedule back-to-back meetings from 8 AM to 6 PM. You'll exhaust everyone and squander the informal time that matters most. Don't make people sit through presentations they could watch async. Don't expect deep, focused work. And for the love of async, don't use onsite time for 1:1s that could happen over Zoom next week.

> **Pro-Tip: The "no laptops in sessions" rule.** For working sessions and discussions, try a no-laptop

> policy. People can take notes on paper, but ban screens. It forces engagement and signals that this time is different from normal remote work. You can transcribe decisions later.

How often and in what formats

At GitHub, we landed on a rhythm: one company-wide summit per year, plus one or two team mini-summits. The company summit was a week-long gathering—talks, unconference sessions, team dinners, late-night conversations. Part conference, part reunion, part culture reinforcement. The mini-summits were smaller: just your immediate team, maybe 5–15 people, for 2–4 days of planning and bonding.

That cadence—twice a year—felt right. More than that and you're spending too much time traveling; less than that and relationships fray. Six months is long enough to accumulate questions, ideas, and tensions that need face time, but not so long that you forget what your teammates look like in three dimensions.

As GitHub grew from hundreds to thousands of employees, the annual company-wide summit became impractical—logistically complex, wildly expensive, and harder to make meaningful at scale. The model evolved. Company-wide summits gave way to department-level and org-level offsites, still large enough to create cross-team connections but small enough for real conversations. GitHub introduced the Hubber offsites program, where groups could self-organize regional or interest-based gatherings with company support. Instead of one massive annual pilgrimage, you had a constellation of smaller, more frequent meetups. The cadence shifted, but the principle remained: regular face time is infrastructure, not a perk.

Different formats serve different purposes

Large-scale gatherings work best when you treat them like internal conferences rather than oversize team meetings. At GitHub's scale, the summit evolved into an internal conference—leadership keynotes, unconference sessions voted on by attendees, expo-style team demos, and plenty of hallway time. These gatherings reinforce company values, share big-picture strategy, and give new employees context they'd otherwise spend months piecing together.

> **Pro-Tip: Try dine-arounds instead of one big group dinner.** Instead of herding hundreds of people into a banquet hall, book tables at several restaurants around the area and let people sign up for whichever one interests them. You end up with intimate groups of 8–12 having real conversations over food they chose, rather than 200 people shouting over each other in a noisy ballroom. Rotate the groups each night, and the cross-team connections happen naturally.

Team mini-summits are your default gathering—your 5-person engineering squad planning the next quarter, your product trio working through a redesign, your leadership team tackling organizational challenges. Cheaper, easier to schedule, more targeted. You don't need a fancy venue. A coworking space or someone's home office works fine.

Ad hoc meetups happen when team members are near each other. If two engineers are both in New York, they should grab lunch. If a PM is visiting the city where three designers live, schedule a working session. GitHub had a policy: if you're near a colleague, expense a meal.

> **For managers: Budget for regular gatherings upfront.** Don't make teams justify travel every time. Set an annual budget—X dollars per employee per year—and make it clear that gathering in person is expected, not exceptional. Remove the friction. Otherwise, managers will skip onsites to save themselves the bureaucratic pain of expense approvals, and you'll lose the benefits.

> **For individual contributors: Push for face time if your company isn't providing it.** If your organization hasn't budgeted for onsites, advocate for them. Volunteer to help plan one. Show leadership this chapter (or the broader research on remote team effectiveness). Make the case that in-person time isn't a perk—it's infrastructure that makes async work sustainable. And if your company won't fund it, organize informal regional meetups on your own.

Planning an onsite that makes more than it costs

Most onsites fail not because the concept is wrong, but because the execution is sloppy. Someone throws together an agenda the week before, packs it with meetings, forgets to account for time zones and jet lag, and treats it like a normal work week with worse Wi-Fi.

Start planning early

At least two months out. Book travel and accommodations before prices surge. Send a survey asking what people want from the gathering—don't assume you know.

Leave slack in the schedule

If your agenda has every hour blocked, you've overplanned. Aim for 50–60% structured time, 40–50% unstructured. The best conversations happen in the gaps.

Mix structured and unstructured

Have a working session in the morning, then a long lunch with no agenda. Schedule a brainstorming workshop, then free time to explore the city or just decompress in the hotel.

Account for different needs

Not everyone recharges by being "on" for 12 hours straight. Some need alone time. Some don't drink. Some have dietary restrictions. Some are juggling childcare back home. Build flexibility into your plan.

Include social activities that aren't forced

Skip the trust falls and mandatory karaoke. Offer options: group dinner vs. small breakout dinners, team hike vs. museum visit, game night vs. free evening. Let people opt in based on their interests.

Capture decisions, but don't let note-taking derail the conversation

Assign someone to document key outcomes, action items, and agreements. Otherwise, you'll forget what you decided by Monday.

Follow up afterward

> **For managers: Capture the decisions before they evaporate.** Within a week of the gathering, post a written summary: what was decided, what action items came out of it, and what the team agreed to try differently. Share it publicly so people who couldn't attend still benefit. Then track whether the agreements actually stick—if the "we'll try async standups" decision from the onsite quietly dies by month two, that's data about your follow-through, not the idea.

Within a week, share notes, photos, and next steps. Treat the onsite as the beginning of a conversation, not a self-contained event.

> **Pro-Tip: The "one day less" rule.** Whatever length onsite you're planning, cut it by one day. Three days instead of four. Four days instead of five. You'll be surprised how much more energized people are when they're not burned out by the last day. Quality over quantity.

The mistakes everyone makes

Treating it like a conference

Your team isn't an audience; they're participants. Don't make people sit and listen for hours. Get them working, talking, and problem-solving together.

Ignoring remote attendees

Sometimes not everyone can make it—visa issues, health concerns, family obligations. If you have remote participants, don't treat them as second-class. Set up a good camera and microphone. Pause for their input. Don't have hallway conversations that exclude them from key decisions.

Mandatory fun

Nothing kills fun faster than making it compulsory. Offer activities, but let people opt out without guilt. Some folks recharge alone.

Not following up on what you decided

If you make plans, assign owners, or agree on changes during the onsite, those decisions need to survive the return to distributed work. Capture them. Create tickets. Add them to the roadmap.

Forgetting that introverts exist

A week of constant social interaction is energizing for extroverts and exhausting for introverts. Build in quiet time, optional activities, and permission to skip events without feeling like a bad teammate.

Making the business case

If you're trying to convince leadership to budget for onsites, here's your argument:

Remote work saves money—a lot of it. Office leases, utilities, office supplies, kitchen amenities, furniture, maintenance, insurance. The average office runs $10,000–$15,000 a year for each employee[83] in major cities. A twice-yearly onsite—even with international flights and hotels—rarely tops $5,000 per employee. You're not asking for new budget. You're asking to reallocate savings.

The real ROI isn't in the cost comparison—it's in how your team works the other 50 weeks. In my experience at GitHub, teams that never met in person had noticeably higher turnover, slower onboarding, more conflict,

83. https://www.commercialcafe.com/office-market-trends/us/

and weaker culture. You can't easily measure "trust" on a spreadsheet, but you can measure retention, velocity, and employee satisfaction.

GitHub treated onsites not as a nice-to-have that got cut when budgets tightened, but as infrastructure—as fundamental to remote work as Slack or Zoom. That's the mindset shift leadership needs to make.

It's an investment in async work, not an alternative to it

You're investing in relationships so that async collaboration works better, so that a terse Slack message doesn't feel hostile, so that people don't assume the worst of each other when things get tense.

Remote work isn't about never seeing your colleagues. It's about being intentional with when and why you gather. Make those moments count.

You've built the practices, culture, and habits that sustain a distributed team. One more force is about to test all of it—and async-first teams have a head start.

Teams that thrive remotely treat culture as infrastructure, not decoration. The chapters in this section cover the foundations—what going remote actually feels like, getting onboarded without flailing for a month—and the practices that keep teams sustainable once the novelty wears off: protecting your own time, making appreciation visible, keeping the work fun, and handling conflict at distance before it festers. The closing chapter on in-person time isn't a contradiction; it's a recognition that distributed teams need to choose those rare hours deliberately. None of this is soft. All of it is what separates teams that compound from teams that merely cope.

Key takeaways

- Nobody tells you this before you go remote: your success hinges on owning your own onboarding, shipping something—anything—within your first two weeks, and surviving the month-one firehose of async communication without panicking. And if you're the manager, your job is to design the experience so none of that depends on luck.
- Remote onboarding can't coast on proximity the way the office did—every unwritten rule a new hire used to absorb by osmosis now has to be written down on purpose. Do it deliberately and it's more equitable and consistent than in-person ever was.
- In a remote world, your growth and well-being won't manage themselves—learn how to set boundaries, document your wins, and run regular "career retros" so your work stays visible and your career stays in your hands. If you don't, burnout and missed opportunities become the default—not the exception.
- Replacing an employee costs six to nine months' salary—and the exit interview rarely mentions the real reason: nobody noticed them. Recognition isn't a management perk; it's everyone's job, and the smallest gestures cost nothing while compounding into the kind of loyalty no retention bonus can buy.

- Fun isn't a perk—it's infrastructure. A 15-minute Among Us session or a meme channel replaces the office water-cooler moments that build trust and psychological safety, and without them, async threads turn sour and top performers quietly slip away.
- Remote conflict doesn't fade—it ferments. Catch the warning signs early (circular threads, escalating tone, withdrawal) and switch from async to a real-time call before a minor misread hardens into a lasting divide.
- Onsites exist to build the trust that makes the next six months of async collaboration actually work—not to cram status updates into a conference room. Treat in-person time as a scarce, expensive resource and spend it on what only co-location can deliver.

AI in Open and Async Work

AI isn't a disruption to the open and async operating model—it's a validation of it. Crafting prompts forces clearer thinking, and agentic workflows let you delegate real work through the same issue-branch-PR-review process you already use with remote teammates.

For years, skeptics dismissed remote and async practices as overhead. Document every decision? Give everything a URL? Then AI agents showed up, and all that "overhead" turned out to be exactly the infrastructure AI needs. Clear written context. Discoverable documentation. Explicit acceptance criteria. Automated tests that define "done." **Good practices don't expire—they compound.** The clarity that helps a teammate in Nairobi pick up your work while you sleep helps an AI agent pick it up while you focus on harder problems. **AI didn't break async work. It vindicated it.**

The teams that struggle with AI? They run on tribal knowledge, undocumented processes, and meetings where decisions evaporate the moment someone closes the Zoom window. If your workflow depends on being in the room, neither humans nor agents can participate from outside it.

> **Common objection: "Isn't this just hype? AI changes every six months."** The specific tools will change—that's guaranteed. But AI tools will always work better with clear written communication, documented decisions, and explicit processes. You're not betting on a technology; you're building habits that make any technology more effective.

Two ways AI fits into the open and async model. First, *AI as a thought partner*—where crafting a good prompt is structurally identical to writing a good issue. The real output is the clarity you forced on yourself. Then, *Agentic workflows*—where you assign AI an issue, it opens a PR, and you review through the same process you'd use for any teammate.

> **For managers: Frame AI adoption as a continuation of your async practices, not a separate initiative.** Point to the issue templates, review processes, and documentation standards your team already follows. The fastest way to lose goodwill is framing AI as yet another transformation program when

> it's really just a new contributor type joining your existing workflow.

> **For individual contributors: Your ability to write clearly just became your most valuable technical skill.** AI tools amplify clear thinking and expose sloppy thinking. The engineers who articulate problems precisely and document context thoroughly aren't just good async communicators—they're the ones who'll get the most out of every AI tool that comes along.

What comes next looks a lot like what you're already doing—just with more contributors who don't need sleep or coffee breaks.

AI as a Thought Partner

> **TL;DR:** Using AI as a thought partner sharpens your thinking by forcing you to clarify problems, challenge your assumptions, and articulate your goals; rely on it as a shortcut and you risk losing the critical insight and judgment that make your work valuable. This chapter will show you how to harness AI to elevate your own expertise—without letting it do your thinking for you.

You're stuck on a design document—specifically, how to explain a database migration to stakeholders who think "schema change" means "the website breaks." So you open a chat with an AI assistant. Not because you need it to write the document, but because describing the problem to *something* forces you to figure out what you actually think. By the time you've finished your third prompt, the document practically writes itself. The AI's response? Decent, but beside the point. The real output was the clarity you gained by putting it into words.

The reflection paradox

The people who get the most out of AI are the ones who'd do fine without it. AI amplifies capability; it doesn't manufacture it.

Ask an AI to help you draft a technical design document:

- You describe the problem you're solving
- You explain the constraints and context
- You articulate what success looks like
- You surface your assumptions

By the time you've crafted that prompt, you've done much of the thinking the document requires. What comes back is a draft to refine, not a replacement for your expertise. **The prompt is the product.**

That's the reflection paradox: you get more from AI the more thought you put in upfront. Better thinking in, better output back. Better output nudges you to think harder next time. As @jonmagic observed,[84] reflection itself often matters more than the report it produces—and AI makes that impossible to miss.

> **Common objection: "Won't AI make us lazy thinkers?"** This gets it backward. AI doesn't think for you—it responds to your thinking. A vague prompt produces eloquent nonsense. A thoughtful,

84. https://jonmagic.com/posts/designing-collaborations-not-just-automations/

> well-structured request produces something useful. The work of clarifying what you want, why you want it, and what constraints matter *is* the thinking. AI makes the quality of your thinking more visible, not less important.

That clarity-in, clarity-out dynamic maps directly to how async teams already operate.

AI in async-first workflows

AI tools slot into asynchronous workflows because they're available whenever you are. Unlike a colleague eight time zones away, AI doesn't have office hours or a sleep schedule. Use it at 3 AM when you're stuck on a design problem, or mid-afternoon when you're deep in flow and don't want to break focus. That's exactly what async work needs: a thinking partner that respects *your* rhythm, not its own.

AI interactions are also inherently written—every prompt and response is text, searchable, shareable, and permanent. That fits the URL-first principle of open work. Your AI-assisted work can link to the prompts and iterations that produced it, creating a transparent record of your reasoning.

> **Pro-Tip:** When using AI to develop important work products, save the conversation. The chain of prompts and refinements often contains as much value as the final output—it documents your think-

> ing process and can help others understand (or build on) your work.

AI isn't a universal solvent. Some tasks play to its strengths; others expose its limits fast.

What AI does well

Drafting and structuring

Starting from a blank page is hard. AI provides a scaffold you then revise, restructure, and improve.

Synthesizing information

When you need to summarize long threads, extract key points from documentation, or spot patterns across sources, AI compresses hours of reading into minutes.

Checking your work

AI is a tireless, ego-free reviewer. It catches inconsistencies, challenges assumptions, and surfaces the obvious thing you missed at 11 PM. It won't replace a human reviewer—but it helps you show up to code review with fewer obvious problems.

Translating between contexts

Whether you're explaining a technical concept to non-technical stakeholders or adapting a message for different audiences, AI helps you reframe your thinking.

Brainstorming and exploration

When you're stuck, AI generates options you wouldn't have considered. The suggestions themselves matter less than how they stimulate your own thinking.

What AI doesn't do well

Original judgment

AI extrapolates from patterns in its training data. It doesn't weigh consequences, remember your last incident postmortem, or feel the cost of being wrong. Decisions still require humans.

Knowing your specific context

AI doesn't know your team's unwritten rules, your organization's politics, or the history behind past decisions. Provide that context explicitly, or the output will miss what matters.

Being accountable

When you ship something, you're responsible—not the AI that helped create it. Review AI output with the same care you'd apply to any other input.

Replacing relationships

AI can help you communicate more clearly. It can't build trust or earn goodwill when something goes sideways. The human parts of remote work stay human.

> **For individual contributors: AI is your always-available rubber duck.** When you're stuck on a design problem at 11 PM and your teammates are asleep, AI is the sounding board that doesn't have a time zone. Use it to pressure-test your reasoning, generate alternatives you hadn't considered, and refine your thinking before you post that RFC or design doc. The engineers who get the most from AI aren't the ones who ask it to write their code—they're the ones who use it to sharpen the thinking that informs their code.

Thinking with AI, not through AI

The distinction between thinking *with* AI and thinking *through* AI is everything.

Thinking *with* AI: you use the tool to extend and pressure-test your reasoning. Thinking *through* AI: you outsource your reasoning entirely and accept whatever comes back.

When you think with AI:

- You start with your own understanding of the problem
- You use AI to challenge, extend, or refine your thinking

- You review output critically, keeping what helps and discarding what doesn't
- The final product reflects your judgment, informed by AI

When you think through AI:

- You describe the problem superficially and accept the first response
- You don't verify facts, check reasoning, or consider alternatives
- You can't explain or defend the result because you didn't produce it
- The work doesn't reflect your capabilities or judgment

The first approach treats AI as a tool in your toolkit. The second treats it as a replacement for your toolkit—and will eventually replace you, too. **Outsource your thinking and you outsource yourself.**

> **For managers: Tell your team exactly where the lines are.** For example: "Use AI freely for drafting and brainstorming, but you own every line you ship—if you can't explain it, don't merge it."
>
> Review AI-assisted work the same way you'd review any other work: judge quality and reasoning, not whether AI was involved. Be transparent about your own AI use so your team knows experimentation is welcome, not just tolerated.

You own the quality. Full stop.

> **For individual contributors: Use AI to raise your bar, not lower your effort.** Reinvest the time AI saves on drafting or research in thinking more deeply and reviewing more carefully. When you share AI-assisted work, be prepared to explain and defend every part of it as if you wrote it yourself—because professionally, you did.

AI and working in the open

In a co-located office, colleagues watch you sketch on a whiteboard, overhear you reason through a tradeoff, and absorb your thinking by proximity. Remote teams don't get any of that. Your thought process is invisible unless you make it visible—and AI interactions produce a ready-made artifact of that process.

> **For managers: Normalize sharing AI interactions as part of your team's open work.** When someone posts a design doc, encourage them to link the AI conversation that helped shape it. This does three things: it shows your team that using AI is welcomed, it gives reviewers insight into the reasoning process, and it creates a searchable trail of how decisions evolved. Model it yourself—share your own AI-assisted thinking publicly.

Traditional knowledge work happens in private—you think, draft, revise, and only share when you're ready. AI-assisted work inverts this: the whole process is already written down by the time you're done. For distributed teams starved of context, that trail of reasoning is exactly the kind of artifact that usually evaporates.

That transparency compounds:

Teaching and learning

Junior team members who see how senior colleagues use AI—what prompts they craft, how they evaluate output, how they iterate—learn patterns they can apply themselves.

Quality assurance

Visible reasoning lets others catch errors in your premises, challenge assumptions, or suggest improvements you didn't consider.

Accountability

Documented process means you can explain how you arrived at conclusions. "The AI told me" is not an explanation; "I prompted AI with these constraints, evaluated the response against these criteria, and refined based on these considerations" is.

AI doesn't change the fundamentals

New tools don't rewrite the rules—they raise the stakes. *Impact still matters more than input,* whether that input comes from you or an AI assistant. *Working in the open* still builds trust. *Async-first communication* still respects everyone's time. AI amplifies these principles—it doesn't replace them.

From tools to practices

Not everyone will adopt AI, and that's fine. For those who do, the difference between effective use and thoughtless delegation comes down to critical engagement and professional accountability.

The value isn't in the AI's output. It's in the clarity that produces good prompts, the judgment that evaluates responses, and the accountability that ships quality work. AI is a mirror for your thinking. Make sure you like what you see.

Agentic Workflows

> **TL;DR:** Treat AI agents as remote teammates—hand them clear issues, let them push branches, and review their pull requests as you would any human's. Get this right, and you'll multiply your team's output without rewriting your workflow; skip it, and you'll waste hours cleaning up confused pull requests.

When I asked GitHub Copilot's coding agent to "add agentic workflows" to my blog repository, its first move was to write a self-promotional blog post about agentic workflows[85]—in my voice and style—and submit a PR. I ended up merging it ironically[86] (with a disclaimer). The failure was instructive: the agent had done *exactly* what I asked, and that was the problem. My issue was ambiguous enough that "add agentic workflows" parsed as "write a post announcing them" rather than "wire up the infrastructure that enables them."

85. https://github.com/benbalter/benbalter.github.com/pull/1687
86. https://ben.balter.com/2026/03/18/agentic-workflows/

The lesson isn't that agents are unreliable; it's that they're literal. **Agent receives task, works independently, hands back a result for human review**—same loop as any distributed contributor. The context you give up front determines what you get back.

From assistance to agency

When AI acts as a thought partner, you're still doing the work—crafting prompts, iterating on output, making decisions.

Agentic workflows flip that model. You assign work to an AI agent and it executes autonomously. There's no pair-programming, no supervising every move. You give it an issue, it does the work, and it hands back a PR for review.

You're no longer using a tool—you're delegating work through the same workflow patterns you use with remote teammates. This works because distributed human teams and AI agents need the same things. Clear written task descriptions, well-documented codebases, automated tests that define "done," review processes that verify quality, and stable URLs so context is discoverable. The overlap isn't a coincidence—both sets of contributors share the same constraint: they can't tap a coworker on the shoulder.

Why agentic workflows fit async-first teams

Teams that already work asynchronously have a head start. If you write clear issues, document decisions, and review PRs carefully, the transition is painless—because you're already working the way agents need you to work.

Here's what happens when you assign work to a remote teammate in a different time zone:

1. You create an issue with clear requirements and context
2. They work independently on a branch
3. They submit a PR when ready
4. You review asynchronously, leaving comments and questions
5. They respond and iterate based on feedback
6. Once approved, the work ships

Swap "they" for "an AI agent" and every step still holds. Same process, same interface—the only difference is who or what is on the other end.

> 🤨 **Common objection: "Won't AI agents replace developers?"** This misunderstands what agents do well. Agents excel at routine, well-scoped tasks with clear acceptance criteria and established patterns. They struggle with ambiguity, judgment calls, and deep system context. They're not replacing developers—they're absorbing the tedious work

> developers always said they'd automate "someday."

Teams that communicate primarily through synchronous meetings have a harder time. You can't walk over to an agent's desk. You can't screen-share to show it what you mean. If your team relies on these patterns, you'll need to change workflows before agents can contribute.

That identical workflow isn't a coincidence—it's inheritance. Pull requests evolved as the open source community's answer to a fundamental challenge: how do you accept contributions from people you don't fully trust, at scale, while maintaining quality? A PR bundles everything needed for oversight into a single interface: a clear proposal, a discussion thread, automated checks, a review mechanism, and an audit trail.

AI agents are the latest class of contributors benefiting from that infrastructure. The open source trust model—propose, review, merge—is the right interface for any contributor whose work you want to verify before shipping.

Agents as remote teammates

Treat agents like remote contributors, not automated scripts.

When you assign work to a teammate, you don't micromanage every keystroke. You describe the problem, explain constraints, and trust them to figure out the details. Then you review their PR.

The same approach works with agents. Give them well-scoped work, provide context, and review their output. Don't expect perfection—agents make mistakes, miss edge cases, and sometimes misunderstand requirements. That's what code review is for.

The comparison runs deeper:

Agents have specializations

Some agents are better at Python than JavaScript. Some excel at tests. You wouldn't assign a front-end engineer to optimize database queries—you'll learn which tasks suit which agents.

Agents improve with feedback

When you leave detailed PR comments explaining why something doesn't work, agents incorporate that feedback into their next attempt. The conversation happens in PR comments, just like with human contributors.

Agents thrive on good documentation

A well-documented codebase helps human and agent contributors understand how things work, why decisions were made, and what conventions to follow. *Documentation as a superpower* pays off even more when contributors lack institutional memory.

Agents can't replace judgment

They implement well-specified solutions, but they can't decide which problems are worth solving or when to make strategic decisions. That's still on you.

> **For individual contributors: Start small and build confidence.** Don't assign your agent the migration to microservices. Start with isolated, low-risk tasks: add tests for an untested utility function, update stale documentation, bump a dependency version. Review the PRs carefully. As you develop trust in what the agent does well—and learn what it struggles with—increase scope. Think of it like onboarding any new teammate: you wouldn't hand them the keys to production on day one.

> **For individual contributors: Your issue-writing skills are now a multiplier.** Every practice in this book—clear titles, detailed acceptance criteria, linked context—directly determines how useful agents are. The engineer who writes vague issues will get vague PRs back. The one who writes crisp, well-contextualized issues will get work that saves them hours. Your async communication skills aren't just career assets anymore—they're the interface to a new class of contributor.

Whatever you assign, though, the results hinge on how well you describe the work.

Clear instructions, better results

The reflection paradox from *AI as a thought partner* applies here too, with higher stakes—because you're not there to course-correct mid-task.

When an agent works autonomously, everything needs to be in the issue upfront:

- What's the problem being solved?
- What are the acceptance criteria?
- What constraints or requirements matter?
- What context might not be obvious from the code?
- Where can the agent find relevant documentation or examples?

A vague issue produces vague work—every time. The discipline that produces good agent issues—articulating requirements precisely, identifying edge cases explicitly, linking to relevant context—produces better issues for humans too. Teams that adopt agents often find issue quality improves across the board: ambiguity that a teammate could resolve in a Slack thread becomes friction that breaks the workflow, so people stop writing it.

> **Pro-Tip:** Write agent issues the same way you'd write an issue for a contractor you've never met: state the problem, define done, link to examples, and list constraints. If the issue needs a Slack conversation to make sense, it's not ready for an agent —or, honestly, for a teammate in another time zone.

Human oversight is the point

Agents submit PRs; they don't merge them. Non-negotiable.

The review process is where human judgment kicks in. You verify that the code works, handles edge cases, follows conventions, doesn't introduce security issues, and solves the problem. Your CI checks run. Your automated tests verify behavior. And then you—a human—make the final call.

This isn't a temporary limitation. This is the design. **Async collaboration has always been about reviewing work product, not supervising workers.** You don't watch your remote teammate write code; you review their PR. Same principle.

That review step does more than catch bugs:

Quality gate

Agents misunderstand requirements, overlook edge cases, and occasionally produce code that compiles but doesn't solve the problem. Code review catches these issues.

Learning opportunity

When you review agent-generated PRs, you learn what the agent does well, what it struggles with, and how to write better issues next time.

Accountability boundary

When you approve and merge an agent's PR, you take responsibility for that code. If it breaks production, it's on you—not the agent. That accountability keeps standards high.

Trust builder

Teams that successfully adopt agents are transparent about what's agent-generated and what's human-written. When your colleagues see that agent PRs go through the same rigorous review as human PRs, trust holds.

> **For managers: Set clear policies about agent-generated work.** Define what types of tasks are appropriate for agents, what review standards apply, and how to disclose agent-generated work. When agents submit subpar work, diagnose the cause—what about the issue or codebase led to confusion? The goal isn't perfect agents; it's a system where agents and humans collaborate within clear guardrails.

How this changes team dynamics

Agentic workflows don't replace developers. They change what developers spend time on.

Routine tasks eat engineering hours:

- Bumping dependency versions and resolving minor conflicts

- Adding test coverage to old code
- Updating documentation when implementation details change
- Fixing linter warnings and formatting issues
- Addressing security scanner findings that need code changes
- Implementing well-specified bug fixes with clear reproduction steps

These tasks matter—they keep codebases healthy—but they're not the best use of a senior engineer's time. They're tailor-made for agents: well-defined scope, measurable success criteria, existing patterns to follow.

When agents handle routine work, humans get time back for work that requires judgment:

- Architecting new systems
- Debugging complex production issues
- Mentoring junior teammates
- Making strategic technical decisions
- Exploring new technologies and approaches
- Improving developer experience and tooling

Agents can *increase* junior developer productivity—seniors get more time for mentoring when agents absorb the routine work juniors used to get as "starter tasks," freeing juniors to tackle harder problems with more guidance.

Agents will handle increasingly complex tasks as they improve. But the dynamic holds: agents excel at well-defined, pattern-matching work; humans excel at ambiguous, high-stakes, judgment-intensive work. The teams that benefit most let this division happen naturally.

As agents handle more implementation, your role shifts toward tech lead—even if that's not your title. The skills that matter most are writing clear problem descriptions, reviewing code critically, thinking at the system level, and knowing when to accept, reject, or redirect agent output. None of this makes developers less important. If anything, it makes *experienced* developers more important—because judgment, taste, and context are exactly what agents lack.

Working in the open enables agentic workflows

Agents can't ask where something is—they need stable URLs. They can't tap a teammate on the shoulder—they need written documentation. They can't intuit what you meant—they need explicit acceptance criteria and comprehensive tests. They can't navigate unwritten rules—they need codified workflows.

Teams that spent years building good async practices accidentally built the foundation for human-AI collaboration. Doing right by your human contributors and doing right by AI agents turns out to be the same investment.

> **For managers: Shore up your fundamentals first.** PR templates, test suites, CI pipelines, contribution guidelines—these aren't nice-to-haves. They're prerequisites. An AI agent is only as effective as the development infrastructure around it. Before investing in agent tooling, invest in the practices that make *any* contributor successful.

From thought partner to autonomous contributor

AI as a thought partner showed how AI forces clearer thinking by making you articulate your ideas. Agentic workflows take the next step: from AI that sharpens your reasoning to AI that executes autonomously while you focus on harder problems.

Agents aren't replacing the playbook in this book. They're the best argument for it.

Here's the twist nobody saw coming: the practices skeptics dismissed as "overhead"—clear issues, documented decisions, structured reviews—turned out to be exactly what AI needs to be useful. Every habit you've built for asynchronous human collaboration doubles as infrastructure for human-AI collaboration.

The two chapters in this section traced a natural arc. First, AI as a thought partner: the prompt *is* the product, because articulating a clear request forces you to define the problem before the machine ever responds. People who get the most from AI are the ones who'd do fine without it—AI amplifies clear thinking and exposes sloppy thinking in equal measure. Then, agentic workflows: same issue → branch → pull request → review loop you already use with remote teammates, extended to contributors that don't need sleep or coffee breaks. The prerequisite list—PR templates, test suites, CI pipelines, contribution guidelines—isn't new. It's the infrastructure you were supposed to have all along.

Key takeaways

- Using AI as a thought partner sharpens your thinking by forcing you to clarify problems, challenge your assumptions, and articulate your goals; rely on it as a shortcut and you risk losing the critical insight and judgment that make your work valuable.
- Treat AI agents as remote teammates—hand them clear issues, let them push branches, and review their pull requests as you would any human's. Get this right, and you'll multiply your team's output without rewriting your workflow; skip it, and you'll waste hours cleaning up confused pull requests.

That's the bet this section makes: you're not adopting a new technology so much as discovering that your existing workflow already supports it. The clarity that helps a teammate in Nairobi at 2 AM helps an AI agent at any hour. The documentation that prevents a new hire from re-asking a settled question prevents an agent from hallucinating an answer.

The next chapter reviews the core shifts that tie every section of this book together—transparency, writing, outcomes, and sustainability—and gives you a concrete checklist to start this week.

Conclusion

Open and async work changes how you measure professional success—and who gets to succeed. Traditional workplaces reward face time, office politics, and proximity to decision-makers. Open and async environments reward what you accomplish and how visibly you share it. That shift creates space for deep work, respects your time and energy, and lets you build a career on the strength of your contributions rather than the luck of your seating chart.

The playbook in review

> **TL;DR:** Remote teams succeed not by buying flashier tools, but by treating writing, transparency, and visible outcomes as non-negotiable—skip these, and even the best tech won't save you. This chapter shows you how to put those habits into action, so your team's results—and each person's potential—are no longer limited by "who's in the room."

Strip away the tools and what's left is what actually made the difference: writing treated as the work, not overhead; transparency, not oversharing; outcomes, not effort; sustainability, not a perk. Miss any one of those and the best async tooling in the world is just expensive furniture.

Working in the open—giving everything a URL, documenting decisions, surfacing problems early—isn't a process preference. It's how trust gets built when you can't rely on hallway conversations and shared lunches. Async-first communication then treats writing as a core skill, not a chore squeezed between meetings: the right channel, the human voice, meetings as escalation rather than default. These aren't workflow tweaks. They're how distributed teams protect focus, respect time zones, and make collaboration inclusive.

Impact over input is the test that ties it together. Measure problems solved, not hours logged. Flow over face time. Shipping over performing busyness. I saw this most clearly with the Papercuts team—GitHub's response to the "Dear GitHub" open letter, a public petition from frustrated open source maintainers. Every fix was public, every merge was searchable, and nobody on the team had to *explain* their impact—it was already documented in shipped pull requests that open source users were thanking them for by name. Careers got made on papercuts.

None of which works if people burn out. Fun isn't a distraction—it's a retention strategy. Self-care isn't weakness—it's operational discipline. Healthy conflict norms, intentional recognition, and real boundaries separate teams that sustain high performance from those that merely sprint toward collapse. **Each of these is a load-bearing wall.** Pull one out and the rest start to lean.

Start this week

Principles don't work unless you do. Here's where to start:

> **For managers:**
>
> - [ ] **Document a decision in the open.** Create an issue or document explaining your next significant decision—the reasoning, the options, why you chose the path you did. Make your thinking visible so others can learn from it.
> - [ ] **Convert one meeting to async.** Review your team's meeting calendar. Find one recurring meeting that could become an async update. Try it for two weeks and ask your team what changed.
> - [ ] **Evaluate on outcomes.** Review how you assess your team. Are you measuring time online and responsiveness, or actual results? Adjust your criteria to reward what people accomplish.

- [ ] **Make work visible.** Set up or improve your team's project board so work in progress is visible to everyone. Every significant effort should have a trackable artifact with a URL.
- [ ] **Upgrade your next 1:1.** Create a shared agenda for each direct report and use it to replace status updates with career conversations and coaching. If your 1:1s mostly cover "what are you working on," you need better async visibility, not longer meetings.
- [ ] **Recognize someone's work publicly.** Send a specific, genuine message celebrating a team member's recent contribution—not "great job" but exactly what they did and why it mattered. Post it where others can see it. Recognition that happens only in private doesn't shape culture.
- [ ] **Start with your team and prove it works.** Pick one practice from this book—async standups, decisions as documentation, a visible project board—and try it for two weeks. Measure what changes, then share results with peer leaders. Change spreads through evidence, not mandates.

- [ ] **Use AI as a thought partner.** Before sending your next important message, ask AI to help clarify your thinking or spot gaps in your reasoning. Treat it as a rubber duck[87] that talks back—a tool for refining ideas, not replacing judgment.

For individual contributors:

- [ ] **Share a work-in-progress.** Post an update in a public channel about something you're working on, even if it's unfinished. Let others see your thinking and offer early feedback.
- [ ] **Document a solution.** Next time you solve a tricky problem, write down how. Put it somewhere findable—an issue, a wiki, documentation.
- [ ] **Start your ship log.** Create a running document of your accomplishments—issues closed, projects contributed to, outcomes driven. Update it weekly.
- [ ] **Surface a problem early.** Next time you spot a risk, a miscommunication, or a flaw in the plan, raise it immediately in a public channel or issue. Raising it early is cheaper than letting problems compound in silence.

87. https://en.wikipedia.org/wiki/Rubber_duck_debugging

- [ ] **Try async-first.** Before scheduling a meeting, ask: "Could this be an issue, a document, or a message instead?" Try the async approach first and see what happens.
- [ ] **Ask questions publicly.** When you need clarification, ask in a public channel rather than a DM. Your question helps others too, and the answer becomes discoverable.
- [ ] **Make your next decision legible.** Next time you make a technical or process decision, write down the reasoning—what you chose, what you considered, why. Even a comment on an issue captures institutional memory that helps future you and your teammates.
- [ ] **Define your boundaries.** Pick one self-care practice for this week—a real lunch break, a defined end to your workday, or protected time to learn something new.
- [ ] **Try AI as a rubber duck.** Next time you're stuck, describe the problem to an AI assistant before asking a colleague. Articulating the problem often surfaces the solution—and if it doesn't, you'll ask a much sharper question.

After your first month

> **For managers:** By now, you should have a few async decisions documented, at least one recurring meeting eliminated, your team defaulting to

> visible work, and 1:1s that feel more like coaching than status updates. Now make it stick. Build recognition into your weekly routine. Update your team norms to reflect what's working. Adjust your evaluation criteria to reward outcomes over responsiveness, and share results with peer leaders. The goal isn't to run an experiment—it's to change how your team operates.

> ■ **For individual contributors:** By now, you should have a growing body of visible work, a ship log that tells the story of your impact, and stronger async habits. You've surfaced problems before they became crises and made your technical decisions legible to teammates who weren't in the room. Keep going—help teammates adopt these practices, bring your documented impact into career conversations, and refine your workflow. If you've done the work, the evidence is already there.

These practices build on each other. The first week feels like extra effort—documenting decisions you'd normally just announce, writing updates you'd normally skip. By the second month, it's just how you work. By the sixth, you'll wonder how you ever operated any other way. **Small practices, compounding returns.**

The future is yours to build

Here's what nobody tells you about switching to open and async: the professional benefits are almost a side effect. Your work becomes more visible. Your contributions speak for themselves in promotion conversations. But the deeper payoff is personal. You stop performing productivity and start doing meaningful work. Those hours lost to unnecessary meetings? Reclaimed. You build a body of evidence that follows you from role to role, company to company—a portable reputation that doesn't evaporate when you change teams.

> **For managers: Open and async practices are a retention strategy.** The best people don't stay for perks or inertia—they stay because the work environment respects their time, surfaces their impact, and trusts them to deliver without surveillance.

> Build that environment and you won't need to compete on salary alone.

> **For individual contributors: Your career is a body of work, not a collection of job titles.** Stop depending on a manager who happens to notice your effort. The practices in this book—documenting decisions, working loudly, shipping visibly—give you agency over your own narrative. You don't need permission or proximity to build one that's undeniable.

These principles shaped how remote-first teams at GitHub worked for over a decade. They're not theoretical—they have the scar tissue to prove it. And they compound. The team that documents decisions today makes better decisions tomorrow. The IC who works loudly this quarter lands the high-visibility project next quarter. The manager who trusts outcomes over activity builds a team that ships more and burns out less.

Pick one practice from the checklists above and commit to it for two months. You don't need organizational buy-in to document a decision, share a work-in-progress, or write a better issue. This model worked for me, and I've watched it work for the colleagues who took it seriously. What I've never seen work is half-measures—adopting the tools without the mindset, or the mindset without the discipline to stick with it when the first sprint feels slower. **The rest follows.**

Keep the conversation going

If something in here changed how you think about your work—or if you think I got something wrong—I'd genuinely like to know. Email me at ben@open-and-async.com, or start a conversation at ben.balter.com/contact.[88]

Found a typo? A broken argument? Open an issue at open-and-async.com/feedback.[89] Yes, this book has a public issue tracker. That's exactly the point.

Enjoyed the book? A short review on your platform of choice—wherever you bought it—goes a long way. It helps other readers discover the book and signals to the algorithm that it's worth recommending.

Reading it with a team? Grab the book-club guide.[90] And if you want to hear what comes next, sign up for updates at open-and-async.com.[91]

88. https://ben.balter.com/contact
89. https://open-and-async.com/feedback
90. https://open-and-async.com/book-club-guide
91. https://open-and-async.com

Acknowledgements

The ideas in this book aren't mine alone. They grew from years of conversations, stolen metaphors, and the occasional well-timed nudge from Hubbers past and present. I owe a debt to:

- @amateurhuman
- @amatlack
- @bkeepers
- @defunkt
- @dmleong
- @holman
- @juliebalter
- @katfukai
- @kcwatkins
- @kneath
- @lizsal
- @lizzysoltis
- @mattnigh
- @mojombo
- @mph4
- @mrry550
- @rtomayko
- @schacon
- @spraints
- @sroberts
- @swannysec
- @tnm
- The Best One Yet (TBOY) podcast—Have You Heard The Best One Yet? (HYHTBOY)
- The early access (ARC) readers, whose notes sharpened the final draft
- That one manager who told me I shouldn't write about remote work

Thank you for shaping how I think about work—and for making sure I didn't get it *too* wrong.

Early developmental and editorial review by The Book Shelf Press,[92] who helped shape the manuscript back when it barely compiled.

Tool mentions throughout aren't endorsements. Use the best tool for the job. See *Choosing the Right Collaboration Tools* for more.

92. https://thebookshelfpress.com/
93. https://github.com/github/how-engineering-communicates

Open source

Thanks also to the maintainers of and contributors to the open source projects that made this book possible:

- **Tailwind CSS** and **Tailwind Typography**, used under the MIT License
- **Pandoc**, used under the GPL 3.0 License
- **WeasyPrint**, used under the BSD 3-Clause License
- **Ghostscript**, used under the AGPL (Affero General Public License) 3.0 License
- **qpdf**, used under the Apache License 2.0
- **Poppler**, used under the GPL 2.0 License
- **Source Serif 4** by Adobe, used under the SIL (SIL International) Open Font License
- **Source Sans 3** by Adobe, used under the SIL Open Font License
- **Source Code Pro** by Adobe, used under the SIL Open Font License
- **Twemoji**, used under the CC-BY (Attribution) 4.0 License
- **ImageMagick**, used under the ImageMagick License (Apache 2.0-compatible)
- **sharp**, used under the Apache License 2.0
- **SVGO**, used under the MIT License
- **PostCSS** and **cssnano**, used under the MIT License
- **Remark** and **Retext**, both used under the MIT License, along with countless plugins from their ecosystems
- **textlint**, used under the MIT License, along with many plugins from its ecosystem
- **markdownlint**, used under the MIT License
- **Prettier**, used under the MIT License
- **Harper.js**, used under the Apache License 2.0
- **Vitest**, used under the MIT License
- **Playwright** and **axe-core**, used under the Apache License 2.0

- **Ace** by the DAISY (Digital Accessible Information System) Consortium, used under the MIT License
- **EPUBCheck**, used under the BSD 3-Clause License
- **htmlproofer**, used under the MIT License
- **lychee**, used under the Apache License 2.0 / MIT License
- **html-validate**, used under the MIT License
- **Pillow**, used under the MIT-like HPND (Historical Permission Notice and Disclaimer) License
- **LanguageTool**, used under the LGPL 2.1 License
- **Vale**, used under the MIT License
- **proselint**, used under the BSD 3-Clause License
- GNU **Diction**, used under the GPL License
- **yamllint**, used under the GPL License
- **js-yaml**, used under the MIT License
- **jscpd**, used under the MIT License
- **just**, dedicated to the public domain under CC0 (Creative Commons Zero) 1.0

If you're curious about the process, here's how I over-engineered this book's publishing process.[94] 😂

94. https://ben.balter.com/2026/08/17/how-i-over-engineered-my-book/

About the Author

Ben Balter spent more than a decade at GitHub,[95] most recently as Director of Hubber Enablement, where he helped thousands of GitHubbers do their best remote work. He's used the time trying to figure out how large engineering organizations actually work—and why the obvious answers are usually wrong.

He also led Technical Business Operations for Engineering and served as Chief of Staff for Security, driving how those organizations planned, prioritized, and shipped. As a Staff Technical Program Manager, he oversaw GitHub's on-premises and SaaS enterprise offerings. Earlier in Trust and Safety, he shipped more than 500 features spanning community management, privacy and compliance, content moderation, and platform health—keeping a platform with over 100 million developers safe, secure, and welcoming.

95. https://github.com/about

Before joining GitHub's Product team, Ben was GitHub's first Government Evangelist, driving open source adoption across nearly 2,000 government organizations in over 75 countries.

The US Chief Technology Officer once called Ben one of "the baddest of the badass innovators"—the single nicest thing anyone's ever put in print about him. A member of the inaugural class of Presidential Innovation Fellows, he served as an entrepreneur-in-residence rethinking how government uses technology to serve citizens. As a Fellow in the Office of the US Chief Information Officer within the Executive Office of the President, he helped draft parts of President Obama's Digital Strategy and Open Data Policy and joined the SWAT (SoftWare Automation and Technology) Team, the White House's first agile development team. His paper Towards a More Agile Government,[96] published in the Public Contract Law Journal, argued that federal IT procurement should look more like modern software development.

Ben's spent nearly twenty years building software remotely—across open source projects, the US federal government, startups, and large corporations. Straddling the line between the world's most bureaucratic organization (government) and its opposite (open source) taught him that almost no one questions the defaults: a form that needs two signatures, a status update that could have been a dashboard, a meeting that could have been a comment thread. Most places

96. https://ben.balter.com/2011/11/29/towards-a-more-agile-government/

never ask whether the work has to happen that way. GitHub did—which is why, when he joined in 2013, it felt less like a new job than a revelation. This book is his attempt to bottle what he found there, strip out what's idiosyncratic to GitHub, and hand the rest to anyone building a team that doesn't share an office.

A lawyer and technologist, Ben holds a J.D. and an M.B.A. from The George Washington University and is a member of the DC (District of Columbia) Bar. Off the clock, he's the kind of person who'll solve an otherwise-impossible problem with nothing but duct tape, version control, and the occasional pack of bubblegum.

Find more of Ben's writing at ben.balter.com.[97]

97. https://ben.balter.com

Steal these lines.

"Hours worked ≠ value created."

"Meetings are where work goes to die."

"Async isn't waiting. It's working."

Found one worth stealing? Scan the code for the whole collection—quotable, shareable, yours.

open-and-async.com/q

Appendix: Reference Materials

What follows are practical references for applying this book's concepts. Everything here is optional—supplementary material you can consult as needed. Each section stands alone, so skip ahead and come back when something becomes relevant—or not at all.

Managers will find ready-to-customize policy templates; ICs will find a GitHub primer and an AI prompt they can drop into their workflow today.

- *Software development for non-technical roles*: A primer on GitHub and its core features—helpful if you're working alongside engineers but don't have a technical background.
- *Example guidance for taking time off*: A sample time-off guidance document you can adapt for your own team.
- *Example extended leave handoff document*: A template for handing off context, contacts, and in-flight work before an extended absence.

- *AI prompt for weekly reporting*: A template prompt for using AI to help summarize team activity from GitHub issues.

If you don't come from an engineering background, don't let the tools intimidate you. Issues, pull requests, and Markdown aren't reserved for people with "developer" in their title—they power collaboration across the whole team.

Software Development for Non-Technical Roles

> **TL;DR:** You don't have to be an engineer to fix things directly. GitHub's core features let non-technical roles propose, review, and ship changes themselves—so good ideas don't sit in a ticket queue waiting on someone else.

What is GitHub?

A product manager spots a misleading error message on a customer-facing page. Instead of filing a ticket and waiting three sprints, they open the file on GitHub, fix the wording themselves, and submit the change for review—it ships that afternoon. That's GitHub: a collaboration platform—think Dropbox or Google Drive, but purpose-built for software development—where anyone can propose and review changes to a project, no coding required.

Repositories

Repositories[98] are GitHub's core unit—each represents a project, initiative, or team. They contain issues, discussions, and pull requests (more on those shortly), plus "code." For non-technical roles, this often means text files written in Markdown (explained below).

Markdown

Markdown is the formatting language used on GitHub. Imagine formatting text in a plain text box—using `*` for bullets or `_` for emphasis. That's Markdown—plain text with lightweight formatting that GitHub renders as styled text. Sounds technical. It isn't. To get started, check out GitHub's official documentation.[99]

Issues

Issues[100] are GitHub's units of work. Each describes a *problem* your team wants to solve, and together they form the "issue backlog." You can comment on issues, assign them to team members, and close them when completed. Labels make issues easier to organize and track. For complex problems, task lists with checkboxes track progress on sub-tasks.

98. https://docs.github.com/en/repositories
99. https://docs.github.com/en/get-started/writing-on-github/getting-started-with-writing-and-formatting-on-github/basic-writing-and-formatting-syntax
100. https://docs.github.com/en/issues

Discussions

Discussions[101] are like issues but without a specific outcome or state (open or closed). Use them to ask questions, collaborate on ideas, and share announcements—a blog post, forum thread, or chat room for your repository.

Pull requests

Pull requests[102] are how you propose changes to a repository. If issues describe the problems, pull requests describe the proposed *solutions*. Others can review your proposed changes—commenting, suggesting edits, or approving your pull request. Once approved, your pull request is “merged” into the repository and your changes go “live.”

Markdown files

Repositories contain files—anything from source code to images—but what you'll most often work with are Markdown text files. You can edit these directly on GitHub's web interface or clone the repository to your computer and edit locally (more on that below). Dragging and dropping files to upload them works too. Filenames are typically lowercase with hyphens instead of spaces. These Markdown files are where teams store long-lived information: documentation, policies, procedures, and the like.

101. https://docs.github.com/en/discussions
102. https://docs.github.com/en/pull-requests

Tracking changes

GitHub runs on a version control system called Git. Git tracks changes to files over time, like tracked changes in Google Docs or Microsoft Word (or, if you're into sci-fi, a time machine for your files). You can see who made each change and when—and "roll back" to any previous version.

Commits

Git tracks changes as "commits.[103]" A commit is a snapshot of one or more files at a specific moment. Each commit should have a brief, descriptive message explaining what changed and why.

Branches

Branches[104] are parallel universes for your files. You make changes on a branch without affecting the "main" branch. Each branch contains one or more commits, and when you're ready, you merge those changes back into main. As a result, you can work freely without stepping on anyone else's toes, then bring everything together cleanly.

103. https://docs.github.com/en/pull-requests/committing-changes-to-your-project/creating-and-editing-commits/about-commits
104. https://docs.github.com/en/pull-requests/collaborating-with-pull-requests/proposing-changes-to-your-work-with-pull-requests/about-branches

GitHub flow

GitHub flow[105] describes the process of making changes to a repository. The basic steps are:

1. Open an issue describing the problem you want to solve
2. Once there is agreement to solve the problem, decide on the best solution
3. Create a branch to work on the solution
4. Make changes to files on the branch
5. Commit those changes
6. Open a pull request "requesting" that those changes be merged back into the "main" branch
7. Your colleagues review your pull request and either approve it or suggest changes
8. Once approved, your pull request is "merged," and your changes are now "live" on the main branch

Notifications

GitHub sends you notifications[106] when someone mentions you in a comment, assigns you to an issue, or requests your review on a pull request. You can also "subscribe" to repositories to get notified about some or all activity, and unsubscribe from individual issues you're not interested in. By default, notifications arrive via email, but you can route them to "web notifications," Slack, or Microsoft Teams.

105. https://docs.github.com/en/get-started/using-github/github-flow
106. https://docs.github.com/en/subscriptions-and-notifications/concepts/about-notifications

@mentions

@mentions let you tag anyone in an issue or pull request by typing `@` followed by their GitHub login. They'll receive a notification and can respond. You can also use @mentions to tag teams, like `@acme-corp/engineering` or `@acme-corp/design`. Always explain *why* you're tagging someone. A drive-by @mention with no context forces the recipient to scroll up, guess what you want, and then ask—turning a one-step interaction into three.

Cross-references

Issue and pull request *cross-references* link related conversations together. In a comment, you can reference another issue or pull request by including its number (for example, `This is related to #123`). GitHub automatically links the two, so others can discover context and follow the conversation.

Desktop vs. web

You can do almost everything on GitHub through the web interface: view, create, edit, or delete files, browse and comment on issues, and merge pull requests. If you'd prefer desktop access, GitHub Desktop[107] provides a visual interface for "pulling" (downloading) repositories and interacting with GitHub.

107. https://github.com/apps/desktop

Advanced-ish topics

Pushing and pulling

If you're using the web interface, you don't need to worry about pushing or pulling. With the desktop client, think of pulling as downloading files from GitHub and pushing as uploading them back. Cloning is the initial download of an entire repository.

Project boards

If you track individual tasks as issues, project boards[108] let you monitor a project's overall progress. They show which issues are upcoming, in progress, and done.

Finding information

GitHub holds a lot of information. Finding what you want can feel like searching through stacks inside stacks. Tips for GitHub's search:[109]

- Use keyword search, just like you would any search engine. For example, searching for `widgets` will find all repositories, issues, pull requests, and discussions that contain the word "widgets."
- Scope your search to an organization or repository using the `org:` or `repo:` qualifiers. For example, `org:github` will find all issues in all repositories in the `github` organization, or `repo:github/docs` will find all issues in the `github/docs` repository.

108. https://docs.github.com/en/issues/planning-and-tracking-with-projects/learning-about-projects/about-projects
109. https://github.com/search

- You can refine your search further to show only threads you're involved in by using the `involves:@me` modifier. For example, `widgets involves:@me` will find all issues, pull requests, and discussions containing the word "widgets" that you're involved in.
- GitHub displays different types of information (issues, pull requests, discussions, Markdown) as separate results. Check the sidebar for all matching results.
- You can limit a "code" search to only Markdown files by clicking "Markdown" in the sidebar to filter results or adding `language:Markdown` to your search query.

For more detail, see the official search documentation. [110]

Checks

You *may* see one or more status checks[111] on your pull request. Checks are automated tests that run against your proposed changes to enforce rules like formatting, spelling, or style. A red X next to a check means something needs fixing before merge. Click "details" next to the failed check to see what.

110. https://docs.github.com/en/search-github/github-code-search/using-github-code-search
111. https://docs.github.com/en/pull-requests/collaborating-with-pull-requests/collaborating-on-repositories-with-code-quality-features/about-status-checks

When to use an issue vs. a pull request vs. a discussion vs. a Markdown file vs. a project board

Project work generally flows in this order:

- **Discussions**—Open-ended conversations without a specific outcome or concept of "done." Often the ideation or brainstorming stage.
- **Issues**—How teams track, discuss, and prioritize problems.
- **Pull requests**—How you propose and review solutions and changes. Pull requests should tie back to the issue or problem they solve.
- **Markdown files**—How teams share and store long-lived information (documentation, policies, procedures, etc.). You change Markdown files via pull request.

As a project progresses across repositories, teams track high-level progress on project boards, which visually organize the state of many issues.

Putting it all together: editing a file on the web

1. Open the repository you want to edit
2. Navigate to the file you want to edit
3. Click the pencil icon to edit the file
4. Make your changes
5. Click "Commit changes" to save your changes
6. Describe your changes in the commit message
7. Name your branch
8. Click "Propose changes" to open a pull request

9. Describe your changes in the pull request, ideally referencing the issue you're solving (for example, `Closes #123`)
10. Reviewers approve your changes—or leave comments asking for tweaks
11. Once approved and checks pass, the pull request is merged and your edit goes live on the `main` branch

If all this process talk feels a bit mechanical, remember: the tools and workflows are here to help you work better as a team and to make collaboration smoother—not to turn you into a robot. Working well together also means knowing when to log off—how, and frankly why, you should actually take time off.

Example: Guidance for Taking Time Off

> **TL;DR:** Unlimited paid time off (PTO) only works if you set clear norms—take at least 20 days off each year, coordinate ahead, and fully unplug—otherwise, your best people will burn out and leave. This chapter shows you the exact steps to make time off real, guilt-free, and sustainable for your whole team.

Unlimited time off sounds generous until you realize nobody knows how much is too much—so people take too little, and call it culture. Here's how we keep that from happening:

You should take time off

Without a bank of use-it-or-lose-it days off, it's natural to feel hesitant about taking time off, unsure of how much to take, or even guilty when you do.

Meet your commitments, manage expectations, and communicate your availability—but don't hesitate to take time off. Whether it's an hour or a week, you need the rest.

This document captures team norms around time off, but it's **not** prescriptive. We trust each other to complete our work and care for ourselves however works best.

When to take time off

- You're going on vacation
- You got a new video game, bike, sewing needle, or similar
- You're not feeling well
- You're not being productive
- You're moving and need time to unpack
- The weather is nice
- It's your birthday
- Your partner has the day off
- You're not sure why, but you need a break

Some people prefer to take time off in large chunks, say a week or two or three at a time. Others prefer to take a day here or there, say Fridays during the summer. Either works.

How much time off to take per year

Take at least 20 days per year. Most people who use this policy well take 25–30. Less than 20 is a sign something's off—either with the workload or with the team's permission to disconnect.

Preparing to take time off

- Coordinate with your team and any stakeholders to avoid conflicts with meetings or deliverables
- Work with the team lead on backup coverage for anything business-critical (no formal approval necessary)
- Let anyone directly affected know about your upcoming leave
- For extended leaves, prepare an out-of-office document with contact information and escalation paths
- Put the leave on your calendar as out of office (and invite the team calendar to the event for visibility)
- Update your chat status (and, optionally, your GitHub status, email responder, etc.)

For more, see the extended leave handoff document template.

Pro tips for taking time off

- Unplug. Log out of chat. Turn off email notifications. Don't check in. Really.
- You're welcome to work from a different location, but that doesn't count as time off.
- Think of time off in quarters to plan around team milestones (quarterly planning, launches, etc.).

Example: Extended Leave Handoff Document

> **TL;DR:** When you go offline on a distributed team, you don't just leave a desk empty—your context disappears with you. A findable handoff document spelling out coverage, contacts, and how (and whether) to reach you is what lets you actually unplug instead of returning to a smoking crater.

In a co-located office, a departing colleague's institutional knowledge lingers—someone remembers what they were working on, who they talked to, what's in flight. In a distributed team, when you go offline, you *vanish*. Your context, your relationships, your in-progress work—gone, unless you deliberately hand it off in writing.

A leave document is the async equivalent of walking your replacement through the office and introducing them to everyone they'll need. It captures not just your responsibilities, but who to talk to, what's in flight, and how to reach you (if at all).

Before you write

Start your leave document at least two weeks before departure—earlier for longer absences. Share a draft with key stakeholders and ask: "What questions might come up while I'm out that aren't answered here?" Their answers reveal gaps you can't spot on your own.

Make the document discoverable. Link to it from your chat status, your calendar out-of-office reply, and your email auto-reply. The best leave document in the world is worthless if nobody can find it. In the spirit of everything having a URL, create a short, memorable link (for example, `bit.ly/yourname-leave`) that colleagues can share.

Sections to include

TL;DR

Lead with the essentials. Someone with a quick question shouldn't need the full document:

> *If your question or request isn't answered below, open an issue in [repository] or post in [channel], and someone will point you in the right direction. Wondering about the status of an in-flight project? Check [project board].*

Dates

State your leave dates clearly, including time zones. If the exact return date is uncertain, say so—"returning mid-March" beats a precise date you'll have to correct later. Keep this section updated as plans change.

Contact preferences

Set explicit expectations: Will you check messages at all? What constitutes a genuine emergency, and how should people reach you? Make clear that *not responding* is the expected default during leave, not a sign that something is wrong.

> **Pro-Tip:** Be honest about your contact preferences—and then honor them. If you say you're fully offline but keep responding to messages, you train your team to expect availability during future leaves. Model the boundaries you want your team to feel safe setting.

Points of contact

For every ongoing responsibility, name a specific person who will cover it. Anything without a named owner will fall through the cracks. Confirm with each person *before* publishing—don't volunteer someone for coverage they don't know about.

What	Who
Widget production	Walter
People management	Paula
Escalation (anything not listed)	Emily

Regular meetings

List recurring meetings you normally run or attend, their frequency, and who will take your place. Include host responsibilities, links to standing agendas, and any context the substitute will need.

Meeting	Frequency	Responsibilities	Covering
Staff meeting	Mondays, 10 AM ET	Set agenda, facilitate	Susie
1:1s with directs	Weekly	Take notes, follow up afterward	Danny

Key contacts

"Who do I talk to about X?" is harder to answer when you can't tap the person who usually knows. Map your cross-functional relationships so others can unblock themselves:

What	Who
HR	Henry
IT	Iris
Legal	Larry
Finance	Fran

In-flight work and project status

Link to your team's project board for current work. For anything not captured there, document what you've been working on, where it stands, and what should be picked up. Frame items as problems and context, not just tasks—your replacement needs to understand *why*, not just *what*.

Important links

Compile everything your colleagues might need: team documentation, reports, planning materials, vendor contacts, and anything else you'd normally field questions about. Think of it as pre-answering six weeks of "Hey, where do I find...?" messages.

What makes remote leave different

Co-located teams handle leave coverage through proximity—you overhear who's picking up what. Distributed teams don't get that, so a few areas need explicit planning:

Time zone coverage

If you're the team's primary presence in a particular time zone, note how that gap will be covered. Will someone shift their hours? Will async processes need to adjust? Without a plan, work stalls for 8+ hours because nobody's online.

Async ritual ownership

If you run async standup prompts, weekly reports, or other recurring rituals, hand those off explicitly. These rituals feel automatic until the person running them disappears—then the team notices immediately.

Institutional knowledge

Leaving a clear trail behind—whether for a handoff or your own eventual return—means spelling out what actually happened, not just what you planned. That habit pays off far beyond extended leave; it's the backbone of async teamwork. If you want that clarity without a weekly writing headache, an AI-powered prompt can help distill your team's activity into reports that are useful, not just obligatory.

Example: AI Prompt for Weekly Reporting

Here's a sample prompt you can feed to any AI tool to summarize your team's weekly activity from GitHub issues—a robot intern for your weekly snippets. The prompt bakes in the writing principles from *Weekly Reporting That Doesn't Suck*—situation-action-result format, specific accomplishments over filler phrases, and so on. Customize it to match your team's norms.

The prompt

> *The user will provide a list of your team's weekly activity in the form of GitHub issues. From that list of issues, create a high-level summary of your team's weekly activity and accomplishments in list form. Write this summary for a technical executive audience and include it in a weekly report for the leadership team.*
>
> *You MUST adhere to the following criteria:*
>
> *The list of summary items should be a bulleted list in GitHub-flavored Markdown.*
>
> - *Each list item MUST refer to completed work in the past tense and work still in progress in the present or future tense, as appropriate.*
> - *Only include the most important activity from the week.*
> - *Each list item should be no more than three complete sentences, using a situation-action-result structure. Focus on specific deliverables and milestones rather than vague progress statements.*
> - *The most critical parts of the list items should be* ***bold*** *to improve readability.*
> - *Combine related accomplishments to show themes of business impact rather than listing each accomplishment.*

How to use this prompt

1. **Gather your team's activity.** Use saved GitHub searches to collect issues your team touched during the week (e.g., `org:github involves:@monalisa is:issue updated:>=XXXX-XX-XX`).
2. **Feed it to an AI tool.** Copy the prompt above along with your list of issues into your preferred AI assistant.
3. **Edit the output.** The AI-generated summary is a first draft—fix anything inaccurate, vague, or that doesn't sound like you.
4. **Publish.** Share the refined summary as your weekly snippets.

AI handles the busywork, not the judgment calls. Always sanity-check the output—AI doesn't know what your team actually prioritized last week.

www.ingramcontent.com/pod-product-compliance
Lightning Source LLC
LaVergne TN
LVHW052015200926
848481LV00005B/1492